JUST LET THE KIDS PLAY

How to Stop Other Adults from Ruining Your Child's Fun and Success in Youth Sports

Bob Bigelow, Tom Moroney and Linda Hall

Health Communications, Inc.
Deerfield Beach, Florida

www.hci-online.com

Columns by Tom Moroney reprinted with permission of The MetroWest Daily News, *Framingham, Massachusetts.*

Library of Congress Cataloging-in-Publication Data

Bigelow, Bob
    Just let the kids play : how to stop other adults from ruining your child's fun and success in youth sports / Bob Bigelow, Tom Moroney and Linda Hall.
    p.cm.
    Includes bibliographical references.
    ISBN 1-55874-927-6 (tradepaper)
    1. Sports for children—United States. 2. Sports for children—United States—Psychological aspects. 3. Sports for children—Social aspects—United States.
    I. Moroney, Tom. II. Hall, Linda. III. Title.

GV709.2.B54 2001
796'.083'0973—dc21   2001039137

Publisher: Health Communications, Inc.
          3201 S.W. 15th Street
          Deerfield Beach, FL 33442-8190

Cover design by Andrea Perrine Brower
Inside design by Lawna Patterson Oldfield

To Nancy,
A wonderful wife, mother,
coach and mentor;
To David and Stephen,
may their games always be fun
and challenging;
And to my parents, Kay and Bob,
who gave me the perfect blend
of encouragement, support
and non-intrusion.

—Bob Bigelow

To our sons,
Tom and Kevin,
and to all the children
who play.

—Linda Hall and Tom Moroney

What People Are Saying About
JUST LET THE KIDS PLAY . . .

"This book is the best available resource for parents, coaches or anyone involved with youth sports. This book offers practical, usable advice to solve the problems of violence and burnout, with clear-cut steps you can take to ensure your kids get the most out of sports."

—**Mike Eruzione**
captain, 1980 USA Olympic Gold Medal Hockey Team

"If you have a child who plays youth sports, your first move is to read this book. Bob Bigelow's voice is finally being heard throughout the country on the issue of sports parenting—his book should be 'must reading' for all parents and officials."

—**Rick Wolff**
chairman, The Center for Sports Parenting

"Instead of sticking one of the hundreds of lists of rules under the nose of every parent and asking them to sign on the dotted line . . . hand them a copy of *Just Let the Kids Play*. This book is more powerful than any code of conduct that I have seen. It speaks to making sure that we are all stakeholders of equal importance in the youth sports experience."

—**Brooke deLench**
founder, *MomsTeam.com*

"We must give youth sports back to the kids. The authors' passion to do that comes through in this book!"

—**Mike Pfahl**
vice president/education
National Alliance for Youth Sports (NAYS)

"When I began researching the ways youth sports influence the moral development of children at Harvard in the early eighties, there were relatively few quality resources to turn to for guidance. Since then there has been numerous research and books chronicling the youth sports phenomenon. *Just Let the Kids Play* represents the best review and analysis of the state of youth sports in America today. In fact, I plan to include *Just Let the Kids Play* as a must read for my counselors at my Sports PLUS Summer Camp.

Just Let the Kids Play offers parents, coaches and community leaders a clear road map on how to return the love of sports to its right owners—the kids."

—**Dr. Jeffrey Pratt Beedy**
headmaster, New Hampton School
founder, Positive Learning Using Sports and
GoodSport models

CONTENTS

ACKNOWLEDGMENTS

B ooks," wrote Charles W. Eliot in *The Happy Life*, "are the quietest and most constant of friends; they are the most accessible and wisest of counselors, and the most patient of teachers." In writing this book we certainly benefited from our own wise counselors and patient teachers. We thank them for their advice and their inspiration.

Doug Abrams, a law professor who has been a youth hockey coach for thirty-two years, and Dean Conway, director of coaching for the Massachusetts Youth Soccer Association, provided terrific ideas about creating healthy, fun programs for children. We thank Doug, a writer whose columns about youth sports have been published in various newspaper opinion sections, for his suggestions regarding our manuscript.

Rick Wolff, a nationally recognized expert on sports psychology and youth sports parenting, offered wise counsel at the start of this project, and has provided inspiration and friendship to Bob Bigelow for many years.

We thank the enthusiastic people whose energy and clear thinking have created wonderful youth sports programs across the country. We appreciate their sharing their ideas with us.

We express our gratitude to those people who have partici-pated, with passionate conviction, in battles over youth sports reform. We appreciate their candor about the controversial and uncomfortable aspects of youth sports politics.

We recognize the contributions of Mike Clark, Martha Ewing and the staff at the Institute for the Study of Youth Sports at Michigan State University for their data and inter-pretation in order to help us all understand what children don't like about youth sports and why they often quit.

This book has benefited greatly from the guidance and craft of our copy editor, Heath Silberfeld of Enough Said, her writing, editing and production company in Portland, Oregon. About her contributions and her commitment we cannot say enough.

We thank Allison Janse of Health Communications, Inc., for steering this book project from conception to completion. Her advice and support helped all of us in many ways throughout our journey.

We thank Nancy Bigelow and our parents, Kay and Bob Bigelow, Alice and Tom Moroney, and Lena Hall Cody, for their love and encouragement. We thank our sons, Stephen, David, Tom and Kevin, for the joy they bring to our lives.

Finally, we acknowledge each other. From our long tele-phone conversations to our multiple meetings in fast-food restaurants to our frenetic e-mails, we have challenged and counseled each other. We have tried to be patient teachers, and we most certainly remain constant friends.

Bob Bigelow
Tom Moroney
Linda Hall

INTRODUCTION

All over the country this week tens of millions of children will play an organized game of youth sports. Tens of millions of adults will watch and cheer from the sidelines as parents and as coaches. There will be joy and triumph, but there will also be trouble.

Many adults will be wonderful mentors, but others will make misguided choices and will end up causing hurt for the children who play. In the worst cases, the adults will create an atmosphere that is neither healthy nor fun.

Except for the most extreme violence or abuse in youth sports, the coaches and the parents who create trouble for our children are not bad people. They are caught up in, and sometimes corrupted by, youth sports systems that have gone astray. Such systems allow misdirected principles and priorities to take over. These are not bad people in charge; these are flawed systems in control.

This book is different from many others you will find about youth sports because it advocates changes that remove the true sources of much of the adult misbehavior and the problems that are created for the children who play. This book confronts the organization and management of leagues, teams and players.

The hot blood of emotions in youth sports, the politics among adults in charge and, sometimes, the outbursts on the sidelines flow from each organization and its management. Structures such as the selection of elite teams at young ages and caste systems that rank athletic abilities in children and stick kids with labels—often unfair labels—that can last throughout their years in youth sports. Management practices that bench children in order to win games, that nurture "the (perceived) best" at young ages but neglect "the rest." Actions that convince children they're not good enough to play.

We need to reform those systems. Behavior pledges and parents' classes, coaches' training and gag orders on spectators' yelling will not go far enough.

Youth sports are my business and my passion. I have been a professional athlete—I spent four years playing in the NBA—but for the past ten years I have traveled the country talking to audiences about what is wrong with youth sports and how we can right those wrongs.

People who speak for a living are often advised to fix on one person in an audience and to talk directly to that person. In talking to one person, the speaker transfers that connection to an entire audience.

That is what I hope to do in this book. I hope you read it and feel as though I am sitting next to you in the stands or standing next to you on the sidelines as you watch your child or coach your team. While I have traveled to hundreds of communities, I hope this book will reach the parents and coaches I have not met.

In writing this book I pictured that mother or father or coach at a hockey game, a baseball game or any other sport on a typical day when there are lots of other things that need to be done, not including the game. I pictured that parent hoping for his or her child to do well, hoping for their team to win. I also pictured, too often, uncomfortable tension and conflicts over what is best for the children. I pictured choices made that cause children pain.

Although I consider myself a specialist on what is wrong in youth sports, my ideas for change would not mean as much were I not also a sports parent. As a parent, and as a coach, I have made the same mistakes that other adults make every day. As a spectator I have felt the mix of intense, and often conflicting, emotions parents naturally feel when they watch their children win, lose, get discouraged or get hurt.

I love what youth sports can do for children. I love competition. I love to win. Sports offer children opportunities to achieve, to develop confidence and self-esteem, to plug into physical fitness, to learn how to be part of a team, to challenge themselves and to make friends. And, oh yes, to have fun. Having fun is where our discussion about youth sports should begin.

To do away with the negatives and to rebuild youth sports systems that are healthy, productive *and* fun, adults need to take three steps: Recognize the true sources of the problems, find solutions and join—or lead—efforts for change. Some of these changes are nothing short of a revolution. But this revolution can be waged in small steps, with day-to-day choices made to serve the wants and the needs of the children who play. This book is a guide to those choices.

You won't agree with everything in this book. That's okay, too. I enjoy a feisty debate about what youth sports should be and how we should get there. I think this book offers great ideas for reform, but this is food for thought and fodder for your own battles. Not all of these suggestions will fit neatly into your community, your team or your family. I do, however, stand fast by these guiding principles, and think they will keep you on the right path.

Chapter 2 takes direct aim at what is perhaps the most destructive force in youth sports today: the misguided efforts by adults to identify and to cultivate sports "talent" at younger and younger ages, to select out "the best" and, in that process, to discourage "the rest."

Throughout the chapters, you will find stories of the boys and girls who play, and stories of the parents who watch and the adults who coach. Some stories have an ugly side. This book tries to unravel the reasons that adults act the way they do. Looking in the mirror, as in chapter 3, will be one of our first steps.

Chapter 4 explores the toll that youth sports can take on the bodies and psyches of the children who play, especially overuse injuries and burnout, emotional abuse and plain old fatigue. It is important that we recognize the depth of the problems created by the current systems in order to understand why we need to fight for change.

This book focuses as much on solutions as on problems. Chapters 5, 6 and 7 focus on how to make informed and healthy choices—step by step—when you enroll your child in an organized sport, when you assemble a team and when you play a game.

Chapter 8 takes you to the front lines of passionate battles in youth sports—from arguments about elite teams to disagreements about the value of trophies.

Chapter 9 introduces you to impressive people who have developed excellent programs in youth sports from New England to California and in between. Some have created programs of their own; others have made meaningful changes in the systems in which they volunteer. All have terrific ideas.

This book concentrates on children from kindergarten through grade eight. Chapter 10 looks at the transition from youth sports to interscholastic sports in middle school and high school, and all the promise that is lost before and during those years. This chapter also considers college and professional sports, and how mistakes during developmental years in youth sports continue to take a toll at the highest levels on players still left in the game.

This book also pays attention to children no longer in the game. An estimated 70 percent of children who play a youth sport end up quitting that sport by the time they are thirteen. It is perhaps in their name that we need to fight the hardest. These are the children who are cut at early ages, who drop out or who are left out by systems that do not do enough to encourage *all* children to play.

We'll have fun in this book, too. We needn't be serious all the time. Poking fun at ourselves is sometimes the clearest method by which to recognize the error of our ways.

I am a public speaker, not a writer. In order to write this book I needed a team. My coauthors bring to this project professional and personal experience. They researched the issues and interviewed many of the people you meet in this book. We have kept this book to a single voice, but this is a united message. My coauthors, Tom Moroney and Linda Hall, are writers. More than that, they are youth sports parents who are, in fact, married to each other.

I first met Tom when we appeared together on a television show in Boston during a segment about youth soccer. Tom is a columnist with *The MetroWest Daily News* in Framingham, Massachusetts. Long before we met he had been writing about the antics of parents at their children's games. You'll find a few of his columns excerpted in this book.

Linda is an experienced newspaper and magazine writer and editor. She is also one of those thoughtful parents who has been sitting on the sidelines for years, asking herself tough questions about what she sees happening on the playing fields and in the gyms. She often focuses on the best question of all: Isn't there a better way?

This book starts with the assumption that yes, indeed, there is a better way. Now, let's find that way.

CHAPTER 1

Youth Sports: There Must Be a Better Way

*At the start of a grueling season
that doesn't seem to have an end, in the
middle of a tirade between coach and
players, at the end of a stressful car ride to
a faraway gym, many parents wonder:
"Am I doing the right thing?"*

Picture the typical youth sports game—a blur of motion and sound. Some parents are busy cheering or chatting among themselves. Others are prowling the sidelines. The prowlers mean business. These parents become field generals, barking orders and commanding their children to excel.

In this world of high volume and hyperventilating, one parent stands out. You can

1

hear him from the parking lot. "Mark your man," he screams to his little boy. Red-faced and nearly breathless, this father runs up and down the sidelines, keeping pace with every play. "See the ball," he growls. And this, his favorite one-liner from the "General Patton Does Soccer" playbook: "Stay within yourself!" The louder he screams, the more he seems to expect from his son.

He is the reason his wife doesn't enjoy going to the games anymore. Today, as she listens to him bellow, she finally asks: "Do you think he even understands what you're telling him out there?"

"Of course he does. I've been telling him this all year. *Stay within yourself!*" the father shouts again. Just then, an opposing player steals the ball from his son, dribbles around him and heads straight toward the goal. Score!

That pushes the father to the edge. As the boy walks off the field, the father makes a beeline for his son. "Why didn't you do what I told you to?" he yells. "Aren't you listening to me?"

"I'm listening, Dad, but I don't know what you're talking about."

Such is often the case in youth sports. There is a disconnect between what adults say versus what children want and need to hear. What adults want and need from youth sports is often not what children want and need. It's as though the adults and the children live in different worlds and speak different languages.

More dramatic and disturbing examples of how far adults stray from their proper roles in youth sports occur every day—from assaults on coaches and officials to brawls among parents, even a fatal fight between two fathers.

The damage is obvious, but the solutions harder to find. And that is where this book begins. The solutions to these problems, and the solution for the hyperventilating soccer dad, is not for the child to figure out how to fit into the adult's world, how to meet adult expectations. The solution is for the adults to look at youth sports through the eyes of the children, and to serve the wants and the needs of those children at play. This will require not only a change in adult attitudes, but changes in the sports systems themselves.

I don't offer you this guidance lightly or without the credentials to back it up. I was a first-round draft pick and played in the National Basketball Association for four years, toe-to-toe and elbow-to-elbow with the stars of the game. I played basketball at an Ivy League college, in high school and in the driveways of my hometown, where children of my generation got the best education in sports there is: from each other.

Today I'm a lecturer, an occasional professional scout, a youth sports coach and an administrator. I'm the father of two sons who have played youth sports since first grade. These days I travel the country talking to parents, coaches and other youth sports administrators about what is wrong and how to give youth sports back to our children.

You won't find advanced degrees in physical education, sports science or child psychology on my résumé. I do not labor over complex theories or reams of statistics. Instead, I take what I have learned from the best men and women of physical education, sports science and child psychology. I apply their work to what is happening in the gyms and on the playing fields all over America, and I hit the road. I travel to cafeterias and lecture halls, wherever schools and sports organizations can find a room. I look parents and coaches straight in the eye and tell them much of what they are doing is wrong.

During these talks, I ask the audience tough questions, questions that I also ask you now. Can you read the headlines about assaults and brawls at youth sports events and still believe we have created healthy systems for all children? Can you look at the startling numbers of children who get fed up or burned out and who quit youth sports at an early age, and still believe we're doing right by them? Can you look at your own children, your friends' children, or the children on your team and feel assured that they are not paying a price—a price that allows the adults in charge of youth sports to get what *they* want?

Not only can the youth sports systems controlling our children's lives ruin their fun, but also they often deny individual children fair opportunities to reach their full potential. With the cruelest irony, these systems rob us of athletes who, had they been given a fair chance as children, might have been terrific players as high school seniors or as adults. As a consequence of these misguided youth sports systems, we sacrifice the present *and* the future.

There is no way to accurately measure that toll. A lot of potentially great players have simply moved off the sports radar screen before high school. We could argue about whether or not today's sports professionals are better than those who grew up without endless seasons of organized youth sports. As I watch games in person and on television, as a scout for colleges and for the pros, I have no doubt that players today are no better than players of previous generations. In fact, some things, such as teamwork, have suffered.

Give Back the Games

This book describes a grassroots revolution, with bottom-to-top changes in the ways we organize and operate our systems of youth sports. These actions rely on common sense and your love for your children. These are changes to be made in your community, on the team that you coach or perhaps simply within your own family.

Organized youth sports involve an estimated 30 to 35 million children each year and, along with them, their parents. Youth sports are second only to school in the amount of interest, investment and involvement of parents on behalf of their children. For some people, strictly measured by those three gauges, youth sports actually come in first.

Youth sports can be a wonderful experience. Consider the joy a child feels learning a sports skill or scoring a winning point. Consider the excitement and the pride of that child's parents watching from the sidelines or from the stands.

Coaches can have great fun amusing themselves by wondering if one of the youngsters on their team will be a star someday. Youth sports, organized and operated with children's best interests at heart, can offer some of the most delightful and memorable experiences of childhood—not to mention all the health benefits that exercise provides.

But in many ways and on too many days, organized youth sports need to be saved from themselves. They have a disturbing side, where troubling motives and unhealthy choices made by adults hurt the children who play.

One Chance at Childhood

Most of the changes offered here are fairly easy to make. In fact, some of them require less adult time and energy than do the organized systems already in place. Yet these changes carry might. Taken together, they can re-create the world of youth sports.

These changes speak to your vision of the childhood you want your child to experience and to remember. These changes speak to the kind of adult life you want to lead and the kind of parent you want to be.

If you listen to these stories and hear this advice, it will help you stop yourself and others from stealing away your child's right to have fun and to find success playing youth sports—and, believe me, for so many children that fun and that success are stolen away.

Let's be clear up front about something else. When you try to make changes, you will meet with resistance—plenty of it. Some adults are so mired in the process, so caught up in "The Way Things Are" that they cannot see clearly to "The Way Things Should Be."

Disagreements and misunderstandings ignite the politics of youth sports. Pulling apart and questioning adults' motives generally exposes a minefield of emotions. Here's how the coach of a highly competitive third-grade boys' basketball team described his efforts to *Dayton Daily News* (Ohio) sportswriter Susan Vinella for a July 7, 1997, story: "We don't want to lose a ballgame because we played kids equally. It's sort of like a business: I'm trying to put the best product on the floor."

Product? These were eight-year-old and nine-year-old boys.

The sportswriter reported that the coach, with his team winning by twenty-one points and four minutes left on the clock, kneeled near a few players and explained why he wasn't sending them in. "There's too much time left. I don't want the other team to go crazy [and catch up]."

When the sportswriter asked the director of this league whether parents objected to the extremely competitive nature of the league, he responded: "We tell them our philosophy right up front. If parents don't like it, it's America and there are other places to play."

After the story appeared, a local radio station named the third-grade coach its "Idiot of the Week," and newspaper readers weighed in with criticism. The coach and the league director fired back with letters to the editor. Their words were taken out of context, they said, and the story didn't mention all the good they do. Both coach and director were outraged that anyone would conclude they didn't have the best interests of the children at heart.

The purpose of their basketball league, they said in their letters to the newspaper, is to "field premier, select" teams, starting in grade three. Their league, they said, is a "feeder system" to prepare children to compete in middle and high schools. They offer a "competitive level" of play, stressing "player responsibility" and improvement of skills, "expecting to win as a result."

The coach and director said those third-graders on the

bench were pulled out because they had made "a few mistakes" and were "struggling" with the defensive "press" the other team had set up. They said the boys went back in after the coach's talk.

One of the team's young players even wrote to the newspaper, defending his coach. He doesn't argue like some coaches do, the boy said. "At one of my games, another coach got double technical fouls and called the ref an idiot."

Taken together, these letters articulate major problems in youth sports systems. The way I see it, these adults—most likely dedicated coaches—nevertheless have got it all wrong. They believe they have the best interests of the children at heart, but believing you do and actually serving children's best interests are entirely different. This is a fundamental split in youth sports today.

This select Ohio basketball team, in my opinion, encourages misguided choices by the adults on behalf of young children. Third grade should be the start of organized basketball games, certainly not a time to field "select" teams for competitive play. "Playing sports is about being prepared and accountable," the director's letter says. When you're eight years old, playing sports should be almost entirely about having fun.

Select systems at young ages feed some of the most destructive forces at work in youth sports today and give rise to some of the most ludicrous adult behavior.

Select systems at young ages feed some of the most destructive forces at work in youth sports today and give rise to some of the most ludicrous adult behavior. We need look no further than the young boy's letter about the other coach, with his double technicals and insults for the sports official.

For those who believe these systems are best for children, people who are committed to coaching and are up front about their goals, arguments like mine often fall on deaf ears. These people are not easily convinced that their misdirected approaches are not in the best interests of the children now or in their futures.

Sports Battlefields

This probably isn't the first time you've heard that things have gone terribly wrong in youth sports. You've seen the stories on television and in newspapers and magazines. Police have been called to respond to fights at games for children as young as four and five. Coaches and parents across the country have been arrested, even served jail time, for assaulting each other, game officials or even players. Coaches, officials, parents and players have been injured in these fights, some seriously enough to require hospital care. In Massachusetts in July 2000, a hockey father died after a fight with another hockey father, allegedly after a confrontation between the two about what one father saw as rough play during a pickup scrimmage involving their children.

The problems are worse than you may realize. I have a friend whose computer search service alerts him to almost every item that appears in any newspaper or magazine around the country about parents' misbehavior and violence at their children's games. My friend receives, on average, more than a story a day, all reports of adults gone over the top.

Across the country people are taking steps to stop this kind of behavior. You may have heard about "Silent Saturday" in Maryland and "Silent Sunday" in Ohio. These communities imposed gag orders on parents, demanding that they keep silent during designated basketball and soccer games.

In February 2000, Florida's Jupiter/Tequesta Athletic Association became the first league in the country to require parents to attend a course on behavior and to sign a parents' pledge before they may enroll their children in youth sports. According to the National Alliance for Youth Sports (NAYS), leagues nationwide have followed with mandatory pledges and courses of their own.

These are good steps, but we need more. We need to reform the youth sports systems in place—including the way leagues are organized, teams selected and players managed. Unless we rebuild systems from bottom to top, we're putting salve on wounds that will not heal.

I've seen sports from all sides now. I was an NBA first-round draft pick out of the University of Pennsylvania. In my senior year of high school, several magazines named me among the top fifty basketball players in the country.

I have run sports clinics for all ages, from kindergarten to professional adults. I have spent more time in gyms, rinks and fields, and watched more children play more games of baseball, hockey, soccer, football and basketball than most adults. I have conducted more talks on this topic in more schools in more communities than anyone I know.

I've met the enemy and, yes, it is us. We have the power to change the way things are done, and the tools are within our reach. My vision of better systems in the future is not a field of dreams. These changes are as close as your next league administrators' meeting, your next season's team signups or your next game.

By following through on these changes, you will cut to the core of the misguided structures adults have developed for children. The changes set down in the following chapters will help to quiet the madness on the sidelines and give our children back the joy of play.

And here's the best part: These new systems will not get in the way of any child's dreams, even the dreams of the most fired-up young competitor. After you make these suggested changes, your kids will be able to take sports as far as they would like, whether that is high school varsity, college or the pros.

These new systems, once in place, will make those children better players if they reach those top levels.

Changes Create Controversy

I'm all for children playing hard, competing in games, and winning and losing, but I believe in programs and teams that serve primarily the children's wants and the children's needs, not those of the adults in charge. However, people like me who espouse such shifts in priorities are often lambasted as being soft or wimpy by the "tough guys."

In 1997 the Massachusetts Youth Soccer Association implemented what is known as "non-results-oriented" tournaments for children under age ten. Scores would be kept, but not standings. In other words, teams would not be eliminated. Most importantly, the results would not be calculated in order to determine an overall tournament winner who then would be awarded the trophy at the end of the weekend.

The idea was aimed at taking some of the pressure off the children (and their coaches). With less pressure to win, the idea was that coaches would allow more children—whatever their abilities—to participate more fully in these tournaments, which are often season-ending events.

I love this idea (in fact, you'll find more about this in chapter 8), but pundits in the media crucified the people who spearheaded this change. John Leo, a usually sensible columnist for *U.S. News & World Report*, decided the move was a bunch of politically correct baloney dreamed up by those who unrealistically seek to protect all children from the heartache of losing. In a June 22, 1998 column in the magazine, Leo got downright sarcastic by suggesting that, instead of not recording the results, soccer officials could make sure all children are happy by simply giving each one credit for a goal "when he or she touches the ball for the first time."

What an unfortunate distortion. The facts are that children play hard at these tournaments and they know who wins or loses. What's taken away is the glorious trophy ceremony at the end that tells children the trophy is the most important reason for being there.

When adults make winning their priority, their choices often hurt at least some players. When they place winning above nearly everything else, their behaviors can escalate to the kinds of out-of-control antics and violence we see in the headlines.

However, if you heed only the bloodletting and the violence, you will miss the point. There are equally insidious but less obvious ways in which adult egos violate youth sports and suffocate children's spirits every day on fields, in gyms and in ice rinks across the country. The harm is usually perpetrated by seemingly well-intentioned but nevertheless self-centered adults who cannot subjugate their desire to win in order to help all children develop as players. These adults lose sight of the value of staying committed to such bedrock principles as allowing all children equal access, meaningful playing minutes and ownership of what are supposed to be *their* games.

Aren't We Good Enough?

Consider this story about my friend's son. It's not the kind of story that invites newspaper headlines or that generates footage for TV. It is instead a story about a private hurt and its impact on a life, in this case a child's life.

In my friend's town, like many others, the boys' youth basketball program has teams that combine fifth-grade and sixth-grade boys. Tradition dictates that two groups of players rotate court time throughout the game. Typically, the group of sixth-graders plays the first quarter, the group of fifth-graders the second, and the groups share playing time in the second half.

My friend was the assistant coach of one of these teams and the parent of a fifth-grader. The team's head coach was the parent of the sixth-grader widely regarded as the "best" player on the team. Throughout the team's so-called "regular season" games, the head coach rotated the sixth-graders and the fifth-graders. All the boys on the team got pretty much equal time on the court. Then came the playoffs.

Playoffs have a buzz. The kids are excited to play. The

adrenaline among players, coaches and spectators is pumping. Coaches are on full alert. Such was the case as the team took to the court and won its first playoff game, all of the boys sharing playing time and sharing high-fives at the end.

The second playoff game was more of a challenge. Things didn't go well from the start. The sixth-graders got behind in the score in the first quarter, and the fifth-graders stayed behind in the second. The coach started to get that panicked feeling that he might lose this one.

Then, with the scoreboard bearing down on him, his adult ego on the line and victory at the top of his grown-up list of priorities, this youth coach turned his back on half his team. He turned his back on tradition and fair play. He benched all his fifth-graders, who watched from the sidelines as the other boys on the team played the rest of the game.

During this period one of the fifth-graders got off the bench and walked over to the assistant coach with a question: "We're not good enough to play, are we?"

This wasn't about how you play the game. This was about whether you win or lose, and this head coach won his game on the backs of those fifth-grade boys. My friend's son, at age ten, had seen these kinds of things before and he didn't want to see any more. He felt as if he never wanted to play another basketball game. In fact, he never did.

It's doubtful that anyone besides my friend and his son recognized what happened in that gym that day. The drama was not obvious to those who watched the game, but for that child's spirit, the consequences of his coach's actions were devastating. He did not recover from the insult. Many children never do.

Emotional Injuries

These hurts happen all the time in youth sports. They may seem small in the larger context of life, but for a young child trying to figure out where he or she belongs, how he or she compares with peers, if he or she is keeping up or falling behind, these hurts have great impact. Taken in their entirety, over the course of countless youth sports seasons, the toll is heavy indeed.

This is not to say that children should never experience disappointment or that we adults cannot be honest and up front with our children. We can be, and children deserve that, but I won't agree with the idea that it's never too early to learn how "the real world" works or that disappointment at an early age in sports is a good thing because it "toughens up" young players.

There is more than enough time for children to learn about "the real world." There is, on the other hand, a great loss in not letting them experience and enjoy the child's world. They won't get that chance again. As for all that "toughening up," can't we agree that children in this culture have plenty of other challenges? Do we really think it necessary that we add more pressure to their lives at an early age out on the playing fields and in the gyms?

When you are an adult in charge of youth sports, you must think of the children first. You must make that promise whenever you take a team under your wing or whenever you sign up your child to play.

Your children play sports to have fun and to fulfill their needs to socialize, work with teammates, try out new skills and grow. Your children are there to be true to their own sense of self, not yours.

Until the varsity level in high school, the primary goal of youth sports should be player development. At every prior level, including freshman and junior varsity teams, player development and equal or meaningful amounts of playing time for each child should trump winning a game.

For the youngest players in sports, even the term "player development" sounds out of place. The aim of youth sports should be to have fun, get exercise, develop skills and foster a love of the game. The more the adults stay out of it, the better off those bouncy bundles of energy emerging from minivans and sports utility vehicles will be.

Here's a promise: If you read the following chapters with an eye toward how you can change your own actions and the actions of adults around you, you will make good things happen. If enough of you make that leap from thought to action, you will change the world.

The Greek mathematician Archimedes said, "Give me a lever long enough and a place to stand, and I will move the Earth." Ladies and gentlemen, this is your lever.

On the Front Lines

I've put thousands of miles on my Toyota, spent thousands of hours in front of youth sports groups all over New England and the rest of the country. Nothing is more exciting than standing in front of a room full of parents and helping them feel comfortable enough to share emotions they sometimes have been brooding over since their own childhood experiences playing sports.

Many parents know instinctively that something is wrong with the way we conduct our children's sporting lives. And make no mistake: Conduct them we do. In fact, the worst of us are not coaches at all. We're puppeteers.

I also have met plenty of people who are accomplishing wonderful things for children. People who are on the front lines, so to speak, fighting for change on their teams, in their leagues, for their communities. There are terrific youth sports programs across the United States.

For instance, a local newspaper recently ran the headline: "Back to the Past (Basketball) League." Games in this league are run by the boys for the boys, with little adult intervention and no coaches. The next chance I had, I hopped in my car and visited that gym. What a time the kids were having!

That's the payoff: giving upcoming generations some of the joy and unbounded play we knew as kids, an experience so many of us knew a generation or two ago.

I am a jock. Basketball is my passion. I have great affection for a quick game of one-on-one or two-on-two with a group of ex-college ballplayers. Yet when I look back on my days at the University of Pennsylvania and my four seasons in the NBA, I wonder: *How did I go from playing pickup games with neighborhood pals in a small town in Massachusetts to being selected in the first round of the 1975 draft?*

The answer: My skills developed naturally. Before I reached high school, no coach or other adult had tried to push me to become something I, as yet, was not. While growing up outside Boston in Winchester, Massachusetts, I was no better at sports than were my playmates. In fact, I was no better than the millions of kids who right now have already been sized up by their coaches as not very athletic, with low potential.

Coaches Need Not Apply

A key point in this modern equation of youth sports is that the rush to judgment is incredible and shortsighted. I was never judged too quickly, never classified at an early age, and I thrived. I was simply one of the kids in the neighborhood who wanted to play. We all wanted to play. We all wanted to have fun.

I grew up in a family of four children. Other families in our neighborhood had five kids, six, even eight. When I walked out my front door, getting a game together was as easy as lacing up my sneakers, and I gave both tasks little thought. We didn't fret over putting games together. We didn't worry about playing times. We didn't schedule drafts, complete with tryouts and chalkboard sessions. We played. And when the sun was shining on the old sandlot, the wind was in your hair, a bat in your hand, and the whole afternoon in front of you, there was no better place to be.

You may have grown up in a neighborhood like that. You headed for a backyard, park or vacant lot. Mysteriously and inevitably, everyone found his or her way to the game. The games themselves were spontaneous and fun. They had no beginning and no real end, except when the chilling reality of darkness set in or your mother called you home for dinner. That was magic that today's youngsters seldom get a chance to know.

"All of my friends either go away or to overnight camp [in the summer]," wrote a thirteen-year-old boy to *The Boston Globe*. "There is basically no one around to play with. I have never played in a pickup game of baseball in my life, and I get slightly envious when my father tells me about them."

Today when children play sports they nearly always do so at a prescheduled time on a soccer field, basketball court, baseball diamond or ice rink with a coach or two at their backs. There are paid sports officials in their midst, a scoreboard set at an intimidating height and a gallery of parents on the sidelines. *That's* pressure.

On the playgrounds and in the backyards of my youth we made our own rules and sometimes our own baskets and bases. We didn't pay fees to play. We didn't wear expensive sports gear. We got muddy, we got tired, but we never got burned out. If we got hurt, we went home.

We chose our own sides and we settled our own fights. We played as long as it suited us. In the fall, we'd play kickball or baseball until the day it got too cold, and then someone would run inside and grab a football. In winter, it was street hockey or sledding. In spring, we'd find a baseball again and we'd play into the summer until the day it got too hot. Then we'd all figure out where to take a dip.

When we played together we didn't have parents screaming at us to pay attention. No coaches growled that we should have cut to the basket, taken the shot, faked the pass or executed the fancy play that was rehearsed, ad nauseum, at the last practice.

When I played sports as a youth, there was no search for "talent" to put together a grade-three team of select or elite players. "Talent?" What is "talent" at age eight, age ten, age twelve? When I was ten, I was the same uncoordinated kid as the uncoordinated kid who lived down the street. My parents let me play with my pals, and I never gave the NBA a second thought.

I played all sorts of backyard sports as a boy, and eventually I became a star player on my high school basketball team. I also spent enough time on schoolwork to earn a spot in the freshman class at the University of Pennsylvania. By the time I hit college, I was six-foot-seven and 200 pounds. By my senior year, I was a first-round draft pick.

Now I watch my own children and others play sports all the time. I see good things, but I also have no doubt that something wonderful has been lost.

I believe we can re-create something just as wonderful. As much as I like to reminisce, this plan to reform youth sports is *not* based on nostalgia. Try as we might, we cannot go back. We cannot create a world of sports for our children that duplicates the one we had. Nor should we.

Our world today is a lot different from our world in the forties, fifties and sixties. For one thing, leaving the house and meeting friends for a game a few streets away was no big deal for me. I don't think I had to tell my parents I was leaving the neighborhood unless I was really going a distance. That security is gone. Today we sometimes worry about our children when they go next door.

When I was a child there was almost always an adult at home and plenty of other kids looking to play. Today neighborhoods usually empty out in the morning and don't come alive again until dinnertime or later.

For today's children, their sports, most of their leisure time, in fact, must be supervised, at least tangentially, by watchful adults. Systems for organizing children are needed, if nothing else but to keep them safe.

However, the youth sports systems we have allowed to develop, and in some cases overrun our lives, are too often flawed systems. We need to fix them according to the best interests of our children. We need to learn to juggle sometimes-conflicting needs: our needs to protect and organize our children with their need to be free to play on their own.

But why? Why put in all this time and effort? Why not, as many have suggested, just tell the parents to keep quiet, to chill? If everyone would just c-a-l-m d-o-w-n, everything would be fine. Right? Absolutely not. The fact is, our children are getting hurt. They're getting fed up and burned out. And they're giving up.

Telling parents to behave on the sidelines does nothing, for example, to address the most insidious development of modern youth sports: the creation of elite or select teams at young ages. These teams, at the center of so many of our systems, create nothing less than caste systems that classify, rank and exclude children too soon.

Telling parents to behave on the sidelines does nothing to address the disturbing trends in overuse injuries, damage that can derail a sports career before high school or result in permanent difficulties. Telling parents to behave does nothing to address the pain of that fifth-grader who watched as his coach played the older boys, while benching him, for the sake of winning.

Youth sports dropout rates are alarming. Within our current town and city systems, by the time kids are thirteen, an estimated 60 to 70 percent of those who began playing an organized sport at a younger age have dropped out of that sport. Some of this dropout rate is a natural reflection of emerging interests in other activities, but I am certain that youth sports had been ruined for a large percentage.

The studies that tracked this dropout rate asked children why they quit. Too many of their answers had to do with the ways the adults in charge had mismanaged the youth sports experience.

If the owner of a business had a 70 percent failure rate on a product, he or she would shelve it. And that's what I'm saying: Let's shelve much of what we have created in the name of youth sports.

There are other consequences of these misguided youth sports systems. I won't cite statistics on this but will draw from the hundreds of conversations I have had with youth sports organizers and participants, with coaches and with parents.

High school coaches and athletic directors are seeing burnout or plain old fatigue in some of their players, and less passion to play. Many of these teenagers have played hundreds of youth sports games before they even get to high school. Some have physical scars to show. They've been shuttled all over creation as children. Many have played in tournaments out of state or even out of the country. Some have seen all kinds of incentives and material rewards sent their way. Heck, the high school uniforms aren't even as good as those of their elite youth teams.

In our haste to build bigger and better youth sports machines, in our rush to select "the best" and weed out "the rest," we have not increased the talent that is reaching the higher levels—whether that is high school varsity or the pros.

Children who have dropped out before that point will never know how good they might have been, and neither will we.

We can see dropout trends most readily in statistics compiled by what has become something of an oracle for information about youth sports participation and attrition: the Institute for the Study of Youth Sports at Michigan State University. Two researchers there, Martha E. Ewing and Vern Seefeldt, the institute's founder, conducted a pioneering study published in 1989, "Participation and Attrition Patterns in American Agency-Sponsored and Interscholastic Sports." The study is a seminal document, quoted widely whenever people look at children's attitudes toward the youth sports systems that adults have created for them.

The study found that children as young as ten years old drop out in large numbers. Both boys and girls said, above all, that they lost interest and sports stopped being fun. They were tired of playing and felt too much pressure. They complained that practices were too long and boring, and that extended seasons did not leave them enough time to participate in other activities.

Ewing and Seefeldt gave us a map of the huge gulf that exists between what the children want and need from sports and what the adults want and need. My mission in a nutshell is to make sure adults put the wants and needs of the children first. In fact, I hope to change adult perceptions so that they end up wanting and needing from youth sports the same things that children do.

Potential Untapped

Step back from the landscape of youth sports, and it looks like a Norman Rockwell painting: a sunny day, a couple of lawn chairs tucked into the back of the van, a few hours watching children play.

When you step closer, though, there is trouble in the details. Listen to the shouting on the sidelines. Look at the faces of the children on the bench. See the anger and frustration that emerge on the ride home after a losing game. These, too, are the realities of youth sports today.

We need to fight, and fight hard, to encourage healthy systems and widespread participation in youth sports. The Centers for Disease Control and Prevention reports that childhood obesity has doubled since 1980—doubled, that is, during the twenty years in which youth sports systems have been in hyperdrive. Given the time that youngsters spend in front of TVs, computers and video games, youth sports offer one of the few refuges of health and invigoration.

Let me say it again: In preserving youth sports and in rebuilding systems, I am not suggesting we round off the sharp edges. I'm not spreading a gospel of docile and uniform cooperation, a world in which no one gets sweaty and no one cares whether he or she wins or loses. I like competition.

When I played sports as a boy, there was passion in our play. It's true that we picked our own teams and played by our own rules without adult interference, but we played our hearts out. The score did matter. Who won or lost did count. I've heard of children who kept "league standings" of their pickup games. The point is children can be as competitive as adults can be, and my intention is neither to ignore nor stifle that. It would be unnatural. If there's anything I want, it's to keep things natural.

Children in youth sports should be able to express themselves fully, as themselves. If they want to win, and they want to win badly, it should come from them. If they live and die for the competition, so to speak, it should be on their terms.

Easier said than done. Youth sports will always need adults as mentors and monitors. Still, let us beware of the Heisenberg Uncertainty Principle, which states that when we measure a process we always, by definition, change the outcome. Put an adult on a soccer field, even the best-intentioned and most well-trained of the lot, and the children will behave differently than if they were there alone. The adults, just by being there, change the outcome. Children will spend some of their time playing for their parents.

We can't get around that, but we can recognize the power we have simply by our presence, and we can think of ways to offer support but, when appropriate, disappear into the background—such as staying away from practices and, now and then, skipping a game.

I chuckle when parents proudly tell me they haven't missed even one practice or game in the seven years their children have been playing sports. Here's a little secret: Whether he or she says it or not, your child doesn't always want you there. He or she doesn't always have the gumption to say so.

It is a great experience watching your children play a game

and, sure, children are proud when their parents are there to see them score. For games far from home, it may be important that you are available in case your child is injured. However, if you are frantic about scheduling all of your children's practices and games into *your* life, too, you are showing them how important *you* think it is for *you* to be there. Sometimes a case of parental guilt or a full-blown example of a parent reliving his or her own childhood through a child's accomplishments is involved. Whatever their reasons, many parents would never consider intentionally missing a game. They think it's a failure; I think it's a good idea.

Radical Moves

Adults are overly invested, overly zealous, overly stressed. It all comes back to the same thing. Adults have taken an increasingly active role in their children's sports, sometimes to the point of manipulation.

As we gaze into the rearview mirror of modern history, we see a ratcheting up of the pressure adults put on children. Radical changes in family structures and suburban sprawl took away key ingredients needed for sandlot and backyard games. Television played a part, too, helping to create new heroes in sports and pushing the ones who play professionally into the stratosphere of mass entertainment, celebrity and hero worship. Professional salaries soared. Soon city and suburban kids dreamed about becoming millionaires by playing a game.

As intently as the youth were watching, so were the parents. Too often, adults took their cues from the highest echelons of achievement; that is, college sports, the Olympics and the pros. Adults dreamed of glory for their children and also for themselves. More and more adults got involved as youth coaches. When they set up structures and systems for their children, they looked at the only models they knew: varsity high school, college and professional sports. With adults at the helm, youth sports teams and leagues grew exponentially. Schedules got more complicated and uniforms got fancier.

At the outset children played inside their communities, against each other. Then parents began to think that having eight teams of fourth-graders, composed of all levels of abilities, was perhaps not the best way to organize their children's sports. They worried about the "better" players. It didn't seem fair, they thought, to hold back these "prodigies" by forcing them to play with children of lesser ability.

Select teams were created. Children were stuck with ability rankings, and a caste system was born. Managers of elite teams in one community challenged elite teams in other communities. The travel-team system intensified. Select teams of children younger than grade seven—which should be the youngest ages for select teams—began traveling outside the boundaries of their communities to play select teams of children in other communities. That, my friends, has made all the difference. It is the core of the problem in youth sports. No other factor comes close in influencing the sorry path we have forged for our children and ourselves.

With select teams in place, winning became the priority. No longer was it simply team against team within the same community. Taking a team out of town almost always makes the competition more intense. You likely don't know the guy coaching the other team. You don't know his kids or his wife. It's no longer just a children's game, but rather a contest for community bragging rights.

Select travel teams are cauldrons of trouble, mixing a brew of emotions that intoxicates even the most level-headed adult.

Everything gets cranked up. This is why select travel teams are cauldrons of trouble, mixing a brew of emotions that intoxicates even the most level-headed adult.

To be deemed good enough to play in these systems, children must be evaluated. As soon as you start evaluating "talent" in order to create select teams at young ages—and to cut children from those teams—you lose. Everyone loses.

"Talent" identified early is often pushed too hard, and that takes a toll on young minds and bodies, often creating a child who burns out at an early age and even quits the sport. Cutting children from teams or keeping them on the bench for most, maybe all, of a game—or the better part of an entire season—robs them of valuable playing time and development. Awarding select players (the chosen) with most of the playing time pumps up their egos to unrealistic highs and discourages the ambitions of kids on the bench who have equal potential to become great players at maturity.

Finally, orchestrating young children's sports games primarily from the perspective of boosting the score overly focuses children on adult-driven strategies—things such as a full-court press in grade-five basketball. That's the defensive strategy those boys on the Dayton select team were struggling with. This approach robs players of the fullest opportunity to develop creativity, individual skills and strong team interaction. Children are so afraid to make mistakes that they often will not take risks—and taking risks is an essential ingredient for developing players.

Nagging Doubts

If you are the parent of a child playing youth sports today, chances are you have wrestled with uncomfortable thoughts. You may have nagging doubts or a feeling that things are not as they should be.

At the start of a grueling season that doesn't seem to have an end, in the middle of a tirade between coach and players, at the end of a stressful car ride to a faraway gym, you may have wondered, "Am I doing the right thing? Is my child happy? Am I happy?"

Look at all the overanxious parents and overscheduled kids and you get the sense that we have lost our compass. Many of us are thrashing about for new directions.

We have laws in this country about child labor. We restrict the age for drinking and driving. We legislate against second-hand smoke. We vigilantly guard for signs of child exploitation, child neglect and child abuse. Yet every day, all over the United States, parents sign their children into youth sports programs that have few if any limits on how many games their children will be forced to play, how hard and at what costs they will be pushed to win, and how young they will be held to adult standards, adult goals, adult-strength stress.

Parents seldom check on their youth league's mission statement. They seldom check out the coach's philosophy or the team's rules about whether all children will be given a fair chance to play.

If you are the parent of a child playing organized youth sports today, chances are your family is feeling the stress. Chances are the adults have organized an unnatural, over-scheduled, ill-intentioned and sometimes irresponsible sys-tem. Chances are that system has created parents who must be ordered to keep silent on the sidelines or enrolled in clin-ics on how to behave at games. Chances are your child is pay-ing a price.

You Say You Want a Revolution?

In more optimistic moments, I envision how this message will convince everyone of the need for change, but long ago I understood just how much preaching to the choir I do. Those who want to listen to suggestions for reforming youth sports are often quite vocal at my talks. I want to reach those who are not speaking up.

The world of adults involved in youth sports is roughly divided into three groups. About 20 percent understand either on their own or because of their background and expe-rience how to make healthy choices for children. Another 20 percent, with due respect, are quite off the mark. Then there's the great majority—often a silent majority—in the middle. Their hearts and minds are generally in the right place, but they are easily caught up in the roar of the crowd. They are easily swayed by the zealots. Many of them may sense things have gone wrong, but they're just not sure what they can do about it. These are perhaps the people we need to reach most of all.

This is nothing short of a revolution. Our troops need organizing. They need to see the power in their numbers.

We need to dismantle parts of the youth sports systems that are in place. We need to rebuild. We have strength in numbers, for sure, but now we need a united purpose to find our way.

With open minds and the best interests of our children at heart, let us begin.

CHAPTER 2

Elite Teams: The Unkindest Cuts of All

*We're putting too much emphasis
on physically gifted athletes instead of
developing all those who want to participate.
It's no wonder that we lose more than
half of them by the time
they are teenagers.*

Gary Allen, national staff coach,
U.S. Soccer

This youth sports revolution has a battle charge, and this is it: Eliminate elite teams before grade seven.

This is a radical move for adults—heresy, to some—but it is essential. If the adults in charge do not make this move, they will do little to solve most problems in youth sports. Elite teams are at the center of those problems and, therefore, must be at the center of the solutions.

Elite teams are those that attempt to select out the top "talent" in a particular age group and travel to play the top "talent" in other communities. They are also known as the select, travel, competitive (versus recreational), "A" (versus "B") and all-star teams. But please keep in mind that what I suggest, even the most radical moves, will not dilute competition, interfere with any athlete's future success or take away the fun. In fact, these moves will do quite the opposite.

When I suggest eliminating select teams before grade seven, I recognize there are differences in athletic abilities among children in the same age group. For the vast majority of children, however, these differences are truly insignificant. The first point is that there are usually only a few children in any age group, especially at young ages, who are noticeably more skilled than the rest. There is very little difference in ability among the vast majority, too little difference to start labeling and eliminating. The second point is that abilities change significantly among children from year to year, sometimes within the same season. Among adults there is a wider discrepancy of athletic abilities, and those abilities are less likely to change year to year. The current relative athletic ability of a young child, particularly a child who has not reached the onset of puberty, is not an accurate predictor of his or her future athletic talent.

The most important thing adults committed to reforming youth sports can do is to put off selecting "the best" and eliminating "the rest" at an early age. We must abolish the youth sports caste systems that rank children according to their athletic abilities and entrap children as young as five.

When you attack the hierarchy of select teams, however, you enter a maelstrom of disagreements and passionate convictions among parents about what is best for children. This issue cuts to the core of arguments over being "more competitive," playing at a "higher level," identifying "talent," getting used to "the way it is in the real world," lessons about winning and losing, tryouts, cuts, playing time, benching, tournaments, trophies, varsity stars, college scholarships and professional contracts.

To find their way out of this whirlwind of divisive issues, adults in charge of youth sports systems must commit to tearing down team structures that feed caste systems at young ages. Parents must learn to say "no." That's right. They must learn to say "no" to an elite team at a young age even if their child is invited to join.

At the kindergarten through grade-two levels, adults should not spend any time evaluating "athletic ability." For this age group, traditional team structures and formal games aren't always the best choices anyway, so there is certainly no need to be selective.

In grades three and grades four, adults—please, not the parents of these children—may conduct general assessments and try to create teams with general parity, mixed groups of children who have ranges of skills in this particular sport. Teams at this level should play each other within their own community. Traveling to other communities to play at this age is a waste of precious time.

In grades five and six, adults—again, not the parents of these children—may conduct general assessments and create teams of mixed abilities which may, if they choose, travel to play teams from other communities that, hopefully, have also been convinced of the wisdom of creating mixed teams. Two rules apply here. The first is this: Don't use the grade-three or grade-four evaluations or previous team placements to figure out where these children belong in grade five or grade six. Children can change radically from year to year, and so can their skills. Start with a clean slate. Do not stereotype, or you will create another caste system. The second rule is that no child should be cut at this age.

In grades seven and eight, adults—again, not the parents of these children—may evaluate players' skills and create stratified teams that place children together according to their similar levels of ability. Set up rules about equal or meaningful playing time in order to develop all players on all teams. Tread carefully in this new territory, though, because adult choices at this critical age that cater to certain players often discourage those children who might be terrific athletes when they mature. Do not cut children at this age from your programs.

At grade nine, children enter high school. Even at the freshman and junior varsity level, where there will likely be tryouts and cuts for interscholastic teams, adults should commit to developing all players who make these teams. These children, some as young as thirteen and fourteen, will continue to change athletically from year to year, sometimes radically, through senior year and even beyond. So-called "late bloomers" are often just coming into their own at these ages. Continue to develop as many young players as possible. You cannot predict the future, not even a future as close as a high school varsity team.

Priorities First

To rewrite youth sports rules in order to bolster sportsmanship principles, but to leave in place a system that foolishly courts elite teams at young ages, is to miss the point of this youth sports revolution.

If adults see their children on a path of "athletic success," they are likely to discount much of this book. If adults have a child who has been cut at an early age, benched or burned out, they are likely to consider a different take.

From whatever perspective you arrive at this discussion, however, please consider all sides. Youth sports systems that are created for the greatest good of the greatest number of children will be the right choices for all children—from the child who appears to have the greatest athletic potential at a young age, to the child who may not show that potential until later, to the child who never shows any athletic talent.

Creating youth sports systems that truly serve all children's needs will offer our future athletic stars the best environment in which to grow up, as well as to develop as team players. These ideas are not about creating a happy place where there is no competition, no one wins or loses, and no one is challenged. These ideas are about creating vibrant competition, invigorating challenge and hard-fought contests in which, yes, there *is* a winning score. But, for sure, the goal is to create a happier experience for our children. They deserve that.

Boy Goalie:
Have Talent, Will Travel

TOM MORONEY

MetroWest Daily News

June 21, 1998

Even in these hard-charging, sports-crazy times, the ad in the paper almost socked me in the eye.

"Goaltender," it said. "Under 10 male relocating July 1. Talented travel goalkeeper seeks team in this area."

A little person, younger than ten, was shopping his services as a soccer goalie? Had the world gone completely mad?

To find out, I called the number in the ad. After several attempts, I hooked up with the parents who placed the ad.

They have two children: a daughter, seven, and a boy, nine. The boy's name is Matthew. And his mother says he's a soccer goalie without equal.

The family was moving from their home in Pennsylvania to Massachusetts by the first of the next month. The right soccer team was a must.

"The ad was his father's idea," said the mother. "But the idea of finding a competitive team in the area is Matthew's."

I must admit, the whole idea of taking out an ad for a nine-year-old first struck me as wacky. But Matthew's father, come to find out, has had quite a bit of success with the technique.

For one thing, he's a corporate recruiter who uses ads to find the right executive for the right job. For another, he also found his wife through a personal ad in *Boston* magazine.

Ads are also used in the Philadelphia area by a number of soccer coaches who post their need for players, Matthew's mother said. "You see it quite a bit down here," she said. "Coaches looking for certain kinds of players to fill out their teams."

Both of their children play soccer, but Matthew is more intense, said his mother. He is so competitive, in fact, that he doesn't even play in his hometown or his home state of Pennsylvania. Instead, he goes to where the competition is better: Delaware. There, he is a member of the Hockessin Lightnings.

He is four-foot-eight, seventy-three pounds. "And he's strong," his mother told me. "He also has great hand-eye," which is short for hand-eye coordination, a valuable asset for a goalie.

Matthew plays soccer nearly all year, and has recently expanded his sports repertoire to include baseball and basketball. But he's only nine and some people may think his parents are pushing him too hard, too early, I suggested.

His mother was pleasant but firm in her response. "If he doesn't want to do it, he doesn't have to," she said. "The only thing we say is that if Matty makes a commitment to a team, he has to see it through." In other words, no quitting in the middle of a season. Other than that, he can quit soccer whenever he wants.

And what about the response to the ad?

"It's been great," she said. "We've had several calls."

Matthew is excited, said his mother.

"Good luck," I said, but, somehow, I didn't think he'd need it. ■

Just Say No

The call to eliminate elite teams at young ages aims directly at community systems that create such squads within their programs and at elite teams that are entities unto themselves.

In many communities adults independently create elite teams in a particular sport and compete within a regional group comprised of other such teams. Some clubs are, by their own definition, competitive or elite clubs.

If you are an adult intent on creating these systems at young ages, I ask you to stop. If you are a parent faced with deciding whether to allow your child to try out for or to join an elite system at a young age, consider not joining.

I call for no cuts until grade nine. Some elite teams and independent systems field only one team; they're all about trying to identify "the best" and, by necessity in their book, there must be cuts. If these systems cut children from programs before grade nine, those systems should go and new ones should be created to take their place.

Select teams, in my mind, are often the creation of adults focused on ways to prove their children are as good as, or better than, the rest of the children. Parents often use select teams to prove that they are good, or better, parents. Select teams are often about not getting "left behind" if you perceive that other children are "getting ahead." Select teams are also about winning.

Okay, let's consider that last point. I know what's coming. I've heard it often before — it's the "I am *not* trying to win at all costs" rebuttal. Let me clarify: I don't think many coaches try to win at *all* costs. I do think they're often willing to pay too high a price. If, as a parent or as a coach of a young team, you make decisions based primarily on how to win a game rather than on how to develop all your players for the future, you make poor choices for children now and foolhardy moves toward that future.

Please don't assume I have tunnel vision on this issue of select teams. Good things do happen on select teams. There are select-team coaches who teach their charges a lot about a sport. There are coaches who care, and there are select-team players who excel. And everyone, players and parents, often have great fun in the process.

The downside of these select systems, though, is heavy indeed. The toll that select teams take on individual children, including those who are cut and those who participate intensely, and on youth sports systems in general, is insidious.

The Heart of the Trouble

Many youth sports reformers shy away from this bold step of abolishing select teams before grade seven. In many ways, this is the third rail of the youth sports debate. Touch it and you might get hurt, seriously hurt.

Some reformers talk around this issue; others try to see if they can throttle down the tension, the anxiety, the pressure involved in the select-team culture. It's no use. The select team is not simply an appendage in most communities; it is the heart of many youth sports systems.

Creating and lavishing attention on select teams within a community program often sets an agenda for the rest of the program. Practice time, number of games, length of seasons, type of conditioning and drills, the very attitudes of the coaches and the parents on the sidelines, are influenced by the possibility that their children might make the elite squad now, at the end of the season, or in the coming years.

Even when the elite squads are independent entities, you often see an impact on the more, shall we say, democratic youth sports systems in town. You hear this impact in the disdainful way some adults say the words "recreational" and "intramural." To those adults, those other sports systems are for children who can't make the cut, not for those who have a real shot at future athletic success.

Children affected by sports systems intent on identifying and nurturing "talent" at an early age pay a price. This selective process can be damning both for those selected early and for those left behind.

I'm not alone in saying this. At the annual National Soccer Coaches Association of America convention in 1998, according to an article in *The Cincinnati Enquirer*, a panel of coaches and former professional players—including soccer legend Pelé—blasted youth sports systems that promote elite teams for children younger than fourteen, saying, simply, that is too early an age to weed out "the best."

Tony Waiters, a former coach of the Canadian national soccer team, told that same convention that most future stars cannot be identified at age thirteen or fourteen. "We tell this ten-year-old she is the greatest thing since sliced bread," added Tom Fleck, director of coaching and player development for the Idaho Youth Soccer Association. "We tell three or four other ten-year-olds they aren't as good as 'she' is."

"We're putting too much emphasis on physically gifted athletes, instead of developing all those who want to participate," said Gary Allen, director of coaching education for the Virginia Youth Soccer Association, in the November 2000 issue of the *Georgia Tech Sports Medicine & Performance Newsletter*. "It's no wonder that we lose more than half of them by the time they are teenagers."

The pressure to win often inhibits the children who are playing from being spontaneous, creative and taking risks during the game.

Select teams, with winning as a primary goal, also often have negative effects on young children learning to play a sport. Coaching choices made to protect the score of a game often stifle natural forces that would serve to better develop more players. The pressure to win often influences coaches to play those children they believe will most help them to win, and to bench or to give less playing time to the rest. The pressure to win often inhibits the children who are playing from being spontaneous, creative and taking risks during the game.

Mistakes are usually not welcome. Adults often manage these teams tightly, with moves closely choreographed and loudly criticized. Children learn by doing, and on these elite teams children too often learn simply to do what adults tell them to do. They get little chance to learn to be themselves as players, or to figure out what that means.

In a *Sports Illustrated* article that analyzed World Cup competition during the year of the NSCAA soccer panel discussion, writer Ian Thomsen described the game between the United States and Iran. The Iranians had grown up playing in the streets or on dirt fields with cheap plastic balls and "no coaching to speak of until their mid-teens. . . . In defeating the Americans for Iran's first World Cup victory," Thomsen wrote, the Iranians "exhibited an ear for the game, whereas the U.S. players seemed to be reading from sheet music."

Spontaneous play. Creativity. A love of the game. Freedom to take risks. These are the ingredients of great games and great players. These qualities do not require a system of select teams. As you've read, these qualities are often stifled by an elite system in which a coach, putting himself or herself under pressure to win, begins choreographing instead of coaching.

Pride Has Its Price

The speed at which youth sports have gone from sandlot to elite teams is stunning. During the past few decades youth sports have become a vast array of interlocking adult-run directorates.

At first youth sports systems were created in communities with city and town leagues generally for nine- to sixteen-year-olds. Quickly systems progressed—or regressed—to a point at which four-year-olds found themselves putting on team uniforms and executing drills.

Once community leagues were in place, adults went looking for a more sophisticated top-down organization. They went looking for more ways to compete against other adult-run teams. That meant league commissioners searched beyond their borders, to other communities. Thus was born the concept of elite or select travel teams.

In most places once a select team was established for eleven-year-olds, within the next year or so a select team was created for ten-year-olds, and so on, "creeping" down to five- and six-year-olds, known in soccer as the U-6 (under six) division. This phenomenon blossomed as the sport of soccer grew, with competitive travel teams creeping downward into lower and lower age groups. I call this "soccer creep," although it is found in most every team sport in most every community.

How far will this creep go? Can't you almost envision the day when "U-0" elite soccer teams will be selected: those children identified in utero as showing the strongest potential to be all-stars? Selection would be based on gene profiles (parents' sports accomplishments and siblings' records) and the strength of the baby's "kick" during his or her ultrasound.

That's an exaggeration, for sure, but here's a reality: A few years ago a Texas TV news station aired a plea for community fund-raising in the wake of devastating floods that caused $15 million in damage to the area. Because the floods interfered with fund-raising plans, a local baseball team was reaching out for fifteen hundred dollars to enable it to travel to a state baseball championship tournament.

The team? All-star T-ball players, boys and girls ages five and six. At an age when even scores shouldn't be important, this community selected elite teams of kindergarteners. Why? "Parents insist on it," an organization representative told Dan Schofield, a youth specialist for the U.S. Air Force, in 1997, and he wrote about it in S.A. *Kids Magazine,* a San Antonio publication.

Any parent involved in youth sports can tell you that select teams are the pride and joy of most youth organizations today. These elite teams field only handpicked kids, deemed to be the best and brightest right now and likely to be the best and brightest in the future. Because of the attention and prestige, most kids aspire to be on these squads, and so do their parents. It's exciting. As a parent, you're proud.

But this badge of pride has its price. And you never know which year you or your child will be asked to pay.

A Troubling Side

At the heart of elite teams are the tryouts: who makes these select teams and who is eliminated.

Let's say your community has a select squad for third-grade basketball. Ten kids make the team the first year. When next year's tryouts roll around for the fourth-grade select squad, who will make the team? The kids from the third-grade squad have had a year of practicing and playing together. Which coach is going to want to call the parents of one of those third-graders and tell them they've been cut from the fourth-grade squad?

If there are fifty children trying out for sixteen spots, you may have two or three who stand out, but the others are all pretty similar in athletic ability. Certain players, though, are almost assured of making the cut: the coach's child, the assistant coach's child and, perhaps, their closest friends.

Once a select squad has been culled from those who tried out, these elite teams are usually self-fulfilling prophecies. Those deemed to be "the best" often receive more coaching, more chances to play, more practice time, even better facilities to play in. They may seem to get relatively "better" than kids who have not been given the chance to play.

These select teams erode the self-confidence of the children who aren't selected. These teams ramp up the pressure on the anointed ones. These teams create false bravado in players who begin to see themselves as prepubescent "stars."

Elite teams also feed into the trend toward specialization in one sport at young ages. If more more more is better better better, then—the thinking goes—playing a sport for more than one season will create a more proficient and advanced player. Play outdoors. Play indoors. Don't miss a tournament. Sign up for summer camp. How about private tutoring? How about getting started in kindergarten?

One night I got a telephone call from a father who said he wanted me to work one-on-one with his son to help him improve his basketball skills. I get these calls now and then, and I have worked with high school and college players, as well as professionals. I asked the father the age of his son. His answer: six.

I laughed at first, figuring one of my buddies had put him up to this, but the silence on the other end of the line let me know quickly that this father was serious. What, I asked him, would you want me to work on with your son? He suggested I could work with him on "defense." I laughed again, but then I got serious.

I was very tough on this father, who most likely had called me in a sincere but nonetheless absurd effort to give his son a head start on his athletic career. If your son, I told this father, discovers over the coming years that he likes basketball and if he wants to work with me—in seven years, maybe—give me a call then.

Listen to me, I told this father. The way you're talking now has me worried about whether your son will make it to eighth-grade basketball. You have already burdened him with the mantle that he's going to be good at this. That is a frightening first step for your first-grader. The father of this six-year-old certainly had anxious expectations.

I always turn down requests for sports tutoring of young children. I know I could pick up a nice piece of change doing that kind of work, but it goes against what I believe. I would never start tutoring a child before he or she is in eighth grade, and even then I would have a talk with the parents and with the child to make sure this is something the child wants to do, not just something the parents want so they can say their child is working with someone who used to play in the NBA.

The Stakes Are Too High

Select teams also pump up the intensity of the adults on the sidelines. The stakes are higher and, therefore, so are the emotions. All the more reason to reiterate: No child before grade seven should be on an elite travel team. Not your gifted slugger who, at age eight, shows he could have the power and grace of Ken Griffey Jr., not the hockey forward who, at age nine, has the potential of a Mario Lemieux-like slap shot.

No children of that age should be subjected to the rigors, the commuting time, the anxiety or, yes, the expense. That whole elite-team culture makes it too easy to lose sight of the fact that these are still simply children playing games.

After one of my talks to an audience of parents in New England, the father of a fourth-grader picked for an all-star basketball team was incensed. "How," he asked, "do I reward my son for excelling at basketball if I don't give him the chance to be on the select team?"

"Excelling," I said, befuddled, "in *fourth* grade?"

It gets better: Every one of those children chosen for the all-star team at the end of the season was the son of a regular-season team coach in that league.

Two other parents in that audience had fourth-grade sons who did not make that select team. One of the fathers spoke up: "My son," he said, "is probably as good as others who were chosen."

"Right now," I told both these fathers, "there are thousands of kids across the country who are much better fourth-grade basketball players than either of your sons. How much sense does it make in this small town, at age nine or ten, for a boy to be told that he's not good enough to make the cut? Your elite team is there for one reason: the adults' egos."

This scenario is depicted in a great cartoon by Joel Pett, a Lexington (Kentucky) *Herald-Leader* cartoonist who won a Pulitzer Prize in 2000. In Pett's cartoon, two parents are walking toward the playing fields at a school. The father wears a sweater bearing the logo "Saint Lordovers Academy." The parents' car sports a bumper sticker: "My kid's an honors student. Your kid's a loser." The cartoon dialogue bubble offers this question from the mother: "But if *everyone's* children achieve, how will we know ours are superior?" Funny stuff, and so true.

The problem for many parents and coaches is that select teams are so ingrained in a youth sports system's mind-set that it is hard for adults to step back and see the error in their ways. It's hard to pull apart the status quo in order to consider how we got to this point, and whether this is a good point at which to be.

If you and your child are among the chosen ones, part of the select-team crowd, how much passion will you have for standing up and saying this just isn't the right thing to do? If you and your child have already been excluded, how much courage will you have to stand up and say this is not about sour grapes, this is not about pride, this is not about my child not making the team? Will you be able to argue that this is about doing the right thing for *all* children?

For too many parents the pressures are daunting. So they go along, year after year, continuing to be part of the problem by not finding the passion and the courage to be part of the solution.

Back Away: Children at Play

When you think about these things, think about a game you played as a child—good old-fashioned tag. It's great fun to play and a game that teaches fundamental athletic skills in a way that children naturally play.

Just imagine what would happen if the adults decided they ought to jump in, help out and organize tag games for their kids. Actually, you know what would happen. Within a few years, they would have sliced, diced and organized tag to death.

The adults would start with their basic needs for organization and management. They would find the fields, organize teams, set schedules. If the kids were going to play tag, obviously they'd need adults to tell them how to play. They'd need coaches. The coaches would need assistant coaches to keep track of tag minutes, tag assists and tag hits. The coaches would need to figure out how to beat the other tag teams.

If they were expected to beat the other tag teams, the adults would worry that their taggers might not improve as quickly as the other taggers, so they would figure they'd need tag practices. The more, the better. Two tag practices and a tag game each week.

During the first season, the adults would notice different levels of tag abilities. Next, the adults would worry about how their best taggers could get better fast enough if they continue to play with their worst taggers.

A mother or father would be sitting in the tag bleachers thinking, "You know, my kid is just a born tagger. I'm sitting next to so-and-so, and his or her child is just not a good tagger. My kid needs more competitive tagging."

Enough adults would start to think this way that they would contact The Town Next To Them, which would have started its own tag teams. Towns would get together and form a tag conference. Another board, more meetings. A regional tag commission. Our tag all-stars against your tag all-stars. That would result in tag evaluations and tag tryouts. Soon enough, some eight-year-olds would be told, "You're just not good enough to play tag."

By that time, the commercial lines of tag shoes, tag shirts and tag caps would already be on the shelves. They'd probably have overnight tag bags for those serious taggers who travel to tag tournaments.

When you force teams of second-, third- and fourth-graders to travel to other communities to play their teams, you create all sorts of negative and unnecessary consequences. Parents and children are forced to spend a great deal of time traveling. Those hours in the car, SUV or minivan are usually wasted hours, and they're often stressful hours because you're late, hungry and have *so many other things to do.*

In addition to the adult energy required to organize and carry out these complicated travel schedules, select travel systems raise adult expectations. Adults begin to see games as more serious, and they feel there's more on the line. Egos and politics take over. All sorts of bad things flow from the added pressure.

A Losing Proposition

Among other ways adults select and label "talent" at young ages is to assign weighted values to squads of players within the same age grouping, as is done in hockey. Most young hockey players, after graduating from pushing the chair around the ice, go into what is called the "mite" system. Mite organizers usually break up the mites into A, B and C teams, based on their relative prowess. Remember, these kids are between the ages of six and nine.

As a mite "A," you are generally considered better than a mite "B" and that much better than a mite "C." It's insidious because, in many cases, the die is cast. You are an "A" for the rest of your young career, as you move into bantam and other hockey age divisions. The same thing happens in soccer, basketball and football, and in baseball's minor and major leagues.

Parents form cliques, in many cases strong political forces with which to reckon. In practical terms, this means that once your child is an A, you're not going to stand by idly if, in the next season, the league organizers want to make him or her a B. You're an A parent; you're not a B parent. You will rant. You will call other A parents. You will find ways to make the coach miserable if he or she persists in telling you that your son is now a B.

Hopefully, you know by now how really terrible this caste system is.

Once young players understand the caste system, they often see that their chances of being "promoted" are close to nil. This drives some of them right out of the sport. It certainly diminishes self-esteem. And for what? Though the As before puberty will not always be the As after puberty, based on athletic ability alone, our caste system is often a self-fulfilling prophecy. Those children anointed as

As get the upper edge and often hold on to it while the Bs who had equal potential get left behind.

You can even feel the pressure placed upon As, the pressure to win. After all, they're the best. Right? A father who had played college football, and thus understands sports pressure better than most parents, told me it was excruciating for him to watch his mite-A son playing hockey. Uncomfortable tension in the stands and the coach's yelling made it all the worse. This father admitted, "I'd rather have my son on the Bs. Maybe he would have some fun there."

Level the Playing Field

As children move into upper elementary and middle schools, teams may be put together based on children's athletic abilities—teams of mixed abilities at first, and ability-level teams later. As an adult, you must commit to taking politics out of this game. You must start fresh each year, evaluating each child based on that child at that time; things change dramatically from year to year.

Another good idea is described in a chapter of the book *The Child and Adolescent Athlete.* Robert Malina, Ph.D., retired director of the Institute for the Study of Youth Sports at Michigan State University, and Gaston Beunen, Ph.D., a professor at Katholieke Universiteit Leuven in Belgium, are the authors. They call on those in charge of tryouts to put the evaluations of children's athletic abilities in the hands of adults who are neither coaching the teams in question nor who have a child who is trying out at the same time. They also recommend considering the qualifications of the evaluators.

"The majority of coaches in youth sports are volunteers," they write. "Many have had personal experiences in a particular sport, but they may not have had experiences with children and youth in the context of sport and in the assessment of skill. Many volunteer coaches also have a child involved in the sport, which may complicate the assessment process."

Parents of children labeled as talented may develop a false sense of potential for their child's success in sport.

Once evaluations are completed, Malina and Beunen write, "Children should then be assigned to a team and then the team assigned to a coach. Drafting players, lotteries, recruiting players and so on often create extreme competitiveness, and at times, ill-will among coaches and parents."

In an article written for the spring 1997 issue of the Institute for the Study of Youth Sports newsletter, *Spotlight on Youth Sports*, Malina also cautions parents of those children who are chosen for select teams: "Parents of children labeled as talented may develop a false sense of potential for their child's success in sport either in the form of a college scholarship or a professional career. Some parents even invest considerable sums of money in early sport training for their children. . . . It must be emphasized, however, that the numbers are many and the probability of success is miniscule. . . . Early identification of 'talent' is no guarantee of success in sport during childhood, let alone during adolescence and adulthood. There are simply too many intervening variables associated with normal growth, maturation and development, and the sports system itself."

How many children do you suppose never get the chance to see whether those "intervening variables" would have turned them into a great athlete at maturity? How many have been discouraged or given up long before that? I'll tell you: too many.

Let Them All Play

Many years ago I was asked to officiate a scrimmage between the two "select" teams of sixth-grade boys' basketball players in my community. I walked into the gym that day to find thirty youngsters warming up. An uncomfortable feeling welled in my stomach.

I asked the coaches how they had selected these squads—in other words, "How many kids did you cut?"

They told me that thirty-seven boys had tried out—thirty had been selected for two teams and seven had been cut. What did those coaches tell those seven boys? They told them there were things they could work on to improve and they could try out again next year.

Have you ever watched sixth-grade boys play five-on-five basketball? My neighbor had the best description: "It's pathetic." Simply put, none of them is very good.

As I officiated this scrimmage of sixth-grade boys, I got angry. Seven boys had been cut, seven boys were likely sitting at home, maybe playing video games while their friends were being given the chance to play basketball. That bothered me.

At the end of the scrimmage, I walked over to the coaches. I told them that I had spent four years playing in the NBA, that I have worked as a professional basketball scout since. I told them that if they had asked me to watch those thirty-seven original sixth-grade hopefuls try out, I could have picked out five, six or seven boys who were the "least worst" of the entire group of players. Notice I didn't say the "best." That would make you think that sixth-grade basketball players are good, and I can assure you they are not.

Then I could have concentrated on watching the other thirty "less than least worst" players. I could have watched them for another three hours—or maybe another three days—and I would not have been able to tell much difference in abilities among them. "How," I asked these coaches, "could you have cut seven of these kids? What criteria did you use?"

While they couldn't give me a good answer, I knew one thing for sure: All their sons made the team. I tell parents, sarcastically, that if they want to make sure their children make an elite travel squad, they have to offer to coach the team.

Instead of cutting seven boys from tryouts and creating two "elite" squads of fifteen players each, my community should have created three teams of about twelve boys, or four teams of about nine boys, established man-to-man defense, and guaranteed each player a minimum twelve minutes of playing time. That would have been in the best interests of *all* the children.

Keep Dreams Alive

In many cases what is seen as a golden opportunity—being selected for an elite team—becomes a painful experience, a defining moment for some young players.

I know a boy who worked hard to make a select basketball team in a town near mine. He loved the game. He loved it so much that even when he didn't make the cut for this elite team in sixth grade, he tried again in seventh. In eighth grade, he finally became one of the ten chosen ones. This was prestige, the chance to walk around school feeling as though people knew he was a cut above.

Once on the team, it was a different story. The pressure to achieve—to win, win, win—killed off any chance for spontaneity and fun. There was nothing spontaneous about this play. Every move up the court, every pass, every shot was thought out and directed by the adults running this squad.

This boy didn't see much playing time, just a few minutes here and there, sometimes no minutes if the game was close all the way through. This boy, after all, had barely made the squad, had been added into a core group of "veterans" who had played together for many of their young years and knew the game plan like the back of their hands. It was difficult for this boy to catch up and fit in.

Toward the end of the season, he had had enough of giving up his weekends to sit on the bench and maybe play for a few minutes here and there. Enough of the insults to his confidence when his few minutes under pressure didn't go well. Enough of all the coaches' and parents' tension, enough of their yelling at the sports officials and kicking of bleachers. This boy finally told his parents he didn't like basketball anymore.

Yet a funny thing happened to him on the way out of eighth grade. He had a chance to play in a *recreational* basketball league. Each team had an adult coach, but they were there basically to get the game underway and to make substitutions. Every boy played equal time. The plays during the games were basically up to the boys—you know, spontaneous. And fun. This boy had a ball. He couldn't wait to get down to that gym.

Playing in that recreational league probably kept this boy in the sport. He didn't really hate basketball. He hated the basketball system that had destroyed everything he liked about playing the game, a kind of destruction that is widespread in youth sports. The more it occurs, and the fewer alternative choices offered our children, the more of them walk away and give up. Remember the Michigan State survey that asked children why they quit? It's just not fun anymore.

Instead of incubators for success, breeding grounds for future stars, elite teams can be dead ends of frustration and wasted potential, particularly if you are a child watching from the bench or the parent watching your child watch from the bench.

Damage to the Sport Itself

The implicit mission of select teams is to nurture and develop the players of tomorrow. The ten who are picked for the select team in boys' basketball in the sixth grade, for example, often carry with them the expectation that someday they will play varsity in high school or play beyond high school. Individually, some of these players—along with their parents and coaches—carry the expectation that they will earn a college scholarship or a shot at the pros.

Yet the ultimate irony of the select-team mind-set is that the system is actually hurting the sport at those higher levels. Select systems sometimes discourage and derail the very children who, had they been supported as young players, might have been sports stars at maturity. Unfortunately, select teams cut those potential stars before bodies and minds have fully developed.

I am living proof of this concept. When I was in sixth grade—I would have been ten years old at the start of the 1964 basketball season—if you had put me in a gym with thirty other boys in my class, I would have been ranked twentieth, maybe even twenty-fifth in terms of skill, coordination and maturity. I could have been cut easily during my preteen years, and eventually I would have caught on to the not-so-subtle message that I wasn't good enough. Luckily for me, when I was growing up there were no organized youth basketball programs at that age level.

If I had been cut or relegated to the bench, I never would have become a player of any distinction. Most likely I would have taken the cue and exited stage right, leaving basketball behind as one of those childhood pastimes I had outgrown. I probably would have shot hoops with friends, watched the NCAA tournament on TV every March, complained about the Boston Celtics' latest acquisition, but by age thirteen or so, my serious playing days would most likely have been over.

If you take my story, and multiply that by the millions of times a child has been excluded in this way over the past twenty years by systems intent on selecting "the best" at young ages, can you still tell me we are making good decisions for our children?

Puberty: A Determining Factor

Although I would allow select teams beginning in seventh grade, tread carefully in this territory because it's still too early to predict future athletic success. Late-blooming athletes are not yet showing their full potential. At ages twelve and thirteen, the ages of typical seventh-graders, children show wide ranges of physical development and the athletic abilities that often come with that development.

Take two thirteen-year-old boys, for instance: one who has developed through puberty and one who hasn't. One may have a body more like that of a sixteen-year-old, the other more like a ten-year-old—a six-year span for children with the same birth year.

That's one reason that children who are "the best" at eight or nine years old are often not the best in high school, and vice versa. Puberty changes everything. Puberty is a major determining factor. It isn't how good you are at age ten but how good you continue to get at age fifteen, age sixteen and up that makes all the difference.

Remember those wiry little boys who so dominated the kickball, baseball and other games at your school when you all were ten years old? How many of them stayed dominant into their teens? And how many were overshadowed and overpowered by new "stars" who used to be gawky and uncoordinated before the arrival of facial hair and deeper voices?

I've watched this scenario play out countless times. Puberty causes such radical changes that child athletes who excel before puberty are quite often not the ones who excel after puberty.

Olympic hurdles champion David Hemery, who won a gold medal in Munich in 1972, interviewed sixty-three of the world's best athletes in the mid-1980s for his book titled *The Pursuit of Sporting Excellence*. He asked these athletes, from a variety of sports disciplines, when they got really serious about their sport. Only five said that it happened before the age of twelve, and those five were in individual sports such as gymnastics and golf.

Speaking of golf, the story of Tiger Woods—a striking athlete and successful businessman—has done much to perpetuate the concept that early, early, early and more, more, more is better, better, better. Tiger had a golf club in his hands at age three. He practiced, competed and excelled throughout his childhood and adolescence. He became a stupendous adult golfer. As far as I can tell he still loves the game.

As Tiger proves, there are wonderful success stories in youth sports—individual children who do well from the start and burn bright into maturity, and beyond. But let's consider two important points. First, golf is an individual sport and youth team sports is a different species. Second, the overwhelming majority of children are at risk of being shut out, hurt or discouraged by their experiences in youth sports.

Early and Late Bloomers

The early bloomer, the child who gains an edge in physical strength and maturity relatively early, often finds success at a young age in the system of select teams. That child often holds a competitive edge in tryouts. Those most at risk for getting shut out or discouraged are the late bloomers, those who reach puberty later than peers born in the same year and attending the same grade. This is the self-fulfilling prophecy theory in action.

Those recognized early are often given more opportunities to play and to excel. They are given more encouragement and more support. Their self-esteem is boosted and their motivation is thereby increased.

The players who are given the most playing time are often seen as the best players. Those who come off the bench for only a few minutes are often seen as less capable. In reality, both players often have equal potential and perhaps even equal ability. What they do not have is equal access and equal time to develop. Seventh-grade athletes, remember, may represent a six-year age span in terms of physical status, with the early bloomers looking more like fifteen-year-olds and the late bloomers looking more like nine-year-olds.

The late-blooming seventh-grade boy, therefore, may find himself at a disadvantage. The adults may believe he has less potential, he may be cut from the team, or he may not be given as many opportunities or encouragement to develop. That boy may have equal potential—in fact, he might have more skill at maturity—but he may be unwittingly discriminated against by systems intent on winning. In the worst cases, he may quit before he or anyone else ever gets to recognize his true potential.

The scenario is more complicated for girls. Early-maturing girls, too, may have some of the same advantages as do the early-maturing boys if their physical strength and abilities are ahead of the curve. However, after puberty the physical changes in body shapes may feed into biases about whether they will be as interested or as capable in sports.

The widest fluctuations in physical abilities occur around the changes brought on by puberty—which arrives at different ages for different children and occurs rapidly for some and less rapidly for others. This time of maturation and growth spurts—sometimes dramatic ones—may continue throughout the high school years, and even beyond.

There's a thread in the life story of basketball icon Michael Jordan that shocks most people when they hear it for the first time. It's the thread about him trying out as a sophomore for his varsity team at Laney High School in Wilmington, North Carolina—and being cut.

We can assume, then, that Jordan wasn't the world's best, or even showing signs of that caliber, until he was well past childhood and the start of puberty. In a January 4, 1998 *Dallas Morning News* story, one of Laney High School's former assistant coaches recalls the high school sophomore Michael Jordan as a "shy ballplayer." Remember, these coaches cut the 1978 Michael Jordan, not the 1988 Michael Jordan.

Between his sophomore and junior seasons alone, Michael Jordan grew from five-nine to six-three. He starred on his high school varsity team, and the rest—from North Carolina's NCAA championship in 1982 to the stunning career, two times over, with the Chicago Bulls—is history.

"I had no idea all this would happen," Michael Jordan's father is quoted in an April 15, 1990, *Chicago Tribune* story, "and maybe that's better. If I had, I might've pushed him too hard and screwed him up. As it is, everything happened very naturally."

●●●

So here's the important question again: Will your sports prodigy be hurt by drastic reconfigurations in youth sports systems and the elimination of elite teams at young ages? No. Odds are he or she will become a better player, with a better likelihood of staying in the sport.

Reconfiguring our systems will help the young athletes, and it will also help the adults—both the coaches and the parents. The intensity of emotion that some of them bring to games and practices can be frightening. In the next chapter we will take a closer look at this adult behavior.

CHAPTER 3

Out of Kilter: Why Adults Lose Control

*I don't think there's been a
single season since my oldest was five
that I haven't been blindsided by unexpected
emotions surrounding my kids' sports.*

Warren Goldstein
author, A *Brief History of American Sports*

By the time the fight was over on that warm afternoon of July 5, 2000, one hockey father was unconscious, his body slumped near a vending machine inside a rink in the town of Reading, Massachusetts. His face was so disfigured, according to a report in *Sports Illustrated*, that his two sons would say they barely recognized him. Two days later, he died. His alleged assailant, another hockey father, was charged with manslaughter. While the two families had unspeakable grief to confront, the national media had a face for a story that had reached a crisis in youth sports: out-of-control parents.

The death, prosecutors said, came at the end of an argument between the two hockey fathers when Thomas Junta, forty-two, a truck driver and father of two, watched from the stands as his ten-year-old son played in a pickup game. Junta's lawyer told the judge at his arraignment that Junta watched as his son was checked hard with an elbow to his nose at the hands of another player on the ice below. Junta yelled to complain about rough play, the lawyer said. The father running the practice on the ice, Michael Costin, forty, a part-time carpenter and single father of four, skated over toward Junta in the stands and, according to the lawyer, said, "That's what hockey's all about!"

After the practice, Junta and Costin met off the ice and fought, according to prosecutors, with Junta ripping Costin's shirt and tearing a chain from his neck. Some said a rink employee broke up that fight and ordered Junta from the rink, but prosecutors said he returned. The two parents met again. This time, prosecutors said, Junta pinned Costin with his knee on Costin's chest, then he pummeled his face and banged his head on the rink floor until Costin lost consciousness.

I live twenty minutes from that ice rink. I remember the media frenzy in the days that followed. It was an awful way to shake us from our summer reveries. Because of my knowledge about youth sports, I was contacted by more than a dozen television and print reporters. It seemed as though they all had the same question: Am I surprised that such a thing could happen?

"Yes," I told them. "I am surprised. I am surprised it hasn't happened sooner."

Read any U.S. newspaper, watch any television newscast for a week, and most likely you'll see at least one instance of over-the-top parents at a youth sports event. It's worse than you may think.

No matter what age group is playing, no matter which sport, parents have left a trail of disgrace. And if all youth sports administrators could be as honest as the recreation director quoted in *The Record* (Bergen County, New Jersey) on November 19, 2000, they would probably agree that every community is at risk for violence. As Jim Oettinger, the Closter, New Jersey, recreation director, put it, "We're just one bad call away from that same kind of thing happening right here."

A Trail of Disgrace

The stories of parents acting up, acting out and being arrested range from ludicrous, to sometimes laughable, to dangerous. Parents have been arrested, even sent to jail, for assaulting coaches or officials and for fighting with each other. Children have been attacked. The local police, even the National Guard, have been called to respond to all-out brawls on the playing field.

Following are some of the more notorious incidents:

- In January 2001 a Northridge, California, father was sentenced to forty-five days in jail, three years of probation and six months of anger management counseling after being convicted of slamming the manager of his son's youth baseball team against a truck. According to prosecutors, the father threatened to kill the manager for taking the eleven-year-old out of a game after only three innings. The judge ordered the father to refrain from "any verbal dispute at any sporting event," according to a January 26, 2001, *Los Angeles Times* story.

- In September 2000 a tied soccer game between eight- and nine-year-old boys that took place in South Brunswick, New Jersey, ended in a brawl among dozens of parents and coaches. It was touched off by an argument about whether one coach should have been allowed to stand behind the goal during the shootout.

- In Torrance, California, the father and the uncle of a high school football player were sentenced to forty-five days in jail for attacking the team's coach in October 2000. Police say the father and uncle were upset that the high schooler had not been given more playing time.

- In February 2001 at a youth basketball game of seven- and eight-year-olds in Fayetteville, Georgia, police say tension that built up during the game, including disputes about the sports official's calls, led to the official slashing a coach with a knife. The wound required seventeen stitches. The official told police the coaches berated him throughout the game.

- A Las Vegas father was charged in November 2000 with trying to poison one of his son's youth football teammates with ipecac syrup, a drug that causes vomiting. Eight players got sick after they ingested the tainted drink, which ended up being available to the entire team.

- In suburban Swiftwater, Pennsylvania, in October 1999 an estimated fifty to one hundred adults came together in furious fisticuffs after a football game for eleven- to thirteen-year-olds. The adults kicked, punched and screamed at each other—a ten-minute melee caught on videotape and shown on the local news.

- In Port Orange, Florida, in September 2000 a Pop Warner overtime football game ended in a brawl involving an estimated one hundred adults and players. Words were exchanged at the end of the game, players began fighting and parents got involved trying to stop the brawl.
- In Miami, Florida, in September 2000 about twenty men fought over an umpire's call at a T-ball game for four- and five-year-olds.
- At a pee-wee playoff hockey game between teams from Port Dover and Delhi, Canada, referees halted the game after spectators pelted them with coins, batteries, a water bottle and even a broom. With less than two minutes left, all 200 spectators were ejected from the rink so that the game could be completed. Police escorted the referees out.

The stories about outrageous behavior in the stands and on the sidelines could fill more than this book, more than three books. The adults, analysts say, are out of control, but those analysts often have difficulty explaining why.

Looking for Answers

Parents are sometimes described as overgrown children who can't keep their tempers in check. It's all part of an angry society prone to violence. There's road rage. Airline rage. And, yes, youth sports rage.

"People bring their own frustrations to the games and they are naturally so protective of their children," former youth hockey coach Paul Dennis told *The Toronto Star* in a March 17, 2001 article. "The two combined are a combustible experience," said Dennis, who is development coach for the Toronto Maple Leafs. "People lose it."

Other analysts attach motives. Parents are driven by ambition for college scholarships and professional contracts. Parents are trying to live out their own thwarted dreams of athletic glory through the achievements of their children.

"Raising kids is the most emotionally evocative experience you will ever have," sports psychologist Alan Goldberg of Amherst, Massachusetts, told *Parents* magazine in an October 2000 article. "And rearing an athlete—no matter how amateur—is particularly intense. Even if you think you're well adjusted, it can bring up a lot of stuff."

The reasons parents behave as they do are obviously complex and far-reaching. Whatever the causes of the damaging adult behaviors seen in youth sports, in order to stop them we must take away what triggers them in the first place.

The ways in which many youth sports systems are organized and run—particularly the ways in which children are evaluated and ranked, selected for or excluded from teams, or subjected to politics among the adults—are often catalysts for explosive emotions.

A Wrenching Experience

Even if they have no realistic thoughts of their children chasing college scholarships or professional careers, adults often feel pressure to help their children excel, and they also may feel compelled to keep up with other adults. The parents of young sports achievers, after all, often have status within a community. Many parents also want to assure themselves that, despite all the stress and juggling in their busy lives, they have not let their children down, that their children have not fallen behind.

Few things feed into these complex emotions more insidiously than do organized youth sports. Consider this solitary image: In Severna Park, Maryland, a father who is a disabled Marine Corps veteran carried signs and protested in front of his daughter's high school for months after she was cut from the soccer team. "If you want to play a sport, you should be able to play it," the father was quoted in *The Capital*, an Annapolis newspaper, on August 24, 2000.

Parents watching their children play in a game are sometimes surprised by the intensity of their own emotions. "I don't think there's been a single season since my oldest (child) was five when I haven't been blindsided by unexpected emotions surrounding my kids' sports," wrote Warren Goldstein, a U.S. history teacher at the University of Hartford (Connecticut) and author of *A Brief History of American Sports*, in an April 6, 1997, article for *The Boston Globe Magazine*.

Even parents who enroll their children in programs with the best of intentions can be easily pulled in by the intensity of other parents in the stands and on the sidelines. "Watching your child compete is a singularly wrenching experience," wrote Bob Katz of Lexington, Massachusetts, in a July 12, 2000, op-ed piece for *The New York Times*. "Nobody is immune from bad behavior. I have watched in disgust as some jerk lambastes a hapless eight-year-old ('Use your left foot!'), only minutes later to hear myself howling an equally pointless rant ('Watch the ball!')."

Nothing makes the point better than an episode of the wonderful hit show *Picket Fences*. The show, popular in the mid-nineties, was one of producer and writer David E. Kelley's early successes, well-written and superbly cast with Tom Skerritt as the town sheriff and Kathy Baker as a physician and the sheriff's wife.

In the opening scene of this particular episode, a basketball game of young boys is in full swing in the local gym. Suddenly, the coach of the Wildcats has a heart attack and collapses. A group of parents approaches Baker's character, whose son is on the team, and asks her to be the new coach. Frankly, they tell her, the team needs change. She is in the stands for every game anyway. She played varsity basketball when she was in high school. What more do you need?

She accepts. Initially, she is the picture of fair-mindedness, a Mother Earth figure who is the catalyst of great fun for all the boys. All of them play the same amount of time and the star shooter is encouraged to pass the ball to his less skilled teammates. Hooray for Mom!

Unfortunately, some of the parents are unhappy with this turn of events. They expected her to be a coach who wants, above all else, to win every game and to get these boys into the playoffs. After all, isn't that the point?

She encounters one of the more gung-ho fathers, who is baffled by her instincts to give every kid an equitable chance. "Are you really going to blow their chances with some Girl Scout notion of fair play?" he asks.

She stews about the criticism and watches her team as the boys perform dismally. In one game, with the score 32–20 and the Wildcats losing with time running out, she is transformed. She sees the light. Gone are quaint rules about equal time. Gone is the idea that the star shooter should pass the ball. Enter Morphed Mother, the new Vince Lombardi of the local gym.

"If they want a fight," the newly transformed mother barks at her team during a break, "we'll give 'em a fight!"

Just as the boys are about to get back on the floor, she exhorts, "Knock 'em down if you have to. Kick some butt!"

Her Wildcats do indeed kick butt. They win with a basket at the buzzer, but instead of being joyfully triumphant, at least a few of the boys are not happy. You can see it on their faces. Even the coach's own son is baffled by her newfound intensity. When the boy's pal suggests that her new attitude is probably "good for us," the coach's son fires back, "Spinach is good for you. Basketball is supposed to be fun." What a great line.

Frustrated and unhappy, a group of the boys organize, hire a lawyer and take their parents to court. They want a restraining order to keep parents out of the gym and off their backs for the rest of the season. No parents allowed. What a concept!

After an impassioned hearing, the judge, played gruffly and pitch-perfect by the late Ray Walston, grants an injunction, telling the boys they have two months without parents in the gym. However, before the judge issues his ruling, the coach's husband, the sheriff, delivers the best line I've ever heard about the problem with parents in youth sports.

The sheriff says his wife is the most caring and sensitive

person he knows. "If she can be transformed from someone who started out wanting nothing but the best for these kids to a coach who wants to win at all costs, then I got to believe there's something terribly wrong with the system. That's all I have to say."

Sheriff, you said it all.

A Permanent Sick Day

Many of the systems we have created to organize and propel our youth sports seasons are overorganized, overscheduled, overwrought. Nine-year-olds can play more hockey games than their counterparts in the National Hockey League. Several years back at a rink in Marlborough, Massachusetts, so a friend told me, boys in an under-ten all-star hockey league had their own locker room with each player's name scribbled onto white tape plastered over his individual stall. Some college hockey players have less elaborate digs.

In a March 11, 2001, *New York Times* article about the Bergen Thunder (New Jersey), an elite baseball team for boys thirteen and younger, the team's head coach described their game against an elite team from Georgia in a tournament played in Connecticut. When the other team "ran out of pitching," coach Art Clyde told the newspaper, "their manager gets on his cell phone, calls down to Georgia. Georgia called a kid in Texas. He was on the private jet that night, and he pitched in the tournament the next day."

Soccer, the first of the youth sports to push toward a year-round schedule, is more highly organized in many communities than local government. Boards, commissioners and other overseers, driven by the idea that more games and more elaborate tournaments make better players, put stress on the individual coach-parent and spectator-parent, pushing them to get overly involved in their children's lives.

Being an involved and interested parent is a good thing, but there should be limits. As much as children should be left alone to be children, it would best serve adults and their children if now and again adults were left alone to be adults, to find fun and to pursue interests that have nothing to do with their children.

A perceptive analysis of this cultural landscape was published in the June 1998 issue of *Gentlemen's Quarterly*, in which author Anthony Giardina writes, "To be a good parent, according to the going wisdom, is to spend a great deal of time not at work, not out there hustling in order to provide for one's children (as perhaps our parents viewed the task), but staying home obsessing about them.

"In the current American equation," he continues, "it turns out that it takes neither a village nor a family to raise a child. What it takes is a permanent sick day."

According to Giardina, too many parents view the world "not simply from the perspective of the child but from the perspective of the *aggrieved* child" and are ushered by cultural forces "toward a single, guilt-ridden vision of life."

"Does our religion of child-centeredness jibe with the experiences we had as kids?" Giardina asks. "I remember being always sort of grateful when Dad wasn't in the stands watching, when I could swing a bat just because I wanted to, not because the family honor was at stake."

When I played organized baseball as a boy, my parents

showed up at games only occasionally. After all, there were three other Bigelow children who needed attention.

Peer Pressure on Adults

For some parents, their adult pursuit of social acceptance and accomplishment is almost completely wrapped up with the achievements of their children.

It's striking that parents who worry about how their children will handle peer pressure fail to recognize those pressures among themselves. You don't read much about parent-peer pressure, but it's equally forceful. Adults are driven to keep up, to be accepted, to be seen as one of the popular crowd, one of the winners. Among today's parents, a hectic schedule is the new status symbol.

"You think you're busy? Wait'll I tell you *my* schedule!"

"You've just signed up your son for hockey summer power camp? Pleeeze—we made sure we signed up last year; you *do* know they're accepting only a few new kids, don't you?"

When you listen to many parents talk about youth sports, you often hear the word "we." "What is your child playing this spring?" "*We're* playing soccer and baseball."

Doug Abrams, a law professor at University of Missouri-Columbia and a youth hockey coach for thirty-two years, says he has seen youngsters in the locker room "chattering after a loss and looking ahead to the afternoon's in-line hockey game or that night's sleepover. Their obsessed parents were still in the rink yelling at the opposing team or the official because the parents could not accept the defeat their children had already put behind them."

For adults caught up in the culture of youth sports, many of their peers are leading them down the wrong paths.

Paying the Price

Some parents need computer printouts to keep their weekends straight. Husband and wife never see each other— they have to be at different fields at the same time. Mothers pull into the fast-food drive-through at seven at night, having been with three children to three different games in three different communities in the same day. Working parents say getting back to the job on Monday is a relief.

We complain about these harried schedules when we bump into each other or while we stand on the sidelines. We sometimes laugh about how ludicrous it all is. Yet we go along in hordes, tired, stressed and overwhelmed. We dutifully send in soccer, baseball and other sign-up sheets when they are due. We fear missing deadlines and being left out. We worry about falling behind. A fair number of parents sign up their children for the next season without ever even asking their children if *they* want to play.

There's so much to do that parents often do not take time to step back and consider the toll, on their own lives and on the lives of their children. The toll upon schoolwork. The toll upon rest and relaxation. The toll upon the family dinner hour. Can parents even enjoy their children's games once they get there? For so many parents, their attention is distracted— after all, they've got to be at another field in twenty minutes, and that community is at least forty minutes away!

The Weekend Vortex

TOM MORONEY
The MetroWest Daily News
September 28, 1997

He looked like a tray of half-eaten lasagna warmed over.

"Tired?" I said as I stood on the sidelines of the youth soccer game.

"Unbelievable," he sighed. "This is my third game of the day, and it's only 12:30. I have another game after this, then football practice.

"Then tomorrow morning, there's a soccer tournament for my youngest," he continued. "Then the football game, which I will have to leave early so I can pick up my other child from the other soccer game. My wife, hopefully, will be at the football game for the second half, although I don't like to miss the second half. But halfway through the season, my wife and I will switch halves so I'll get my chance. By December, we should be a little less busy."

"By December? By December, you should be dead," I said.

Sadly, my own weekend schedule wasn't much easier. Soccer, then a birthday party later. Then, on Sunday, our reputed day of rest (remember that), more soccer, basketball, then a whole afternoon of Cub Scouts.

By then, I'd be ready for my own merit badge: Human Rickshaw.

We boomers are quickly turning ourselves into a nation of caffeine-powered zombie idiots. We get up on weekends, travel great distances to shuttle our children from soccer to football to hockey to dance, whatever, until our eyes are the color of a foggy day in London town.

"I was up at 5:30 this morning," said the man with the itinerary to rival Madeleine Albright's.

"Slept in, huh?" a second parent chirped. "We were standing in front of the coffee shop at 5:30, waiting for it to open. We had a soccer game thirty miles away. And then my husband had to leave in the second half to bring my other daughter to. . . ."

As one parent would spill his or her litany of weekend activities, a full run of stuff that would exhaust Alvin and all the chipmunks, another would start right in. If you listened closely, you would swear each parent was trying to one-up the parent who had just spoken.

He who dies with the most miles on the odometer by Sunday night wins.

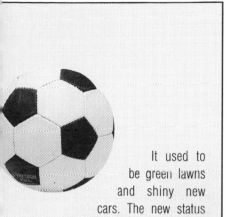

It used to be green lawns and shiny new cars. The new status symbol is the weekend schedule. The strangest part of all is trying to figure out why.

I assume most of these people grew up like I did, at least the males. As a boy, you got up on Saturday and watched a bunch of really bad cartoons, then you went to the hardware store with your father.

You didn't especially like the hardware store, but it was better than staying home. If you stayed home, your mother might ask you to actually do something, like clean the garage.

Years into this routine, you discovered your father didn't much like the hardware store either, but he had made the same discovery you had. If he stayed home, *he* would have to clean the garage. ■

Practices or games for young children are sometimes scheduled for two hours midweek. "Does anyone say, 'Gee, this is a school night'?" said one youth sports coordinator quoted in a May 24, 1998, *Minneapolis Star Tribune* story. "No, everyone goes along with what's been decided. And if you don't agree with something being done, it's difficult to speak up for fear of your kid being blackballed."

Parents get sucked in, caught up. They've signed away their entire spring or their summer and winter vacations before they even ask what their family will need to give up in order for their children to play youth sports.

One youth hockey club in Maine, for instance, takes nine- to twelve-year-olds and travels to Boston every Sunday for twenty-six straight weeks. That's half a year! Does anyone ask, "Do we really need to do this for twenty-six straight weeks?"

Living Through Your Children

Some youth sports parents are motivated by what is best described by medical experts as "achievement by proxy," that is, adults living vicariously through the success of their children. This trait, the experts say, takes on varying levels of intensity. The most extreme form is nothing short of child abuse, the willful neglect or harm of a child in order to serve an adult's needs.

If you are an adult driven by these tendencies, even in their subtle forms, it is really you as much as your child who is out on the field, the rink, the gym. That was you who scored. That was you who lost.

Psychiatrist Ian Tofler, who is secretary of the International Society of Sports Psychiatry, describes parental involvement as going from healthy to obsessive to dangerous along a spectrum of progressive overinvolvement. In "The Achievement by Proxy Spectrum in Youth Sports," published by the Child and Adolescent Psychiatric Clinics of North America in October 1998, Tofler and his coauthors describe what's at work in each stage.

In the beginning, parents feel pride and offer their children support. Then the dynamic moves to what Tofler calls "sacrifice." Here, parents are skipping work and letting other responsibilities go. After this, adult commitment turns into obsession. The child's identity is lost in the goals set forth by the parent. I have read about parents who put so much pressure on their daughters trying out for an elite basketball team that at tryouts some of the girls vomited or fainted. These parents would cuss and swear at the coach, demanding nothing short of perfection, even though he was a coach who had brought them to national titles.

You think that is bad? There's an even more unsettling stage, the last along Tofler's spectrum. He identifies it as "strong parental encouragement of a potentially dangerous endeavor for the purpose of gaining recognition or financial reward." This is the kind of behavior that can be classified as child abuse.

This more extreme form would include a parent forcing a child on an unhealthy diet or weight-loss method in order to make the weight-class restrictions in youth football. This would include a parent encouraging a child to play while injured. This would include turning down needed surgery because that would look bad on the child's sports résumé.

Wow, this is getting serious, isn't it? Most parents, of course, never go that far. It is important, however, for us to talk about the extremes so that we might recognize more subtle expressions of unhealthy tendencies: pressuring a child to stay in a sport if he or she wants to quit, neglecting to recognize the stress of overscheduled sports seasons, failing to speak up when your child is unfairly treated by a coach, and so on.

Overwhelmed

We are a nation under stress. Lack of time is an enormous and pressing problem today for most parents and children.

We're really trying to do too much. We're overscheduled. We're sleep-deprived.

Parents are worried that their children will fall behind if they aren't engaged in as many activities, on as many teams, playing in as many seasons as their peers. Coaches worry that their teams will suffer if they don't practice as much as the competition.

Maybe, maybe not. But we have to ask at what price? Would you prefer to feel better about what your children are doing with their lives, or would you prefer to win a few more games?

"If most of us think back on our lives and to the turning points," Michael Lafavore, former editor of *Men's Health* magazine told *USA Today* in a June 6, 1995, article, "few of us are going to say, 'If only we had won that Little League game in '58, life would have been different.'"

The Root of the Problem

How did we get to this point in our culture? We have already talked about the shift from backyards and sandlots to a society, without the security of the streets, in which children at play must be supervised. Television has played its part, first with the fanfare and adulation of Olympic heroes—the Dorothy Hamills, the Mark Spitzes, the Mary Lou Rettons. Here on a pedestal for all to admire are examples of those who practiced and trained hard from childhood, devoted to the pursuit of sports and wildly rewarded for their sacrifice.

We have talked about the differences between individual and team sports, but this model of zealous pursuit from an early age under the watch of overly involved parents and coaches rubbed off on how we approached team sports for children. If Dorothy and Mark and Mary Lou could achieve unprecedented heights by showing up at the rink or the pool or the gym at dawn each day, that model could be imposed on team sports, or so the thinking went. More, more, more. Younger, younger, younger. Win, win, win.

Television also turned sports into mass entertainment with mass merchandising. Professional salaries skyrocketed. Sports stars became even more important.

At the same time, the look and feel of neighborhoods changed, as did the typical patterns of which parents worked and for how long. While two-working-parents households became more the norm, parents also found time and flexibility in their work schedules so that many of them, notably many fathers, volunteered to manage youth sports leagues, coach teams and attend games.

As these adults headed out into the world of youth sports to build league structures, organize teams and manage children, they brought an outlook best described as Management 101: What works in the workplace will work with the kids.

Parents involved in youth sports also brought along what they knew about playing, coaching and watching sports — namely, high school varsity, college teams and the pros (for the most part these parents didn't have a lot of organized youth sports when they were growing up). What the grown-ups lost sight of, however, was that they had brought along ways to coach and play adults, not children.

Adults brought along tactics designed primarily to win games, not necessarily to develop young players just learning a sport. They brought along notions about training and practices that fit adults who have contracts to do a job, not third-graders there to have fun. If the college coaches and the professional coaches in suits stand up and scream at their players, we'll do that, too, they figured. You can almost hear some of them thinking: "Get in line, little one. This is serious stuff. You'll thank me for pushing you this hard in third grade when you make that elite team in fourth grade. Believe me, you will." Totally absurd. Totally misguided.

The Mirror of Parenthood

Many of the adults who run our youth sports programs, many of the coaches who lead our teams deserve our great respect and admiration. They are volunteers and, as such, they deserve our gratitude. Some of them have got it quite right, too, but far too many have got it wrong. While their motives are not sinister, their methods are misinformed, and much of the time they do not recognize the error in their ways.

Timothy Harper, a New Jersey writer who has confessed to some overbearing moments of his own as he has watched his children's games, tells a story in the April 1997 issue of *Sky* magazine about a public relations executive in Washington, D.C. The executive was the father of a boy and a girl, fourteen and nine at the time. This father would show up for his children's games to cheer them on, but after a few outings he noticed he wasn't really cheering. He was yelling at them. His comments were more negative than positive. The executive finally realized, in a moment of painful self-revelation, that he was one of *them*, a bizarro wacky sports parent.

Harper quite accurately calls the biggest such offenders "Sideline Saddams." The executive admitted, "I needed to be saved from myself."

So he found something to occupy himself at the games. At soccer he volunteered to run up and down the sidelines with the flag, signaling which team gets the ball after it has gone out-of-bounds. In basketball, he ran the clock. In softball, he kept the score book. He rescued himself from adult impulses that seek to control and to impose adult order on what's happening on the field.

That's one way to do it. The problem is, as Harper notes, we can't all hold the flag, run the clock or keep the score book. We can, however, start by doing what that public relations executive did in the first instance. He took a good long look at himself in the mirror of parenthood. By doing so, he came up with powerful observations.

He saw what I see and hear every day in this business of helping to put parents back on the right road. Many adults realize that they have, essentially, lost their way. The adults, so wrapped up in the systems that exist, have overlooked the perversion of the process. That is, what started as an effort to delight and motivate our children has swung into a new reality, one that stands as a way to delight and motivate the adults.

We must continually look for and consider how much the adults in our children's lives see youth sports through the eyes of an adult, not through the eyes of a child. We need to stop treating children like high school varsity, college or professional athletes. Check out this snippet from an article that appeared December 29, 1995, in the *Derry News* (New

Hampshire): "Despite the posting of a losing record, the team's efforts have been unbeatable throughout the initial portion of the season. Each of the team's marginal losses was at the hand of an anticipated rival. Each game has also remained well within the team's grasp throughout the last minutes of play. . . . With an unfaltering spirit, energy to match and two-thirds of the season left to play, it appears that a solid league finish is within their reach."

Pretty exciting, isn't it? It has the requisite drama, the requisite sympathy for a struggling but feisty and certainly noble squad. It's the kind of peppy sports journalism you'd expect to read about a high school, college or pro team. The problem is that the team in question is comprised of third- and fourth-graders.

Invest in the Process

Adult coaches often show up at games—with all that Management 101 mind-set, all that desire to achieve—and they try to manage the outcome. If there's a scoreboard, so much the worse. Their coaching is almost solely based on the outcome, which is the score.

Outcome is not what the children are solely there for, nor is it what they solely should be there for. They are much more interested, as polls and surveys have shown, in investing in the process. The score is not the most important thing to them. Of course they want to win, but most of all they want to have fun and to play. Surveys show that children would prefer to play in a losing game than to sit on the bench and win.

Children are different from adults, different enough to

want different things. In surveys in which children are asked to rank "winning the game" among the top ten reasons for why they play, it usually comes in at number seven or eight. Sometimes it doesn't even make the top ten.

If you are an adult willing to take a hard look at your priorities and your motives for being involved in youth sports, you may find the actual games to be your toughest test. Coaches may pressure themselves to win or they may feel that pressure from the parents.

In most cases, parents who become coaches start off doing pretty well at managing the process. At that early stage, they are more in sync with children's wants and needs. The season is new; the win-loss record is clean. Optimism abounds.

For what happens next, let's imagine that there are two teams in the same league. Team One wins its first two or three games. That team is undefeated. Spirits are high. Those torturous rides in the minivan to and from practice, to and from the games, don't seem so torturous at all. Team Two loses its first two or three games. Team Two is winless. Everything that can go wrong is going wrong. And the rides to and from practice, to and from the games, become for some coaches a struggle to convince themselves that they are having fun.

Finally, it comes to that point in the season when undefeated Team One plays winless Team Two. As the coach of Team Two, the winless bunch, you are having a tough time with all those principles of fair play and equal time that you promised yourself at the beginning of the season. You're starting to ask yourself nagging questions. Should you still manage the process—giving as many kids as you can as much playing time as possible—even though it may interfere with winning? Or are you going to say, "Heck, I'm not going to lose any more games"? If you do say that, it is the beginning of the end. You will start to figure that if you alter things just a little—that is, swallow your idealism and do some things in order to win—everybody will feel better. It'll all be worth it. So you start shaving the playing time of your least-skilled players and you increase the playing time of your better-skilled ones.

Lo and behold, you get results. You beat Team One. Your team notches its first win, then its second and third. Suddenly you are no longer managing the process. The less-skilled players are seeing less time in the games and more time on the bench. Boredom sets in and they begin to question their self-worth. You're winning games, but at what price? And with all those high-fives and pats on the back, do you even recognize the price you've paid?

You no longer care as much about the process. Your interest is in the outcome. You try to tell yourself that the trade-off is worth it, that everyone seems happier now that you're headed for the playoffs and you can savor the unimaginable glory of yet another plastic trophy to stuff into the trophy case in the den.

But don't look to me for empathy because, in a phrase, you have failed. You have failed yourself, your players and every other parent for not sticking up for what's really important: to create a safe and happy haven, a place where every child has a fair chance to play and to develop in the game.

If you are motivated primarily by a desire to derive something for yourself from sports played by children, then youth sports is not the place for you.

Reform the Process

Parental overreaction and destructive zealousness, whatever you want to call the out-of-kilter behaviors, are symptoms of deeper problems. Those problems are embedded in the systems themselves. Too often the adults are out of touch with the children's wants and the children's needs. We need to get inside those systems, discard what isn't working and build upon what is.

Training for youth coaches will help ensure that the right people come into the game or at least that the problem people are exposed to the right ways. Behavior classes for parents and ethics pledges will do much of the same thing. But neither training classes nor pledges will solve all the problems. If we do not reform the youth sports systems themselves, we're just putting a muzzle on a dog that still wants to bite.

Consider an August 1, 1994, *Wall Street Journal* article on the antics of youth sports parents in Texas. A head official told the reporter that he introduces himself to police or security guards before he starts any game. He tells them which section of the field or court he'll be leaving from. When the game is finished, he takes off his whistle to reduce the chance that someone will grab it and try to choke him.

At the time the story was written, he was teaching a class in the Dallas-Fort Worth area called "The Fears in Officiating." He would advise his student officials to drive up to the facility where the game is to be played and have a good look around, checking out the best places for quick exits. "Tonight there's going to be a riot here," he would suggest they think to themselves, "and you're going to be the central focus of it."

If you read the newspaper stories about brawls, threats and assaults at youth sports events, you will know that this official was not exaggerating the risk. Assault insurance is now offered by the National Association of Sports Officials. States have already passed or are considering tougher penalties for assaults against sports officials.

Plotting your getaway route may be good advice for officials these days, but it does nothing to reduce the crime rate in the neighborhood, so to speak. Pledges, too, set boundaries in much the same way that good fences make good neighbors, but if those neighbors still can't figure out how to talk with each other, how much has been solved?

These efforts at penalties, pledges and training do much to bring attention to the problems and to sensitize and to educate the adults, but we need to do more to take away the compulsion to scream, to act out or to become violent in the first place. Photos of "Silent Saturday" or "Silent Sunday"—in which spectators are ordered to keep quiet—show us adults with tape over their mouths, others sucking lollipops or holding up signs (DEFENSE!).

Those communities across the country, led by Jupiter and Tequesta, Florida, that require parents to take behavior classes and sign ethics pledges before they can register their children for youth sports, are taking important and valuable steps.

Now we must get inside the systems themselves. We must reform the process—from tryouts and cuts, to playing time and benching—in order to change adult attitudes and decisions about how children playing sports will be evaluated and treated.

We must be careful not to simply ask parents to behave in

any system that is overwrought and misguided. We must create environments that motivate parents to behave on their own, pledges or not.

A Passion in Their Play

How do you create environments like that? You begin by listening to some of the really good people in the business of youth sports. I mean "business" in the best sense of the word, people like Dean Conway, head state coach of the Massachusetts Youth Soccer Association (MYSA). Of all the intelligent and fair-minded people I've met in this field, Conway stands out.

When he talks about soccer, his passion, he talks in terms of the innocence of the game. He may ask you, for instance, where you think the best soccer in the world is being played right now at the youth level. On the finely manicured fields of Virginia? Not even close. The best soccer in the world is being played where it's always been played, on the streets and in the neighborhoods, most often in the cities and towns of Europe and South America.

Children hit the streets, for hours at a time, kicking and wheeling around, weaving and dodging. Not a single parent or other adult intrudes on this process. After ten and eleven years of this childhood play minus the adults, guess what happens? Some of those children emerge as the most formidable and elite soccer players of the world.

Sometimes too much training, too much coaching and specialization at young ages develops bad playing habits that are harder to fix at older ages. Keith Lieppman, director of player development for the Oakland Athletics, told the *San Francisco Chronicle* in a December 10, 2000, story that he thinks "less instruction is better at the younger levels. That's why a lot of times the Dominicans are easier to work with. They haven't had a lot of instruction."

The Dominican ballplayers also become some of the top stars in the big leagues despite the fact that they don't have the expensive training equipment or highly organized tournaments available to their American counterparts.

"If you have ever been down there, it just blows your mind," Grady Fuson, the Athletics' director of scouting, told the *Chronicle* writer. "You go to a park in the Dominican and you will see ten kids playing catch, running around like scatbacks. They are active, live athletes.

"You go to our parks," Fuson continued, "and, number one, you don't see ten kids period. Then you see our kids and they are so thick and slow at eighteen that they are already cooked. You don't see active, live bodies."

When More Is Less

In America today, youth league schedules frequently exceed those of the professionals in length of season and number of games. To that, adult organizers often add playoffs and tournaments, all of which can increase the pressure on young players.

A schedule that includes a lot of organized games, particularly a lot of travel to other communities, does not necessarily translate into better player development. In fact, that kind of schedule can have the opposite effect.

"Parents will say, 'A lot of kids are going to this camp, so I want my child to go there,'" says Dean Conway in a February 1999 article that appeared in the MYSA's newspaper, *The Bay Stater*. "Or a coach will say, 'Gee, if we want to have a better record in

> **Skip a game now and then, go home and cook dinner or have the take-out all ready so there's time to relax at the family table after the game.**

the spring league everyone needs to play indoors this winter.' Pretty soon kids are playing all over the place and parents are driving them everywhere."

Conway cautions about the price children may pay when forced to travel so much in order to play other communities. "Think about it," he says. "You get up early, drive for an hour or two to get to some field, and then the player maybe gets fifteen to twenty minutes of actual playing time in the game. Then you have to drive all the way back. So for four or five hours of hassle, you barely get a good workout or any soccer action. And if you do that every week of the year, it's easy to see how youngsters get sick of the game."

"People are obsessed with results and games," says Conway, "and I don't think young players learn enough from playing in organized leagues all the time."

Conway recommends that young players themselves or their parents sometimes organize pickup soccer games at local fields. No officials. No screaming parents. Just kids playing a game. "Get everyone to pitch in and rent an indoor field for an hour or go to a schoolyard and just put the ball out there and let the kids play. They will pick sides and do their thing."

"And if you're a parent," Conway says, "I recommend grabbing *The New York Times* and staying out of the way. That kind of soccer is what the game is all about."

This idea is echoed in a newspaper column by Terry Marotta in the *Woburn Daily Times Chronicle* (Massachusetts). She wrote about her dentist who, she says, was a very good hockey player in his youth, all through high school and into college. Toward the end of his college career, his widowed mother said to him, "I hear you're pretty good at this game. Maybe I'll come watch you once." And she did. Marotta's dentist describes this mother-son relationship as "the perfect amount of parental involvement in what was, after all, his passion, and not hers." Marotta's column had another fascinating note. Her dentist, at age sixty-five, was still in love with the game and still lacing up his skates to play.

Watching your children play, being there to support them, can be a wonderful experience both for you and for them. You should do it right, but you needn't do it every time. Consider balance in your life. Put things in perspective. These are ways in which you can purposely turn down the intensity and involvement you have in your children's games. Skip a game now and then, go home and cook dinner or have the take-out all ready so there's time to relax at the family table after the game. Every now and then, isn't that worth as much as being able to say you saw your child play?

For the past two years, the Aurora Youth Soccer Club in Ontario, Canada, has asked parents of players who participate in a Saturday program of pickup games to simply drop off their children and leave. Mark Marshall, who coordinates the program, says the no-parents rule is popular with the children, but not so with the parents.

In all kinds of ways, adults send messages—sometimes subtle messages—to their children about how and why they should play sports, how important are these games and these scores, their achievements on the field, in the gym and in the rink.

By taking purposeful steps to tone down the attention and the seriousness, parents can make substantial headway toward releasing some of the pressures that take hold in the stands and on the sidelines.

I'm not crazy about national youth sports championships televised in prime time because they take the playing too seriously. Communities should delay media "coverage" of their youth sports events—scores and standings included. Parents should think twice before they automatically buy into too many of the novelties that youth sports offers, from the mock magazine cover customized with a picture of their child in uniform to the mock sports cards to the pins with their child's photo to be worn at every game.

Don't hesitate to take photos of your children. Cherish your memories, and theirs. But consider buying your children a disposable camera and letting them snap photos of their friends being themselves. Aren't those the memories you really want to preserve?

· · ·

If you are serious about reforming youth sports, you must consider the cold reality of the consequences created by out-of-kilter, adult-driven youth sports machines. Many children pay a price every day, in many different ways. Emotional and physical hurt. Repetitive-use injuries and burnout. Children giving up on sports entirely.

This damage is measured in reports and statistics, and also in the stories told by the children themselves. We must pay attention to the mounting evidence of concern. In the next chapter, we'll do just that.

Injuries: A Toll on Body and Soul

*I see a lot of burnout. It used to
be high school, but now it is ten-, eleven-
and twelve-year-old kids. The kids get fried.*

Erik Johnson, former professional baseball
player, San Francisco Giants

This chapter could begin by revealing a shocking story of a child who has been victimized physically or psychologically by a youth sports system, a coach or even that child's own parents. Those stories are easy to find. But then you would probably say, "Those are extremes. They have nothing to do with my child." And you would be right: Those are the extremes. But you would also

97

be wrong because the pressures within youth sports systems that lead to such extremes have a lot to do with your child.

These pressures not only can hurt children physically, but they also can damage children's self-esteem and discourage their ambitions. That kind of hurt happens in big ways and in small ways in youth sports everywhere every day.

Sometimes the hurt is in what a coach says. Sometimes the damage is done because there is too much pressure to win. Sometimes the pain is in being told, either directly or by being cut, that you're just not good enough to play.

Things happening at home can be as damaging. Perhaps you don't force your child to participate, but do you apply subtle pressures that let him or her know sports participation status is important to you, that *you* like being part of an elite team? Do you ask your children often enough if playing sports continues to be fun for them? You never strike your child because of a poor sports performance, but do you offer rewards for a performance that makes you proud? Do you pay your child for hits, goals or other scoring accomplishments? Maybe you don't yell about your child's performance, but do you spend most of the ride home from a game analyzing his or her play? Does your child's coach do these things?

In subtle and not-so-subtle ways, youth sports systems built by adults have been killing the desire in many children. Research by the Institute for the Study of Youth Sports at Michigan State University found that between 60 and 70 percent of all children who play a sport in organized youth systems will drop out of that sport by the time they are thirteen years old. A number of factors influence this dropout rate, but there is no doubt among these researchers that the overheated youth sports systems—the way they operate and the way they demand so much—are among the principle forces driving children to quit.

If these systems "were structured differently, there's every reason to expect that the dropout rate would be significantly lower," Michael Clark, a key member of the institute's team and an assistant professor at the university, said in an interview for this book.

"We just force a lot of kids out," he said. "That's all there is to it."

The Damage Done

By talking to parents and children, by watching adults and children, I know there is a long list of ways in which your child may be hurt while participating in youth sports. Chances are one or more of these problems will affect your child.

There I go again—"chances are"—but that is really the most accurate way to describe the risks and the toll that youth sports can exact on our children. Chances are they will be hurt in at least one of these ways. Do you want to take those chances? Or do you want to reform systems, change methods and create better ways to help *all* children to succeed and have fun?

National foundations and agencies are studying these risks, and you'll read about that research later. Yet in many ways I don't need data to tell me what I can see and hear for myself. Children have told me these things are true, and so have many of their parents.

Here are some of those risks:

- Youth sports systems that select elite teams at young ages may undermine your child's self-esteem if he or she is not selected. Your child may not want to try out again.
- Select teams that set winning games as the priority may effectively eliminate your child from playing, either by cutting or keeping him or her on the bench.
- If your child is made to feel that he or she is not good enough to play, or if the games and practices become more like a chore than fun, your child may quit entirely.
- Your child may quit before finding out how good he or she really is, or might have been.
- Intense competition and year-round schedules may put your child at risk for overuse injuries that can damage your child's developing muscles, joints and bones, sometimes in permanent ways.
- Heavy-handed adult involvement in youth team sports may take away critical opportunities your child needs in order to learn how to organize on his or her own, to make rules and interpret rules, to truly learn how to contribute as a member of a team.
- Being coached to win above all else may stifle your child's inclination to be creative, spontaneous and a risk-taker, the best ingredients of the most successful team players, whether on youth teams or in the pros.
- All your efforts to have team sports teach your child about fair play, commitment, sportsmanship and leadership may be for naught, because your child's actual participation on those teams may teach him or her the opposite.

- All these pressures may destroy your child's love of the game.

Perhaps you're thinking, "Not all experiences in youth sports are bad experiences." Wonderful things happen all the time and every day across the country. There are terrific youth coaches and memorable times on the fields, ice rinks and gyms in which children eagerly and happily participate. I hope your child is lucky enough to be part of something like that, at least once.

Some athletes start young, play all the games the adults schedule for them, go to all the tournaments, play multiple seasons on multiple teams, go to high school and on to college, and are quite successful in sports all along the way. However, those success stories are in the vast minority. For sure there is a troubling number of children who end up being part of something in youth sports that is not wonderful at all.

Emotional Injuries

One of the most disturbing concerns in youth sports, sometimes hard to identify but definitely widespread, is what can be loosely called "emotional abuse." The National Youth Sports Safety Foundation (NYSSF), a nonprofit group based in Boston, is so concerned that it chose "emotional injuries in youth sports" as the centerpiece of its 2001 campaign for National Youth Sports Safety Month (April of every year). "Certain behaviors and philosophies [in youth sports] have been found to create a destructive environment, causing some children to be scarred for life," NYSSF Director Michelle Klein states in NYSSF publications posted on its Web site (*www.nyssf.org*).

Listen closely to how the NYSSF defines emotional abuse: "rejecting, ignoring, isolating, terrorizing, name calling, making fun of someone, putting someone down, saying things that hurt feelings and yelling."

Don't count yourself or your child out too quickly. The foundation says that emotional injuries do not occur only when a child is assaulted or threatened. Emotional injuries occur also with more subtle behavior, such as verbal put-downs, ignoring and yelling.

When exhibited by adults at youth sports events, assaultive behaviors have significant impact on a child who is forming deep feelings about his or her ability and self-esteem, about whether he or she is accepted and belongs or doesn't belong to a social group, namely a team or sports in general.

The NYSSF cites other examples of emotional abuse:

- Forcing a child to participate in sports.
- Not speaking to a child after he/she plays poorly in a game or at a practice.
- Asking your child why he/she played poorly when it meant so much to you.
- Hitting a child when his/her play disappoints you.
- Yelling at a child for not playing well or for losing.
- Punishing a child for not playing well or for losing.
- Criticizing and/or ridiculing a child for his/her sports performance.

Read that list again, and pay attention to the kinds of behaviors and attitudes that skirt the more extreme and obvious forms of abuse.

The Power of the Coach

In "Sports Competition and Its Influence on Self-Esteem Development," a winter 1989 article in the journal *Adolescence*, researchers at Bowling Green State University reported on a study that examined the factors that contribute to or take away from a child's self-esteem. What is so interesting is that more obvious factors, such as whether the child's team won or lost or whether the child had a particularly productive outing, didn't have nearly the effect as did what the coach thought of the child.

What a coach says, how he or she addresses a player, and whether there is praise or scorn make all the difference in a child's sports life. The study also cited effects from other teammates and the influence of parents, but the study added that "these are minor elements in comparison to the total impact of the coach."

Survey your adult friends. It probably won't take you long to find adults who remember those kind of "scarring" statements by former coaches.

Name Calling

A survey conducted in 1993 by the Minnesota Amateur Sports Commission and posted on its Web site (*www.masc. state.mn.us*) cited the following incidences of abuse in youth sports in Minnesota:

- 45.3 percent of males and females surveyed said they have been called names, yelled at or insulted while participating in sports.
- 17.5 percent said they have been hit, kicked or slapped.
- 21 percent said they have been pressured to play with an injury.
- 8.2 percent said they have been pressured to intentionally harm others.
- 8 percent said they have been called names with sexual connotations.

In youth sports, as in any relationship in which adults wield power over children, parents must guard for signs of sexual abuse, including improper touching. This book doesn't address those issues; it concentrates on emotional abuse that is more a byproduct of the ways in which youth sports systems are organized and managed.

The line between motivating players to win games and abusing them is sometimes not easily recognized. As the NYSSF reminds us in its publications, "People may not be clear what behaviors constitute maltreatment or abuse. Young athletes may not recognize what's happening to them is abusive."

Parental Rage

In its literature, the NYSSF cites another form of emotional abuse, namely parental rage at youth sports events. "What are the psychological effects on children who witness atrocities such as parental rage?" asks Dr. Leonard

Zaichkowsky, head of sport and exercise psychology at Boston University, and an NYSSF board member. Zaichkowsky warns, "Abuse will turn the child off to exercise and sports participation and prevent the development of healthy lifestyles that will promote wellness through the life span."

NYSSF literature includes suggestions for young athletes: "Number one: The most important thing is to have fun. Number two: Remember youth sports are only a game designed for your enjoyment. Play to please yourself and have a good time."

Can anyone doubt the toll that adults have taken on children playing games when national organizations have to remind children to have fun and to play for themselves?

Stolen Childhoods

Some of the attrition of children out of organized youth sports is, for sure, a natural consequence of adolescence. Children explore new interests and want to exercise their independence. There is the attraction of the opposite sex and, later, a license to drive.

Of course, not all the reasons young people quit sports have to do with the fact that they are growing up. A great many reasons have to do with those who are already grown up—the adults who have been in charge of their games since early childhood.

Chances are, a fair number of parents never really understand why their own child decided to drop out of a sport. Chances are, there are some parents who don't even ask why.

I mean *really* ask, in a long and careful conversation in a quiet place, with time for the child to open up.

One of the most poignant stories I ever heard about a child's experiences playing youth sports came from an adult who approached me at the end of one of my talks. This man was about twenty-five at the time. I could tell by the look in his eyes that he had a story he needed to tell.

He started playing youth hockey, he said, when he was three years old. It was the kind of hockey a lot of young children play. They learn how to skate first, and then some of the basics follow. It can be great fun to watch the tiny ones as they slip and slide. If you're serious about ice hockey and want your child to progress to higher and higher levels, as this man's father did, those pleasant interludes are quickly replaced by conditioning, practice and games. The expression I keep using sums up the mind-set you find in many other sports, too: More, more, more at younger, younger, younger will mean better, better, better.

By the time this young man was six years old, he was the most proficient hockey player in his small world. By age thirteen, this young "prodigy" had probably been in every rink in New England, at every hour of the day. Right by his side, every step of the way was his devoted father.

At this point in his story, the young man said, "I looked in the mirror at thirteen, and I said to myself, 'I hate hockey.'"

He was toast, burned-out, sick of all the time and effort he was giving to the sport. The trouble was, his father had invested so much time, so much effort, so much money into making his son a star that his son, then only thirteen years old, found it impossible to approach his father about how he truly felt. The young man started high school with one goal in mind: finishing four years of high school so he could go off to college and get away from hockey for good.

Those were tense years for the boy. His anxiety and dislike for the game slowly began to show. Gradually his father realized that his son had lost the fire in the belly. The father took it hard and took it with anger. The bitter climax came when the boy left for college and his father realized that his son wouldn't be playing hockey at all. That decision made for a lasting awkwardness between father and son.

Now that he is twenty-five, this young man had recently taken up hockey again for the first time since high school. He said he was playing one or two times a week with friends. No slap shots. No checking. He was having a ball.

Then he said something that stopped me cold. "This," he said, "is the hockey I should have been playing when I was eight or nine years old.

"Hockey," he said, "stole my childhood."

As much as he realized the toll that his father's heavy hand had taken, the son still could not bring himself to talk with his father about it. "He's not ready to hear this, and I'm not ready to say it." The wounds, as old as they were, had not yet healed.

Keep those wounds in mind as we continue to look at the toll that organized youth sports can exact on the minds and the bodies of our children.

Just Kids Being Kids

The worst thing we adults do in youth sports is to forget that these players are not miniature adults or high school stars in some kind of larval stage. They are children, with bones that have yet to develop, with minds that are not thinking the same way that we are thinking.

In that survey done by the Institute for the Study of Youth Sports at Michigan State, children were asked why they quit a sport or a team. For both boys and girls, the top two reasons were (1) they were no longer interested and (2) it was no longer fun.

The boys and girls each said the following were the top ten reasons they quit:

Boys

1. I was no longer interested.
2. It was no longer fun.
3. The sport took too much time.
4. The coach played favorites.
5. The coach was a poor teacher.
6. I was tired of playing.
7. There was too much emphasis on winning.
8. I wanted to participate in other non-sport activities.
9. I needed more time to study.
10. There was too much pressure.

Girls

1. I was no longer interested.
2. It was no longer fun.
3. I needed more time to study.
4. There was too much pressure.
5. The coach was a poor teacher.
6. I wanted to participate in other non-sport activities.

7. The sport took too much time.
8. The coach played favorites.
9. I was tired of playing.
10. Games and practices were scheduled when I could not attend.

You'll probably agree that most of these reasons have to do with adults not meeting the wants and needs of the children. Adults are creating too much pressure, demanding too much time, failing to appropriately support and motivate the children. The children's comments that they feel too much pressure is most troubling. Whether or not they tell you, children often feel that knot in their stomachs before games. For some children, soon that knot is sticking around after games, through practices and maybe throughout the week.

Look at the reasons why children quit sports, and the door seems wide open for adults to solve most of the problems that turn children away. A lot of the trouble centers on whether the children see the process as fair or the participation as fun.

The children who answered the Institute for the Study of Youth Sports survey also were asked what kinds of changes would make them consider playing again. The top change, according to both boys and girls: if practices were more fun. The second reason on the boys' list, and number five on the girls' list: if I could play more.

Our youth sports systems fail our children in many ways at different ages, perhaps most profoundly when they are in the throes of puberty and its emotional upheaval and physical changes. Their self-esteem is fragile at this time in their lives, and they have an intense desire to feel as though they belong. They also have an urgent need then for safe activities.

Chapter 10 presents middle schools that are taking strides toward keeping the most children possible involved in sports and other activities for as long as possible. One school's "no-cuts" programs even include what is perhaps the most stereo-typical clique of all: cheerleaders.

At these schools, if you want to join almost any team — from track to wrestling to swimming — you join. The only requirement is that you show up to play. For certain other sports, different ones at different schools, there are tryout squads but also an extensive intramural program that keeps kids in the sport long enough to get to high school, where some of the intramural players beat out the others to secure places on the varsity squads.

Too Much Pressure

Think about the dynamics of many competitive youth sports systems in terms of a big machine, a big machine that easily overheats and races out of control. The fuel that runs this machine is made up of the parents and the coaches who may start with good intentions but get caught up more and more in feeding this big machine.

The new soccer league in town, for instance, may start with a simple league structure of teams — especially at young ages — that play each other in town. After a few seasons, some parents of children who appear to be "the best" in this sport begin to feel something is missing. Their particular kids, they start to think, are showing real talent and they are losing out on better competition. There's a team in the next town or the next county or even the next state that has players about the same age, and they're just aching for fresh competition. The big machine is soon on overdrive. Parents organize travel teams and elite squads. Road trip! Parental egos and a full tank of gas—a frightening combination.

Talk about pressure. The big machine is soon spitting out schedules that are longer than professional seasons. Playing seasons set up in the spring begin creeping into the summer months. Tournaments prolong the seasons. All the while, parents and coaches are at the helm demanding nothing less than total dedication.

For most parents the pressure to go along, the lure of being included in the "select" group, is tremendous. Can you imagine the courage it takes for a parent, especially the parent of a child who has been selected for an elite squad, to suggest that schedules be cut back? Cutting back, coaches and league officials might argue, would mean losing valuable practice and playing time. Other teams, other communities, will get ahead and stay ahead. "We can't take that chance," they would cry.

Many ten-year-old hockey players participate in a hundred or more games in a season that runs from August to May. Remember that youth hockey program in Maine I mentioned that travels to Massachusetts every Sunday for twenty-six straight weeks? Those children would be just fine—better off, in fact—playing half that time or less.

Will your team be just as good if the children practice or play less? Maybe yes, maybe no and maybe just a little. But which would you choose: winning another game or two, or giving your children a more balanced childhood?

Long seasons are sometimes put together unwittingly by youth coaches. My hometown belongs to a loose association of surrounding communities that establish A- and B-level basketball teams to play each other. During one night each year, the coaches of all the teams travel from table to table, booking games against other teams. In a few hours some coaches manage to book thirty to forty games for their twelve-year-olds.

I once talked to a Babe Ruth baseball coach confused about the lack of enthusiasm among his thirteen-year-old players. "For you and me," I explained to this coach, "the number of organized games we played before high school numbered in the teens. How many games do you think a typical player in youth sports has played by the time he or she becomes a teenager? For some children, the games number in the hundreds. Who wouldn't lose interest?"

"I see a lot of burnout," former professional baseball player Erik Johnson told the *San Francisco Chronicle* (December 10, 2000). "It used to be high school, but now it is ten-, eleven- and twelve-year-old kids. The kids get fried. They quit," said Johnson, who played for the San Francisco Giants and now runs a personal-training program. "They resent the game. They don't want to see the game.

"The all-star kid, that 5 percent, will always be there," he added. "Where are the other 95 percent? They want to go to practice a couple of times a week, play a game, get a snack and make some friends. Those are the ones we need to pay attention to."

Specialization

When seasons are prolonged, when schedules are lengthy, when youngsters play the same sport from one season to the next and eventually year-round, they often end up specializing in one sport. If you want to be truly great, some adults say, you need to focus, then do more, more, more and you'll be better, better, better.

Specialization is one of the most prevalent and disturbing trends in organized youth sports. The big machine doesn't stop eating until it has chewed up all twelve months of the calendar year.

"Specialization." It sounds so serious, so conducive to a serious young athlete, so perfect for creating an unbeatable team. Yet specialization and all the sacrifices that youth sports organizations make to get there can end up burning out even the brightest stars.

The American Academy of Pediatrics, which represents fifty-five thousand pediatricians and pediatric specialists nationwide, has issued a policy statement warning against specialization in a sport at an early age, year-round training and competition on an "elite" level for young athletes.

In its statement, published in the July 2000 edition of the journal *Pediatrics*, the academy further advised that children be encouraged to participate in a variety of different activities and to develop a wide range of skills. The risks for children who specialize or train year-round range from overuse injuries to emotional stress and burnout. "Those who participate in a variety of sports and specialize only after reaching the age of puberty tend to be more consistent performers, have fewer

injuries, and adhere to sports play longer than those who specialize early," the academy advises. The academy concedes
that there is a need for more scientific research to support
these risks, but the academy nevertheless urges caution.

In a July 14, 2000, Associated Press story, Dr. Steven
Anderson, a University of Washington sports specialist and
chairman of the academy's committee on sports medicine
and fitness, says waiting to specialize helps to ensure children
will pursue an activity that really interests them, rather than
just their parents.

In my own experience, specialization would have been a
dreadful mistake, probably a fatal blow to my chances of a
professional career. What interested the scouts and coaches
about a forward from the University of Pennsylvania who
didn't peak until his senior year in college? I had several
abilities, I suppose, but one of the more important ones was
my ability to catch a ball.

My childhood sports activities were about as diversified as
you could get. By the time I was ready for serious high school
varsity ball, my hands were ready because I played so many
varied games as a youngster, and not because I had specialized in basketball. I didn't even play organized basketball
until high school.

Dean Conway, the Massachusetts soccer coach, agrees.
"Shoot a basketball, play some hockey, take violin lessons,
add some variety to your life and try something new instead
of just playing soccer all the time," he says in a February 1999
article in *The Bay Stater*. Specialization, he counsels, should
wait until age fifteen or sixteen.

Overuse Injuries

Pressure on young players and specialized year-round play in one sport can cause injuries, notably overuse injuries. In an article posted on the *WholeLifeHealth.com* Web site, Dr. Lyle J. Micheli, director of the Division of Sports Medicine at Boston Children's Hospital and a nationally recognized authority on youth sports injury, writes, "The fact that most of these injuries are preventable raises troubling questions about children and organized sports."

The developing bodies of children are more susceptible to such injuries. During growth, children's developing bones are softer and weaker; their ligaments, tendons and muscles are tighter. Particularly at risk in children are growth plates, areas of developing tissue at the ends of growing bones. A bruise or a sprain that might not be a significant injury for an adult athlete might result in a serious growth-plate injury in a growing child.

Injuries that are the result of overuse develop slowly, and thus may be overlooked or not properly treated. Evidence suggests some of these injuries may cause permanent damage or pain, including arthritis.

Micheli sees large numbers of children suffering from such ailments as bursitis, tendonitis and stress fractures, ailments that used to be confined almost entirely to adult locker rooms. "Until recently, runner's knee (pain caused by the kneecap not tracking or sliding along its groove properly) was unheard of in kids. Now it is the number-one diagnosis in my practice," Micheli said in a November 6, 2000, article in *USA Today.*

Traumatic injuries, referred to medically as acute trauma or macrotrauma—such as broken bones, sprains and contusions—cannot be avoided, whether they occur in organized sports or in the backyard, although they can be reduced with the use of effective equipment. Increasingly, however, medical specialists and national groups are concerned about high rates of certain kinds of injuries that they did not see in significant numbers before organized youth sports hit the fast lane.

When children participated in free play, these experts say, they typically quit playing or went home when they got tired or they got hurt. Now experts fear that intense and specialized participation in organized sports causes what is medically referred to as "repetitive microtrauma" that may go unrecognized by untrained parents and coaches who may allow or even encourage a hurt child to stay in a game. A child, on the other hand, may be afraid to disappoint a parent or coach and may not ask to be pulled when hurt or tired. Experts also worry that training practices set up by untrained coaches may lack appropriate safeguards and may put children at risk.

National and international authorities urge more research to determine the rates and risks of overuse injuries in order to encourage efforts to prevent such damage. The National Institutes of Health has sponsored research on youth sports injuries and provides access to information for parents. The International Federation of Sports Medicine and the World Health Organization issued a joint position statement in 1998 which called for studies on the benefits and risks of organized sports for children. The National Athletic Trainers Association (NATA) Research & Education Foundation based in Dallas considers youth sports injuries a "public health issue" and has committed $250,000 toward research.

"As more and more children participate in organized sports every year, it is important that a study of this type be undertaken to determine who is at risk and enable more effective injury prevention and management," Micheli said in a July 28, 1998, press statement released by the NATA. "In addition," Micheli said, research is needed to "help identify the consequences of intense physical activity on developing young adults."

At the forefront of medical research on techniques and equipment intended to prevent sports-related injuries is the Institute for Preventative Sports Medicine in Ann Arbor, Michigan (*www.ipsm.org*). Founded by Dr. David H. Janda, an orthopedic surgeon, the institute has conducted studies on the effectiveness of such protective equipment as soft-core baseballs, breakaway bases and chest protectors. The institute's research, details of which are posted on its Web site, generally found that heavier soft-core baseballs were no more effective in reducing chest-impact injuries than traditional hardballs, although the lightest weight baseballs produced better results.

The institute is also conducting research on such issues as alternative coaching techniques in football, prevention of cervical spine injuries in hockey, the effectiveness of soccer shin guards and padded goalposts as well as the risks of "heading" soccer balls.

Janda is one of the expert contributors to an Internet resource for youth sports parents called MomsTeam (*MomsTeam.com*), which offers a wide range of information and advice on youth sports issues from safety to sportsmanship to politics. Read more about this site at the end of chapter 8.

In his book, *The Awakening of a Surgeon*, Janda also looks at the politics of sports safety, as he describes his crusade to make playing safer for children and adults, including battles with equipment manufacturers, insurance companies and the government.

Micheli, of Boston Children's Hospital, says that when he cofounded the country's first pediatric sports medicine clinic in 1974, "Many people scoffed at my ambition to not only treat sports injuries in children, but to prevent them." Since then, according to an article for *WholeLifeHealth.com*, Micheli reports seeing alarming rates of overuse injuries, including minor fractures and minimal muscle tears, especially in elbows, heels, ankles and knees. Of the children who come to his Boston clinic seeking treatment for sports-related injuries, he said, 80 percent suffer from overuse injuries.

In calling for more accurate nationwide collection of data on youth sports injuries, experts recognize challenges. There is no central collection agency, community programs are not required to keep such data, overuse injuries often go unnoticed or unreported, and such injuries may be treated by a pediatrician rather than a sports medicine specialist or hospital more likely to track such data.

Experts also worry that youth sports systems and coaches, either because they are misinformed or have entrenched attitudes about the inevitability of sports injuries, may fail to see this as a significant or preventable problem. In an article published in October 2000 in *Pediatric and Adolescent Sports Injuries*, Micheli along with Michelle Klein and Rita

Glassman of the National Youth Sports Safety Foundation, cite one such barrier, which they call "tradition-bound resistance." This kind of resistance may surface, for instance, in youth baseball leagues that refuse to consider the lightest weight baseballs and breakaway bases because they part from tradition.

Youth baseball also may present a risk for child pitchers who throw too many pitches or certain kinds of pitches. Throwing curve balls, for instance, puts tremendous torque on young elbows. By now most leagues have guidelines about the number and types of pitches that can be thrown by a child. Even then, the guidelines aren't always a safeguard. I believe children are throwing the ball harder and faster than they ever did, mostly because this is the great expectation, begun with the radar gun used by networks for major league pitchers. Seeing a fastball clocked on TV at ninety-five miles per hour inspires untold numbers of youngsters to throw that ball as fast as they can.

In an article for the journal *Sports Medicine and Arthroscopy Review* published in 1996, Micheli and A. Ross Outerbridge, M.D., reported another relatively new and significant injury pattern: anterior cruciate ligament tears in the knees of adolescent females. More study is needed, they say, to determine whether and why this population is at increased risk.

Micheli, Klein and Glassman also outline critical needs to be addressed by those who make decisions about youth sports participation. These guidelines are based on recommendations from the American College of Sports Medicine, of which Micheli is a past president, as well as from the

International Federation of Sports Medicine and the World Health Organization.

They recommend more education for parents and coaches about injury risks and child development issues, as well as national standards for coaches' training and certification. Adults also need to recognize that children are often not physically fit. Training for youth sports should focus not just on sports skills but also on general physical fitness in order to prepare children to participate in practices and in games.

The guidelines also caution adults not to place too much emphasis on winning. Children should be encouraged to participate in a variety of sports, and adults should be reminded that children on their own, without adult pressure, will typically—and wisely—quit playing when they are hurt or tired.

The recommendations suggest that rules for adult games be modified for children, as should the length of playing times, and the size of playing fields and equipment. Chapter 7 suggests specific adaptations.

"On the one hand, we are trying to encourage physical activity, and on the other hand we're seeing the problem with uncontrolled organized sports for kids," Micheli told USA Today in November 2000. "We're all in favor of sports. We just have to do them well. We can't afford to have these kids turned off to physical activity and sports. That's a lose-lose situation."

The Obesity Epidemic

Sometimes the toll of youth sports systems—particularly those that eliminate children at young ages or discourage them from participating—can be seen in those who no longer play sports at all. Remember the reminder from the Centers for Disease Control (CDC) that the percentage of young people who are overweight has *doubled* since 1980, an "unprecedented epidemic of childhood obesity"?

To be sure, the problems in youth sports are not alone to blame for an increase in obesity. The attractions of video games, computers and television also contribute heavily. School systems are cutting back or cutting out physical education classes in, I think, misguided pursuit of more time for "academics." Eating habits are a problem, too; American diets are too high in fat.

The U.S. secretary of health and human services and the U.S. secretary of education presented a report to the president in the fall of 2000 titled "Promoting Better Health for Young People Through Physical Activity and Sports." The report calls on those involved in youth sports and other activities to do their part to offer a range of opportunities for children and adolescents to be active. "Our young people . . . will not increase their levels of physical activity and fitness unless they are sufficiently motivated to do so."

Children need to "develop confidence in their physical abilities" and be "guided by competent, knowledgeable and supportive adults," the report to the president says. *Supportive* adults helping *all* young children to *develop confidence* in their physical activities: If I were putting youth sports systems on trial, these words would be in my closing remarks. As the report says, "enhancing efforts to promote participation in physical activity and sports among young people is a critical national priority."

As you look to change youth sports systems, remember this chapter. Come back to it for the best reminders about why you fight. You fight because children are being hurt under the current systems. You fight because, in the extreme cases and the not-so-extreme, children are being used and abused in the form of physical injury and emotional abuse. That happens when you, the parent, may not be paying attention, and it lingers sometimes until that child of yours is a man or woman with his or her own children.

●●●

Now that you've had a chance to consider the destructive forces in youth sports, it's time to begin writing some of them out of the equation. In the next chapter, we look at factors that shape better systems—better for you and better for your children.

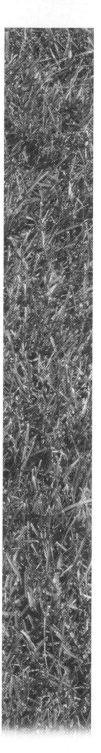

CHAPTER 5

Organizing Teams: Starting Off Right

If you are not committed to serving all who sign up to play, you have started off on the wrong foot. Don't cater to the few at the expense of many.

When adults organize leagues, assemble teams, and manage games and players, they often forget to consider these activities through the eyes of the children who will play. There are step-by-step ideas in this chapter to help adults pay attention to the developmental needs of each age group. I figured out some of these ideas the hard way.

Here's one of the snapshots from the scrapbook of my life's most awkward moments: a basketball clinic in February 1988 with me surrounded by boys not much taller than the hems of my basketball shorts. That's me in the middle, trying to teach basketball's equivalent of calculus to a bewildered group of third- and fourth-graders.

Actually, my topic that day was the pick and roll, a two-player basketball maneuver that, executed well, sets up one player to take a better shot. The problem, which I didn't realize at the time, was that my audience of players—about a hundred eight- and nine-year-olds—wasn't ready for this lecture.

At my clinic four boys tried to demonstrate the techniques involved in the pick and roll. They attempted it again and again. And again. I could tell the boys didn't get it, and I knew the rest of the young audience also had no idea what I was talking about. One look at their faces told me.

I left the gym that day feeling embarrassed because I knew the kids hadn't learned a thing. I had a sense that I had been trying to teach something they simply were not ready to learn, but I didn't understand the entirety of the challenge.

My sense of how ridiculous my pick and roll clinic had been for third-graders was confirmed years later when I stopped by a Boston Celtics practice. There I saw then-coach Chris Ford's frustrating attempts to get his professional players to master the subtleties of the pick and roll. These guys had multimillion-dollar contracts, and they were having trouble, too.

An Epiphany

For years I had known things weren't quite right with youth sports, but the defining moment—an epiphany that helped launch my crusade—came during a trip to Maine in August

1992. I had gone there to lecture at the New Sport Experience Camp for boys ages nine to fifteen.

New Sport was located on the campus of a private preparatory school about twenty miles north of Augusta. New Sport campers learned skills in a variety of sports and competed in games against other camps throughout the state.

As I walked around, a lot of the activities looked pretty familiar to me: the typical sights and sounds of summer youth sports. Yet I was struck by something unfamiliar.

Adult counselors were continually asking children what they liked or didn't like about the activities, what they wanted to do and what they needed. And the kids, even the youngest, had definite responses.

I went to the camp's founder, Jeff Beedy, who at the time was studying for his doctorate at Harvard, and I asked about what I had watched occur between camper and counselor. His explanation was simple: This camp belongs to the children, the counselors are the children's counselors, and those counselors are asking their customers what they want and what they need. Beedy had based the camp's curriculum on the children's wants and needs, and that curriculum was continually being adjusted to serve exactly that.

Beedy said, "When I founded this camp what I wanted to do, ultimately, was to give sports back to the children."

During my three-hour drive home, the idea of "giving sports back to the children" played over and over in my head like lyrics you can't get out of your mind. So much of what I had been feeling and thinking during the previous four years began to gel. I thought back to that awkward clinic, with me trying to teach the pick and roll to third- and fourth-graders.

In youth sports, the kids are the customers. The adults should meet their customers' needs. A pick and roll clinic for nine-year-olds is not good customer service.

As I look around at the entirety of youth sports as it has evolved over the past twenty to thirty years in America, I realize that so much of what the adults are doing truly does not serve the wants and needs of their customers—*all* the children.

The Most Important Question

When you organize a youth sports program, when you sign up your child, or when you watch him or her at practices or at games, continually ask yourself a question: Is this program, practice or game primarily serving the needs of the children in this age group—*all* the children—or is it primarily serving the needs of the adults? Your answer to that question will guide you toward making good choices in the best interests of your children.

If winning is not the children's top priority—and they have told us time and again that it is not—then making choices about which children play and which children do not play based on how best to win the most games does not serve primarily the children's wants. It serves primarily the adults' wants.

Kids want to have fun—that *is* their top priority. If all the drills, all the yelling and screaming from the sidelines and the pressure-packed schedules ruin the fun, the adults have missed the quintessential mark.

Kids want to play. They don't want to sit and watch other

kids play or watch adults coach. If you are making choices that keep kids on the bench, you are making choices that do not serve the wants, the needs *and the rights* of *all* the children, rather than just a select few.

Kids deserve the chance to succeed. If you are intent on identifying "talent" at an early age, selecting elite teams and discouraging those who are cut, you are damaging what is every child's right to have a chance to succeed. You are doing it for no good reason because until children are more fully developed, their "talent" should not be and cannot be accurately evaluated.

Kids learn best by doing, not just by listening, and they learn by being spontaneous, creative and by taking chances. Thus, practices and games do not serve children's needs if they discourage those natural instincts and create fears about making mistakes.

Kids need time to relax, time for their bodies to recharge, time for their minds to wander. Kids need to daydream now and then. They need a day off. If their youth sports schedules overexert their bodies, overtax their energies and rob them of their free time, those schedules are not meeting children's needs.

You see the point. You see the pattern. So much of what adults create in the name of youth sports violates the very nature of being a child, the natural wants and needs of children.

Watch Children Play

To design programs, schedules, practices and games that meet the needs and wants of children, you need to understand them, talk to them, listen to them, watch them.

Find a group of children playing a game on their own and watch how they play. You will see that they like to compete, they want to win and they have a pretty good idea who's better than others.

It's difficult these days to find a group of children able to organize their own games because our culture does not create many opportunities to learn how to do that. If you can find such a group, you will see that children on their own make choices that meet their wants and needs. They don't want a weak or a dominating team; they want a close game because it's more exciting, more fun. They want to make the rules, but they want to bend them, too. They're creative. They take chances. They're always moving. And they're inclusive: You won't see children in a backyard game agreeing to sit on the bench because they're simply not good enough to play. If they are excluded, they will most likely look for another game.

Here's the kicker: If adults choose programs that truly meet the needs of children, those choices will eliminate the roots of much of the preposterous, angry and sometimes violent behavior in the stands and on the sidelines.

The behaviors of adults who are coaching or watching children's games grow out of the nature of the youth sports program in which they participate. Adult behaviors are often responses to those pressures. Take the adult ego out of that process and you remove much of that pressure.

You cannot expect to solve all the problems by sending parents to behavior class to teach them how to respect systems that are essentially inappropriate and unhealthy. And you should not teach children how to maintain a positive attitude in the face of adult choices that violate children's basic rights. Don't seek out magazine articles on "The How To's of Being a Most Excellent Benchwarmer." Get the children off the bench instead.

Establish a Good Governing Board

A great place to begin reforming youth sports systems in the interests of the children is at the administration level by asking yourself this question: Who is developing and overseeing this program for the children?

I hope, although it's rarely the case, that you would have help from professionals who are experts about children, such as physical education teachers, pediatricians, psychologists, child development specialists. They understand the needs of children, how children learn at different levels and in different ways, and the wide range of physical attributes and skills within each age group.

Isn't being a parent good enough? No. Everyone thinks, "Well, I'm a parent of a kid. I know kids." But parents have not been kids in a long time. They've forgotten what it's like to be a kid. They probably didn't give it much thought when they were kids. Most parents are not trained and experienced in all aspects of the development of *all* kinds of children.

There are dangers in having parents alone create and administer youth sports programs. Parents tend to look at programs already in place, such as high school varsity, college, the pros. Too often they create youth sports programs modeled after high school, college and professional systems. They forget that those programs were developed to meet the needs of fourteen-year-olds, eighteen-year-olds, twenty-five-year-olds—some of them elite athletes, none of them in elementary school.

This is not to say that parents should be left out of the administration process. They should be actively involved, but they should seek the guidance of experts.

One of the best resources in this regard is a new effort underway on the Internet, called the Center for Sports Parenting (*www.sportsparenting.org*), which is housed on the campus of the University of Rhode Island. At the center's Web site you will find direct access to about twenty leading experts in the field of youth sports, from pediatricians to psychologists to coaches. Among the experts is Rick Wolff, a specialist in sports psychology and sports parenting issues, who also cofounded the center. You'll find me at the center's Web site, too. Ask us your questions via e-mail, and you will get our answers within a few weeks. You'll also find online forums that address new topics each month. (You can read more about the center in chapter 9.)

Put Your Mission in Writing

The first order of business for any reformer is to write a clear mission statement. A well-crafted mission statement gives you and all the other adults involved a reference point that sets the tone and goals of your system. If your current league doesn't have a mission statement already—it's amazing how many don't—this is your chance to start fresh.

A mission statement shouldn't be fancy or wordy. You could use something like this: "We, the adults who establish this league for our children at play, commit ourselves to the fundamental proposition that we will meet the age-appropriate needs of *all* those children we serve."

But there's one important rule. Each time you use the word "children," make sure you put the word "all" before it. If you are not committed to serving *all* who sign up to play, you have started off on the wrong foot. Don't cater to the few at the expense of many.

Doug Abrams, law professor and youth hockey coach, says a good league measures its success by how it treats its least talented player. In other words: If you're involved in a league, ask yourself if your least talented player wants to come back the following year.

It's a great yardstick. The way we succeed is to commit ourselves to meeting the age-appropriate needs of *all* players. It means we acknowledge that five-year-olds are not miniature eight-year-olds, and that eight-year-olds are not miniature twelve-year-olds. It means we never forget that children are not miniature adults.

Be Specific

If you are a coach, you should make sure that your organization has written a clear mission statement. Your next step is to add details to that statement in order to create a plan of action for your team for this season. Put that in writing, too. One way to avoid some of the tension among adults on the sidelines is to make sure clear goals have been written that support a commitment to all of the children who sign up to play. As the coach, you must be specific. It is in the ambiguity between the lines that some of the worst infighting breaks out.

Explain how teams will be chosen. Establish rules for tryouts. At what age will children be subjected to tryouts in order to determine team placements? How will the results be used? Who will be in charge of evaluating the children? Make fair rules. And make a written commitment, as much as you can, that you will start each new season with a clean slate: Children will be evaluated each year based on their skills at that time, not based on their résumé, their placement from the previous year or who their parents know.

Explain how playing time will be determined. Don't offer a general statement that your system gives "all kids a chance to play." Be specific. If you commit to giving every child playing time that equals at least half of every game, say exactly that. Explain how scores will be kept and reported. Define your league's vision of a winning season. Explain whether or not standings will be compiled. Describe how the season will be structured: Will there be playoffs? How will it be determined who plays in those playoffs? Will the rules about equal or meaningful playing time apply to those playoffs?

Print out that mission statement and those rules and include them when you mail home a simple parent's and player's survey. No one has a lot of time these days to fill out paperwork. The surveys should simply ask your customers what they want and what they need.

Poll parents: How many practices would they like to see this season? How many games? Is there anything about their child that would be important for you, the coach, to understand? How do the parents define a successful season?

Poll your players: What is their favorite thing about playing this sport? What is their least favorite? Ask your players how important it is for them to win games. Ask your players how important it is for them to play equal time or minimum meaningful time. Ask your players to suggest five ideas to make practices and games more fun. Ask each player to define what would be a successful season for him or her. For very young children, the player's poll should be super simple, something to be filled out by their parents who would ask the child the questions.

Poll yourself, the coach: Why did you sign up to coach this team this season? What is your favorite thing about coaching this sport? What is your least favorite? How will you organize your team? How do you define a successful season?

You may be surprised at some of the answers you get, including from yourself.

Write a Plan and a Pledge

Gather the information received from players and parents and then draft a plan for this team for this season. Put your plans, your commitments, in writing—your coach's pledge, if you will. Make a copy for everyone and let them know the time and place of your preseason meeting. You may want to forgo one practice to have your preseason meeting in that time slot instead. Time spent with parents will be worthwhile time, essential time.

Write a pledge that states how playing time will be divided. If everyone will get a minimum of twelve to fifteen minutes in a basketball game, put it on paper. It will keep you honest during the pressure of the game. The parents who want you to play only "the best" can see in advance, in writing, how this team will be played. The parents who want to play "everyone the same" can see where you stand. This will cut off some of the anger and the resentment from both sides during the heat of competition.

Explain how positions will be assigned. This can be difficult, but the more of this you can plan in advance and commit to in writing, the better off you will be during the season. This helps to take personalities and politics out of the picture.

Tell parents and players—after taking into account their answers to your surveys—how many games and practices will be scheduled, how long each practice will be and how many weeks the season will last. If you've got plans for postseason playoffs or tournaments or round-robin competitions, let your players and their parents know from the start.

Schedule in writing—yes, in writing—a few days off. Everyone deserves that. It provides balance and gives players and their parents a break now and then, a scheduled break. It also lets everyone see that youth sports is just one part of what is, hopefully, a balanced family life.

Be clear about the commitment expected from parents and players. State your rules about sanctioned excuses for missing a practice or a game, the procedure by which to notify the coach (emphasize the need to know this in advance) and the consequences of missing a practice or a game. Will the player be asked to sit out the next one? Tell your players under what circumstances they will be asked that, and under what circumstances they will not.

Honor Thy Families

Suggest to parents that they consider something along the lines of a "Family Impact Statement." You may be cringing because this sounds dreadfully serious. It's not. It is simply a direct look at how much time this child and his or her family will be expected to commit to this sport during this season.

Suggest that families sit down together, all of their children included, and decide if this schedule is good for them. What will they have to sacrifice in order to make the commitment to this team and all the other teams to which they may belong?

Encourage your parents to come to you, the coach, or the league individually or as a group if the kinds of schedules you are drawing up do not meet their families' needs. Maybe everyone agrees there should be fewer events, practices or games. Wouldn't that be something? Parents are trying to keep up with an exhausting schedule because they don't want to confront coaches, and the coaches are trying to create an exhausting schedule because they think that's what all the parents want, or that's what their opponents are doing and they need to keep up. By the way, is anyone going to ask the children what *they* want?

Sometimes a team's overall approach does not work well for an individual child. Sometimes adjustments can be made for a particular player. This team of yours is a collection of individuals, very different individuals growing at different rates and discovering different things about themselves. Honor those differences.

Time to Play

The preseason meeting at which you describe the plan to parents and players needn't be long and needn't be complicated. Allow twenty minutes for your talk, and then take questions until there are no more. Parents are about to place their children in a coach's hands for six to twelve weeks of a season. The least they can do is to get acquainted, listen to the plan and share their own ideas. Attending this meeting should be mandatory for at least one parent of each child.

However long your meeting goes, leave some time afterward for a pickup game in your sport—parents versus kids. What good this kind of activity can accomplish.

First, it helps show your children that you and they are all involved in youth sports primarily to have fun. Second, it breaks the ice and brings everyone on the team a little closer. Third, it reminds parents how much they know, or don't know, about the game their kids will be playing for the next few months. Last, but certainly not least, maybe it will give Mom or Dad something to think about the next time they're tempted to scream, "Caitlin, can't you do *anything* right?"

Draft Dodging

In addition to tryouts and cuts to select elite teams, adults wield their power over children in youth sports in other essentially unhealthy ways. One of the most insidious adaptations for children based on professional sports systems is the concept of preseason drafts. There are much better ways in which leagues can establish procedures to ensure fair access and good choices for *all* the children who sign up to play.

Drafts happen everywhere in youth sports. The intention — to balance the varying athletic abilities of players on teams — may be generally appropriate at most ages because close games are the most fun. Yet the results of drafts are often damning, not to mention ludicrous in the way they're done.

Prior to these drafts, leagues generally hold evaluations, at which point the children and their "talent" are sized up and labeled. The adults who get to the negotiating table with the best information have a leg up. That means a lot of coaches "scout" talent and play politics. This is when a "savvy" coach enlists the father of one of his best team prospects to be his assistant coach. That's a lock.

Now, locked and loaded, the coaches go to the drafting table. Left to their own devices, adults compete against other adults for the best young "talent."

Once the teams are fielded, the coaches show up with their roster, their equipment and often some emotional baggage, too. A lot of these coaches are just dying to win their games against the other coaches who have already "beat" them at their first competition, the draft. The adult ego reigns over such coaches' decisions, particularly about which children play in which games and for how long.

The solution? Take the adult egos out of the draft by having a blind draft. It's simple. First, pair up your head coaches and their offspring. They will eventually go as a unit to an assigned team. Next, take the rest of your players and evaluate them by relative ability. An easy way to do this is to assign

Memo to Parents and Ballplayers

TOM MORONEY
The MetroWest Daily News
April 5, 1998

As coach of this year's Dust Devils, the greatest Little League team under the sun, I'd like to introduce some of the procedures and ground rules for the season ahead.

1. Practice will be held not once, but five times a week. That leaves us a day for the game, plus a day off (usually Sundays). On our "free" day, each ballplayer will spend at least an hour or two in the batting cage. I'll have sign-up sheets ready at the first practice. If this should interfere with church or church-related activities, let me know and I'll send a note to the clergy in question.

2. Dust Devils players are encouraged to make use of their spare time by working with strength trainers and/or dietitians. Beads, spiritual advisers, gurus, holy men and other sources of stress relief are acceptable, as long as they do not interfere with practice time. See me for a list of professionals in the area.

3. The league has scheduled us for twenty-five games. The coaches who love baseball got together and opted for a few more, fifty-seven to be exact. We now have an eighty-two-game season, one more game than a professional baseball team's homestand. This takes us through to Columbus Day. With any luck, we should have the playoff season wrapped up the week after Thanksgiving. Please make your holiday plans accordingly.

4. Generally, both family vacations and sick leave are frowned upon in the Dust Devils organization. Short of a death in the family, and only a close family member at that, it is unlikely I would give permission for any leave once our season is underway. If you think the sacrifice is too large, I would remind you of those brave Cuban ballplayers who recently cast themselves adrift in unfriendly seas in order to play baseball in America. Kind of puts things in perspective, don't you think?

5. In the spirit of better communication, I'm asking all families to send me their e-mail address ASAP. My address is *coach.macho@dustdevils.com*. I'll be using e-mail to issue all players instructional video clips on hitting and fielding. If your computer cannot download video clips, contact your local dealer for the equipment necessary to upgrade.

6. HELP WANTED: a parent, preferably with an accounting degree, who can update the Dust Devils' exhaustive storehouse of individual stats. As you may remember from last year, one of our boys lost the batting title when we could not produce authenticated documentation of our seasonal averages calculated to the ten-thousandths place.

This will not happen again!

7. Team photos will be taken this coming Thursday in the high school gym. In order to use our time wisely, tell your children to bring their gloves. The coaching staff will be on hand to hit them ground balls as they wait in line.

8. Playing time. This is always a difficult topic, one that leaves many families emotionally drained. Baseball, as I see it, is one of our last bastions of pure democratic activity, a place where all children, regardless of ability, can come and enjoy the fresh air and the invigorating sense of competition. Therefore, I try to be fair and give even the lowliest player on the squad as much playing time as the best—unless, of course, we're way behind. ∎

each player a number from one to three—the ones being the most skilled, the twos in the middle and the threes at the lower end. Next, have adults who are not the coaches—maybe the league board members—create rosters by divvying up players. This is done by putting an equal number of ones, twos and threes on each team. This should create some parity among the teams. As a last step, put the name of each team into a hat and have your head coaches draw a team from the hat. To complete the roster, add the coach's child. There you have it: an entire league created without politics, jockeying or infighting, or at least we can all hope so. The following year, start from scratch—including "clean slate" tryouts and evaluations.

The Beginnings of Change

Throughout the process of evaluating the capabilities—incapabilities, really—of children, we often encourage pompous and officious adults with clipboards, those who think they are some sort of big deal just because they're in charge of—wow!—the *ratings*. We often create a tense atmosphere for the kids because these are—take a deep breath!—*tryouts*.

With drafts driven by adult egos, some coaches build youth sports dynasties year to year. There's no mystery to these forces of human nature at work. These are natural behaviors. You can't easily change human emotions, so you have to change the systems that encourage these negative behaviors. Like my father used to say when my brothers and I were fighting over the biggest share of something that had to be divided, "One of you cuts, the other ones choose." If your cuts are unfair, you'll lose out in the end because everyone else will choose a bigger piece of the pie.

Children as young as kindergarteners are evaluated and subjected to adult competition in drafts. I know of a first-round soccer pick who was six years old. Is there any six-year-old child who should be labeled as a "superior athlete" compared with his friends? No. In any group of children at any age there are always some better, some worse, but the so-called "better" players are truly just "less awful," and adults would do well to remember that.

The problem is that adults approach these issues with adult minds and egos: How can we take what is done with higher level sports and use that for our children? When we set up programs, are we meeting the needs of the adults or are we meeting the needs of the children? That's the question we must never forget to ask.

Close Games Are More Fun

Paul Diguette of Acton, Massachusetts, has a passion for baseball. He translated that into years of active participation in the Acton-Boxborough Youth Baseball Association.

He began his volunteer efforts when his son was eight. Two years into it, with his son on his team, Diguette had the kind of season professional baseball coaches long for. He and his co-coach, who was the head of the league, discovered they had been phenomenally lucky in the preseason draft.

Sure, they had intimate knowledge of most of the players and they also realized that a fair number of coaches were newcomers to town who did not know these boys. Since both Diguette's son and his co-coach's son were early-round draft picks for their team, they didn't draft other boys until relatively late rounds. To their surprise, they found many of the "better" players still left for the taking. When the drafting was completed, they had snagged what they felt were six of the ten "best" boys in the entire pool.

Their season played out in predictable fashion. They went 16–1. Their one loss came when they pulled their pitcher, who was pitching a shutout, in order to give a lesser skilled pitcher a chance. They lost that game 5–4.

Interestingly, what should have been a celebratory and gratifying season didn't turn out that way for Diguette. The worst record that year was for a team that went 1–16, and

Diguette felt badly. This isn't much fun, he remembers thinking, when one team dominates and another team suffers. It isn't that much fun to win when it is so easy to win.

When his son was eleven, Diguette decided to push through a change in the way teams were configured. He abolished the draft. As co-coordinator of the league, he sat down on a Sunday afternoon and tried to draw up teams with parity. First, he decided who he thought were the ten "best" players in the league and he gave each of the five teams two of those boys. Then he went to a second tier of players who weren't as well-rounded and divvied them up according to their skills and according to which teams could benefit from their particular strengths. Finally he hit the third tier, a group of players who, if picked on a playground by their peers, probably would be picked last. He spread them around as well.

Diguette ended up creating more evenly matched teams and, in his mind, more exciting baseball. The best team that year was 7–5 and the worst team 5–7. The others were in the middle with .500 winning percentages. To top it off, the 5–7 team ended up winning the townwide playoffs. And, Diguette says, he felt that everybody had more fun.

This abolition of the draft continued for several years until Diguette gave up his position on the baseball board. "When I left," he said, "there was no one there to protect the beachfront," an allusion to the battle zone that this can become. Too many adult coaches feel the draft is where they can flex their muscle and outwit other adult men and women. It ends up again being about serving their needs to be competitive among their peers, and not the children's needs.

Diguette loves competition, fierce competition. The point

is, with drafts that create dominant teams, the competition can be sucked out. Diguette says he was able to pull off the no-draft seasons because he had clout, political influence built up over years spent on the baseball board. Newcomers trying to reform do not have that clout.

Diguette says the best way to end drafts is to write that rule into the group's bylaws. "That's really the only way," he says. Diguette suggests newcomers volunteer to help organize and administer their leagues. There are always openings. When you find you have power, Diguette counsels, use it for the good of the children.

Group Appropriate Ages

I recommend, and many child development experts and organizations agree, that teams in any sport cluster children in groups that represent only a two-year difference in chronological age. In other words, a baseball team would have eleven- and twelve-year-olds, but not ten-year-olds. A soccer team would have twelve- and thirteen-year-olds, but not fourteen-year-olds as well. The only exception may be in rural communities where it's difficult to put together enough children in a particular sport within two-year age spans.

One of the worst actions taken in recent years is youth baseball's practice of moving some children up into what are called "major league" teams, which often contain three- or four-year spans, such as ten-, eleven- and twelve-year-olds, sometimes even nine-year-olds. It's too much.

Adults involved in youth sports should take into account

the wide swings, not just in chronological age, but in "developmental" age, that can occur in any age grouping. Children enter puberty at wildly different times. A child's birth certificate may suggest one likelihood, while the hormonal clock inside that child says quite another thing, especially from the ages of nine through fifteen.

Medical experts, as already mentioned, generally agree there can be as much as a six-year developmental difference between children of the same chronological age. That means an eleven-year-old may have a body like that of an eight-year-old or like that of a fourteen-year-old. That's the difference between a child and a near-adult. It's the adults' job to remember this as they go about designing systems.

Also, children of widely different ages may appear more similar to each other in physical strength and athletic skills. An early-blooming ten-year-old looks much like a late-developing thirteen-year-old. That does not mean, however, that these two children should play together on the same team, because they can be far apart emotionally and socially.

Sports Skills May Be Complex

It's important to keep in mind the challenge of learning, and of teaching, serial skills. This challenge is described clearly in *Beyond X's and O's*, a groundbreaking book written by sports activist and author Jack Hutslar, who is also founder and director of the North American Youth Sport Institute.

In this book, Hutslar breaks down seemingly simple maneuvers on the playing field or court in order to show how immensely more complicated they are than most adults realize.

Serial skills, says Hutslar, require "linking related skills together in a flowing motion." For instance, in dribbling a basketball up the court, a child needs to know how to dribble, how to run and dribble, how to dribble and look up while running. It also wouldn't be a bad idea if he or she could keep track of all the other players on the court, too. That's at least four different skills in one action. These are serial skills, meaning you have to juggle and link them together if you are to be successful.

Hutslar reminds adults that for many children, especially young children, serial skills are nearly impossible to remember and to execute, particularly during the added pressure of games. Even for many adults, serial skills mastery is quite difficult. Remember those Boston Celtics players struggling with the pick and roll?

Your job as a reformer of youth sports is to recognize this truth, to understand that children need time, patience and good instruction in order to master serial skills. By the way, some of these, such as that infamous pick and roll, should not even be attempted until high school. If you're a coach, seek the expert help you need in order to ensure that you and your assistants can effectively teach the serial skills you expect from your players and that those serial skills are age-appropriate for the children.

Understanding serial skills will help you to understand that each age group should play team sports in slightly different but no less significant ways. The whole idea is that we no longer simply "child-size" instruction and game plans that work well for the high school, college or pro ranks. Rather, we come up with systems that are unique for each age grouping.

Put Limits on the Season

Through the fifth grade, children should play only one sport per season. To try two in one season—soccer and lacrosse in the spring, for example—wait until the child is in sixth grade or higher.

I venture to guess, though, that any attempt at double-dipping—it might more honestly be called "overachieving"—will take its toll. For one thing, Mom and Dad will be in their cars moving young athletes from games to practices and back again at a more demanding pace than that of New York City's cabbies.

Until about age ten or eleven, children should play only one season of any particular sport in a calendar year.

Until about age ten or eleven, children should play only one season of any particular sport in a calendar year. Yes, you're quite right in recognizing that this drives a wooden stake into the heart of sports specialization. That's the intent.

Also, children need diversity in their interests and in the use of their rapidly changing and developing bodies. Today this diversity is called cross-training. Don't allow your children to play soccer outdoors in the fall, indoors in the winter, outside again in spring, and again at summer camp, only to start the same cycle over in the fall.

All the games I played growing up—spud, kick-the-can, touch football, baseball—had nothing to do with basketball and everything to do with my basketball career. Don't short-change children by keeping them in one sport all year. It will not hinder their progress. Please remember there have been thousands of world-class athletes who played multiple sports through their teenage years.

Forget the Playoffs

Once you have eliminated elite and select teams at young ages, reconsider playoffs. If you do not have elite teams, of course there will be no playoffs at that level. But do not feel the need to schedule playoffs within your community league in order to determine that season's winning team. That's an adult want, not a child's.

That adult want sets the stage for some of the worst behavior of coaches and parents. The desire to win takes over. The stakes are higher, and stress, anger and outbursts follow suit. If making the playoffs is on the line at the end of the season, adults will put standings ahead of player development. The choices adults make, particularly about playing time, are often more damaging once playoffs get underway.

Skip the playoffs. When the season is over, congratulate your young players on a great effort, and have a pizza party instead. If you do schedule playoffs, make sure all regular-season teams get the chance to participate.

Tournaments Run the Right Way

If a parent or coach is interested in having children participate in a tournament, understand that tournament's format and its rules before you join.

For children under the age of ten, look for tournaments that do not eliminate teams and do not declare an overall tournament winner with a fancy trophy and closing ceremony.

If you are in charge of organizing tournaments or if you intend as a coach or as a parent to participate in tournaments, there are few better people to talk to than Rich Irving of Laconia, New Hampshire. Irving is an optician by trade and the father of three children under age nine. He's been involved in coaching children since he was in high school. He recently began a consulting business named Character Through Sports (*CharacterThroughSports@TTLC.net*).

> For children under the age of ten, look for tournaments that do not eliminate teams and do not declare an overall tournament winner with a fancy trophy and closing ceremony.

In the years since he became president of Laconia's Lou Athanas Basketball League, Irving has led the charge for the kinds of rules that can make tournaments fundamentally appropriate, fair, and—yes—fun for all children who attend and all parents who travel to watch their children play. Among these rules are stipulations about minimum playing time, gender equality, and civility among the players, toward the officials, and among parents in the stands.

Irving said he first started thinking of changing tournament guidelines when he asked himself a basic question: "If these are things we truly believe we should be doing during the regular season, why do we throw everything out the window when it comes time for our tournament?"

One question bothered him the most: "For any child who's traveling up here or any family who's going to spend the weekend here, do we want to have the situation—which we know happens—where a kid doesn't play?" There is no reason, he concluded, that every child who attends the tournament should not be guaranteed at least one unsubstituted quarter of playing time.

So that became one of the tournament's fundamental rules. Playing-time decisions were no longer left up to individual coaches. Any player who comes to the tournament gets the chance to play. To prevent coaches from skirting the spirit of the rule by sending in players for a collection of short intervals of essentially meaningless minutes of playing time, the rules specifically stipulate that quarters must be unsubstituted, in order that all players experience the flow of the game.

Here's another refreshing principle: If your community sends a boys' team to this tournament, it must also send a girls' team. According to Irving, that's done because many towns treat boys' teams preferentially.

The tournament makes a family-friendly effort and schedules one community's girls' and boys' teams to play back to back so that families don't have to spend the entire weekend at the gym. "It's all designed to bring common sense and perspective" back to tournaments, said Irving.

Tournament organizers have also taken the younger ages out of tournament competition. In the past, third-graders through sixth-graders were invited. Now the tournament is exclusively for seventh- and eighth-graders. This effort took direct aim at the pressures to identify select players and teams at young ages, which he believes discourages too many children who are not selected.

Most of the communities involved in the tournament select "all-star" teams to send to the competition, but Laconia has moved away from that pressure, too. The city now allows all of its regular-season teams to compete in the tournament, scheduling those teams against each other in early rounds so that all but two will be eliminated. Those two move on to compete against the other communities' teams. Says Irving, "We're out of the tournament all-star selection business."

The Laconia tournament also has rules about defense: Only man-to-man defense is allowed, no zone defenses or traps. This choice is the most developmentally appropriate at this level, according to Irving, allowing players to better develop their offensive game.

A few more wonderful rules can be found at this tournament in Laconia: All players shake hands at the start as well as at the end of each game. All players' names—not just the starters—are announced and applauded at the start. And parents are reminded that they are guests at their children's games. In the tournament booklet, on a separate piece of paper handed to spectators, on signs posted around the gyms and in public-speaker announcements between games, adults are reminded of the code of conduct.

This code has to be specific, Irving says, or spectators may not recognize that their particular behavior is over the designated line. For example, the code stipulates that there will be no arguing with the officials, nor will spectators be allowed to distract a free-throw shooter.

Lead, and Others Will Follow

As if these efforts underway in Laconia weren't terrific enough on their own, here's something even better: Irving says that a lot of the communities that send teams to this tournament are bringing these ideas back to their cities and towns and instituting changes in their regular-season leagues.

Show people a better way, and they may follow.

One of Irving's favorite stories is of overhearing two fathers chatting in the men's room during a break in the tournament. "Hey," says one father to the other, "Did you see how much playing time my daughter got in that game?" (Mind you, the tournament rules stipulate minimum playing time.) "It's funny," the father says, "but she hasn't gotten that much playing time all year. We have to travel in order for her to see that kind of action."

Although Irving has heard the questions about whether to even have a tournament at all, he sees the Laconia tournament as a vehicle for change and healthy competition. He also views the players at this level and the importance of their athletic success in the right context. "There's really no justification at the middle school level for not giving every kid on the team fair and meaningful playing time," he says.

Irving also is conducting an informal survey of the boys who participated in this tournament years ago, presumably considered to be the "cream of the crop" at their age at that time. He's trying to determine how many of those tournament players made it to their high school varsity teams. So far Irving has studied only two teams of fifteen players each, but the early results don't surprise me. On each of those teams of fifteen, only two boys made it to high school varsity. All the more reason, Irving says, to make sure that coaches who bring fifteen players to this Laconia tournament don't play only seven or eight of them. That kind of mind-set, Irving says, often "develops the wrong kids."

Irving calls himself a "lightning rod" and enjoys the challenge of spirited debate. He believes a lot of the poor choices adults make are the result of a lack of training and education in youth sports and child development. In addition to ensuring that adults are trained and educated, Irving recognizes the critical importance of taking action, of instituting changes that people can see at work. "You've got to walk the talk," he says.

People like Irving offer hope in this business of reforming youth sports and finding better ways to organize these games our children play.

●●●

The toughest test for some of these principles comes during the heat of the games themselves. In the next chapter, you'll find a plan of action and a pep talk for making changes in the middle of all that action.

Managing Games: Rules to Play By

A coach should tell the children:
"I know you'll make a lot of mistakes.
I'm not going to yell at you. Otherwise, you
won't try things you should and you're
not going to learn the game."

Dean Conway, Massachusetts
Youth Soccer Association

Have you ever seen the tee used in the game of T-ball? Picture a golf tee, only fifty times bigger, something King Kong might use on the links. The baseball tee is usually made of plastic, stands about waist-high to a six-year-old and, because of its prominence in T-ball's name, one can safely assume the tee is a valued piece of equipment. Right?

Not always. One T-ball coach, Jack Voykin, got himself into all kinds of trouble involving the tee. His transgression? He decided to use it. That's right. The T-ball league in question had determined that young players should first try to hit thrown pitches—try for five times—and only then resort to the tee. My guess is that the league figured that would develop "real" baseball players quicker.

The problem for our T-ball coach Voykin, who lives in British Columbia, was that he kept seeing his six- and seven-year-olds frustrated and unhappy trying to hit pitches served up by adults. He had read about the value of using a tee, something professional players advocate even for themselves. So Voykin decided to use the tee throughout the game: no pitching. Bingo, his kids started to hit. And that's when things went wrong for our coach.

In the first inning of a game in which he used the tee exclusively (the other coach had refused to do so for his boys), Voykin's team scored ten runs in ten minutes. The other team took twenty-three minutes and scored only six. At the top of the second inning, one of Voykin's players hit a grand-slam home run. His team was running away with the game. The opposing coach yelled out an expletive that even the children could hear. A parent from that team approached Voykin after the inning, saying, "What is this? Do you have something personal about hitting off a tee?"

"It still gets better," Voykin wrote in a letter he posted on the *Youth-Sports.com* Web site. "I get a boy that walks up to me and says we are cheating and that whatever we score does not count." After the game, Voykin said, he got a call from the league's executive director, who asked what he was trying to do and if he had lost his ability to reason. Voykin has since hung up his spikes as baseball coach. He and his two sons moved on to soccer.

Too often the adults in charge of managing children's games make all sorts of misdirected decisions about how games should be played, how to best develop young players and how to show children what competition is all about. When those adult decisions are put to the test under the pressure of a game, with parents yelling on the sidelines and scoreboards standing on high, things can get worse.

There are ways to manage games that are productive, developmentally appropriate and fun. That said, I already hear some parents complaining: "These ideas of yours sound like recess. Certainly not the rough-and-tumble world of American sports. How do you expect our children to be competitive? How do you expect them to keep up? Do you really think they'll get better if they play fewer games and we don't let these children know from the get-go who's better and who needs work?"

Yes, wholeheartedly. Actually, I expect more children will be competitive. I expect fewer children will give up or burn out at an early age. Teams of mixed abilities at young ages, for example, will not soften the "better" children or ruin the athletic futures of developing athletes. Before our society created these selective youth sports teams at young ages—before all this intensity and specialization—the United States managed to produce some pretty fantastic players in every sport. Are we producing more amazing athletes these days? I don't think so.

We can create youth sports systems that will give all children —including the most skilled player and the most intense competitor—a sense that this is their young sporting life, not their parents'. That kind of ownership can spell only good things.

"Okay," you say, "I'll listen. But how are these great ideas going to look in the gym or on the playing fields?"

Don't Organize Too Much

These ideas will look different in different sports and at different ages and in different communities, but let's consider an example. Let's pick a sport—soccer, for instance—and an age and gender—in this case, seven-year-old boys.

Under these systems, you would have signed up your seven-year-old son about eight weeks prior to the first day of the new season. Most administration-heavy, paperwork-buried youth sports organizations these days feel compelled to cut off sign-ups sometimes six months before the start, no exceptions!

Think about how much a child's interests can change in six months, not to mention a family's plans and obligations. It is difficult to commit appropriately so far in advance. The changes we will make in how the season is run will not necessitate so much advance commitment and effort.

In our new youth sports system, you and your son would arrive at the field on the first Saturday of soccer season along with about twenty other boys and their parents. Your group would have the 8:00 A.M. slot. Four more groups of twenty would be rotated throughout the rest of that Saturday morning—at 9:00, 10:00, 11:00 and noon.

The twenty boys are wearing T-shirts and shorts, not uniforms. These are seven-year-olds. Did you need uniforms in your backyard when you were seven years old?

Four adult supervisors have been assigned to this time slot. The rest of you adults are free to go. Do your grocery shopping. Play with your other children. You've driven your child to his life. Now enjoy a life of your own.

The twenty boys, meanwhile, are told that this is their time to play. This is their field. They're in charge. Here are the soccer balls. Have fun.

Let them make some of their own rules, even if they make no sense to you. Let them switch teams or reconfigure themselves if one team gets too far ahead. Some of the better-skilled players on one team can be exchanged for lesser-skilled players on the other team.

You may remember making your own rules as a child. I remember any hit to right field in three-on-three baseball was an automatic out because there was no one to play right field. Designing our own games was part of tradition, passed down by our older siblings, by other kids around the neighborhood. Let's renew those traditions, giving children the power to call their own shots.

If you add adults into the equation, sooner rather than later you get games designed around the convenience and the needs of adults to organize, to control.

School Recess Model

Let's take a close look at something that happens every day at hundreds of thousands of elementary schools worldwide: elementary school recess, which revolves around children's needs, not teachers' needs.

This new youth sports program is based on the elementary school recess model. The adults organize the time—that's the need for the modern family. We set the time at which the kids will meet, the amount of time they will play, the place where they will play. We schedule them and we schedule ourselves. We need to know where our kids are. This isn't *Leave It to Beaver*, when parents sent their kids outside and told them to be home by supper. That's not our world anymore. But in this new order of youth sports we don't organize the process. We bring it back to the playground model.

At our soccer game for seven-year-olds, the adult supervisors stand around ready to help when needed: A child has to go to the bathroom, one needs some encouragement to join in, another needs to be cautioned not to be too rough. These are the kinds of situations teachers on recess duty take care of every day when elementary schoolchildren go out to play. The same should go at this age for our roles as parents and coaches in organized sports. This spirit is embodied in the words of U-6 soccer coaching coordinator Bill Walthall of Westborough, Massachusetts, who suggests his coaches treat soccer games for young children like "birthday parties with soccer balls."

With this elementary school recess model, adults on the sidelines—now pressed into service to supervise playtime, rather than to devise plays, scout other teams, shuffle positions and play politics—will volunteer easily and in adequate numbers.

Children Learn as They Play

By the end of the hour in this recess model, twenty kids will have played soccer. They will have run around, kicked the ball, fallen down. In five hours on a Saturday morning, a hundred kids will have played as much soccer as they would have on organized teams—probably a lot more. They will not have been coached, just organized and supervised, like at recess.

You repeat this process week after week throughout the season, mixing up the Saturday groupings each week randomly, which is easily done with computers.

By the end of the ten-week season, you ask yourself if the kids are learning how to play soccer. Yes, but here's the key question: Have they been taught how to play soccer by adults? Not necessarily. They have done more learning through each other.

When your seven-year-old's soccer season ends, don't be ready, pen in hand, to immediately sign the forms and pay the check for the indoor soccer league that starts the very next week. Give your child a break from soccer. Let his or her soccer muscles relax. Now's the time to try something else, use different muscle groups.

Okay, you ask, will a seven-year-old in our elementary school recess model have learned as much, will he or she have become as "good" a soccer player as he or she would have become under a traditional adult-coached model of organized youth sports?

The answer makes note of the fact that there are two types of learning: learning you do on your own and learning that's hammered into you from someone on the sidelines. A lot of the "teaching" that coaches think they are accomplishing, particularly with very young children, is truly a waste of energy. Sideline blather. Pointless rant.

Additionally, learning game strategies—multitasking—is an advanced-level skill, something young children are cognitively not ready to understand.

Think about it: You're seven years old and you've got a ball in your hands or at the end of your foot. There are other players all around you; a second later they're in different positions and everything's changed. By the time you're ready to make a pass, they're all in different positions again.

Understanding how to react to all that is what we call "court intelligence" in basketball, "field intelligence" in soccer and "ice intelligence" in hockey. It's multitasking. It's what a friend of mine calls "moving chess." These are advanced-level skills. But because the adult ego wants to believe it is making a contribution, adults plot strategy and yell commands.

Kids playing a sport of near-continuous motion (basketball, soccer, hockey, lacrosse) make two decisions each second, according Dan Whitham, a Boston-area coach and children's physical education teacher. Do you, as coach, think you will help by adding yet a third piece of information to each second? The kids may hear you, but can they understand you? If they can understand you, by the time they can act on it, your command is probably obsolete. Everyone else has moved to a different spot. Also, the younger the child, the less he or she can understand about the "coaching" coming from the sidelines.

You've got a kid looking around for what to do, you've got the coach yelling directions, and maybe you've got parents on the sidelines telling him or her to do the opposite thing. "Pass!" "Shoot!" "Over to Caitlin!" "Michelle is open!" "Slow down!" "Pick up the pace!"

For far too many adults, coaching is barking orders at a child while he or she is already trying to make two decisions a second. Such coaches are satisfying their needs as adults. They are trying to micromanage children who cannot yet process that kind of complex cognitive information, particularly in the heat of a game. The adults in charge or on the sidelines see the children making many mistakes, and they feel an adult need to point out and to correct any or all of them. They make their children feel as though mistakes are to be avoided, instead of embraced as a way to learn the game.

These coaches and parents have all watched sports—and coaches and managers—on television. They see them yelling on the sidelines, and they think that is how to coach. What they forget is that those folks on TV are coaching professional adults, not children.

If you've ever driven a car with three kids screaming and fighting in the backseat, think about this: Does it tend to pull your attention away from the task at hand? Do you ever feel overloaded? If you add more pressure to that car ride, such as an icy road, can you handle all that at once? That's exactly what coaches do when they yell at kids to do something: They distract them. They create "cognitive overload."

Eleven-year-old Michelle has the basketball. She's dribbling down the court. Her four teammates are yelling at her to pass the ball to them. The coach is yelling his choice of her next target. There may be a mother or father in the stands yelling their choices. Michelle has a lot of choosing to do. The choice she makes most often is to throw away the ball as soon as it touches her. It's too much of a hot potato. Why do this to Michelle?

Parents and coaches often forget that children cannot perform like adults. Thus, when an adult yells out a command and a child does not follow through, things can get tense.

Jay Coakley, a sports sociologist, makes the following point in his book *Sport in Society: Issues and Controversies:* "This inability of children is frustrating to parents and coaches. Without understanding why children have such a difficult time conforming to team strategy, adults accuse them of not trying hard enough, not thinking, or having a bad attitude. This, in turn, is frustrating to the young players who are trying and thinking the best they can. Like their parents and coaches, they do not realize that their inabilities conform to normal developmental processes."

When my son was in first grade, the coach of the opposing soccer team, clipboard in hand, called his players into a huddle, furiously drawing X's, handing out numbers for all the positions, and then sending his team onto the field. My son's team kicked off and all five of clipboard-coach's kids stood still. "Moooooove!" he screamed. One little boy cried out, interrupting the coach's rant: "But, Coach, I'm *standing right where you told me to!*"

So many coaches don't understand what it's like to be six, eight or twelve years old. That's why they need to talk to the physical education instructors and other schoolteachers.

When you add adults, particularly adult male coaches, to youth team sports, they tend to move toward the strategic, away from the technical; it's management theory in action. Ask the high school coaches, though, and they'll tell you this: Young children don't understand much of this strategy because they can't picture it. That would rely on spatial skills young children probably have not yet developed.

Embrace Mistakes

One of the most difficult things for adults to do is to learn how to welcome children to make mistakes, even during games. Even during "important" games. That's how children will learn to play well. Children will make mistakes, lots of them. If you can't deal with this, don't coach. Leave it to someone else with more patience.

Too many adults act on their tendencies to want to point out and to correct every mistake a child makes during practices and games. This intimidates developing players. They are afraid to be creative and to take risks. They often play a game that is less about themselves and more about what their coaches say.

A coach of young children should "get the game started, give them some elementary thinking about what to do. Then say, 'Go have some fun. Make a lot of mistakes because that's how you'll learn,'" says Dean Conway, the Massachusetts soccer coach.

Conway says that at one of his daughter's U-10 games, three coaches from the other team were positioned at three points of the field. "The guy next to me was keeping up a nonstop series of bellowed directives at the two players in the back. 'Move up. Move back. Stand right there—there, that's good.'

"Excuse me for addressing you this way," Conway declared to the coach, "but this is a kids' soccer game. It's not such a good thing what you're doing.

"He looked like he was going to hit me," added Conway.

"U-10 soccer players are *supposed* to make mistakes," according to Conway. An adult coach should tell his children, "I know you'll make a lot of mistakes. I'm not going to yell at you. I'll try to keep your parents from yelling at you. Otherwise you won't be relaxed, you won't try things you should and you're not going to learn the game."

Too often, Conway says, coaching becomes "manipulation," moving children around at the directive of the coach, with little to no input from the kids. "When you're a little kid this should be your world and it should be not intruded upon, not manipulated, not distorted. Just left to you," Conway says.

Of course this elementary school recess model will change year to year, with significant changes by the time children are in middle school and older. Still, this example of soccer for seven-year-olds is important for underscoring the dramatic differences between what this book suggests and what the reality is today for many children in organized sports.

It is not uncommon nowadays for seven-year-olds to be facing tryouts and pressure to make a select team. Some have already played three or more full seasons of organized soccer by the end of second grade. Some adults have already judged, at least in part, these seven-year-olds' athletic potential.

The recess model changes for older children; they can be taught more advanced skills, games and practices can and will be more structured, and more of the decisions will be made by the adult coaches. Hold on to as many of the recess-model principles as you can, for as long as you can. It will do the children good.

As an adult, never usurp complete control. Let the

children, no matter how old, take charge of some of the practices. Let them come up with some of the game strategies they would like to try. Let them figure out who should play which positions. And never, ever, allow things to get so serious that anyone stops having fun.

Trust the Children

> Let the children, no matter how old, take charge of some of the practices. Let them come up with some of the game strategies.

Let's be clear about this idea of leaving children alone. This is not an effort to tone down the competition.

"If I go onto the field and I'm a hard-charging, aggressive nine-year-old and pretty athletic and coordinated, and if I'm left to my own devices, what I'm going to do is charge hard, scrap around, run and score some goals, do my own thing," says Dean Conway. "If I'm a shy kid, that's probably going to be my take for awhile. I'll probably get beaten to the ball and have to learn to fight harder. Maybe I'll be hesitant and miss a few that I should have gotten, but that's how it goes. And as it should."

On the other hand, he says, if you take those two children and put them into a game "where the coach and the parents are yelling all the time, one of the things that's going to happen if I'm that hard-charging kid is that I may hesitate because now I'm thinking 'He's yelling at me to slow down.' On the other hand, if I'm already a hard-charger and everyone's screaming and yelling, I may get overstimulated."

"The first soccer game I ever refereed was a perfect example," Conway recalls. "These parents had these kids in such a frenzy that they basically spent the game running into one another and kicking one another. They couldn't think straight because there was so much emotion. . . . These kids have to be trusted to learn the game on their own. You learn the game when you're left to play it and think about it and react to it as you see it."

There may be instances, Conway agrees, when certain children need a few pointers or reminders during a game, even a "sharp yell" to get into the game more. What Conway is trying to stop is that "constant barrage, the scripting of the game, the highly emotional shrieking" that is too often heard on the sidelines as young children play.

Put Me in, Coach

If your children are involved in a more traditional youth sports system that leaves most decisions up to the adult coach, one of the most divisive issues to face will be decisions about who plays in each game and for how long.

Decisions about playing time are the most important decisions adults make in youth sports. Remember, the number-one reason children get involved in youth sports is to play, not to watch adults coach, and not to watch other kids play. As Jack Hutslar reports in his book *Beyond X's and O's,* "It's not whether you win or lose but how much you get to play."

Few things violate a child's basic wants and needs—and his or her basic rights—more than sitting on a bench. Think of the millions of children, and their parents, who have suffered silently through a discouraging, insulting and hurtful season with a coach who did not let those children play.

Through sixth grade, every child on a team should get equal playing time. After that age, my rule is "minimum meaningful minutes" until high school varsity.

With the agreement of their parents, some children may prefer an exception to the rule about equal playing time. A child who has physical or cognitive special needs may find extended game action to be challenging. Some children may join a team as much for the social experience as for the athletic competition. Practice times, if they are more fun and more relaxed, present opportunities to participate fully in scrimmages. If you see, however, that pressure during the season's games is difficult for a particular child, do not make assumptions on your own and simply cut his or her playing time. Talk with the parents and talk with the child. Let them decide.

When the focus on winning displaces the focus on developing players, playing-time decisions are easily corrupted. If you are a coach, do not make poor decisions about this. If you are a parent, do not allow the adults in charge to deny your child a fair chance to play. Children lose confidence whether they are told outright (by not making a team) or indirectly (by not getting playing time) that they are not good enough. When playing time is denied, children don't get the chance to fully develop their skills, and often they are unable to hold on to the passion to keep trying.

Do not break the equal-time rule because of your assessment of any child's athletic ability or perceived ability to help your team to score. Your little "superstar" player who can make eighteen points for you in a basketball game in which the team's total is likely to be around twenty-six is probably going to want to be on that court the entire time. His parents will want that, too. In the presence of such a "prodigy," most coaches succumb to the pressure from both sides and allow the little guy to play to his heart's content. For no other reason than it's fun to watch.

Don't do that. Don't give in to the little voice in your ear that tells you to play "the best" and appease "the rest" with a few minutes here and a pat on the back there. Play the good, the bad and the ugly all the same. You'll be a better person for it, and your players will be better players. Also, your budding "superstar" who plays too much will get a much-needed dose of empathy and humility by watching and cheering the others.

Equal-playing-time rules are actually simpler for a coach to follow. They take the emotional struggle out of the picture. No more internal tug-of-war about who to play and how long to play them. No more glares from angry parents on the sidelines because you're not giving their children a chance to play. No children relegated to being benchwarmers and made to feel they're just not good enough. This is a win-win-win situation. It's so simple and so right that it is shocking how often the adults in charge go wrong when it comes to deciding which children will be allowed to play.

Children who are put into a game for two or three "meaningless" minutes will know it's their only chance to shine. They'll be pressured and frustrated if things don't happen immediately because—oh my gosh!—they've only got a minute left to prove themselves. They'll make mistakes, probably the same number that their teammates are making over a longer period of time. However, the benchwarmer's mistakes will seem more obvious. When a benchwarmer who comes into a game cold for a few minutes of play is judged by his or her coach, that brief playing time is often used as justification for why the coach should not put this player in more often.

Adults bench kids to win games. That's the adult want. The children's need to is have a chance to develop as players. You can't do that sitting on a bench.

And for all anyone knows, that benchwarmer may become a high school varsity starter or a college or professional star. The elitism that is courted by so many youth sports leagues — that is, selecting "the best" of these children early on, playing them more often, concentrating on them in hopes of breeding a better high school or college crop — often does quite the opposite of what is intended.

Equal playing time is the best way to ensure that you will send a larger group of more talented players on to the greater glory of your secondary schools. In that case, the athletic directors will thank you. The parents whose children did not wash out because they sat on the bench in their early years will thank you, too.

Minimum Meaningful Minutes

Adults should commit to rules about "minimum meaningful minutes" of playing time for every child on a team. This is fitting through middle school, as well as for freshman and junior varsity teams, since lower-level high school teams should still be developing talent for the varsity.

The high school varsity level is the first time that winning should trump playing time and player development. Too many people look at eighth-grade, seventh-grade and sixth-grade teams as feeder programs for high school varsity. They are not. You cannot select your elite players, those who are headed to your varsity squad, when they are in middle school. You should develop all players and start assessing their varsity potential during high school. Obviously, this bears mentioning again and again.

Even freshman and junior varsity teams that act as feeder systems or minor leagues for the varsity include players who are as young as fourteen or thirteen. The bodies and skills of these children are far from fully developed, and giving them an equitable chance to play is well-advised.

> In order to learn to play in a game setting, a child needs at least twelve minutes of play in each basketball game.

Let's take basketball to further illustrate minimum meaningful minutes. In order to learn to play in a game setting, a child needs at least twelve minutes of play in each basketball game. My preference is fifteen or more.

Even with that slim amount, however, problems can arise. There are only so many playing minutes per game. For a 24-minute game with five players out on the court at any given time, you have a total of 120 minutes to distribute among your players. But if you have fourteen players on the team, each one entitled to a minimum of 12 minutes, you need 168 minutes of playing time. What to do? You must reduce rosters so that there is more playing time and increase the number of teams so that no youngsters are cut. This will mean more coaches and more gym time.

To figure out what minimum meaningful minutes are in any sport, consult those people who work in the state and regional chapters of the relevant youth sports organizations. Information is accessible on the Internet, too. (See chapter 7 for details about recommended team size in different sports.)

Create More Teams

Here's a guideline for determining the sizes of youth soccer, baseball/softball and basketball teams: If there are more players on the bench than in the game, chances are your team is too big. A good rule of thumb is to take the number needed to play in those sports, multiply that by 1.5 and assemble your teams according to that number. You will have players on the bench. The trick is to rotate all players regularly so that none are sitting for too long. Football and hockey, because of how they are played, should be exempted from this 1.5 rule. Football teams can carry thirty-three players and hockey seventeen.

My hometown belongs to a regional system of A-level and B-level boys' basketball teams that play against each other. Typically, each team has about twelve players, which means that during any given game five boys are playing the game and seven boys are watching the other children play or watching the adults coach. That's not my idea of fun or effective player development. So I look for ways in which the most children can play the most time in any scheduled game. Isn't that why the children want to be on a team?

Before their teams arrive at our town's gym to play a game,

I talk to opponents' coaches about my philosophy. I don't always get the chance to make that earlier contact, and such was the case one day when we were scheduled to play a team from a larger community nearby.

That community's coach showed up with fourteen kids (one boy was sick that day). I suggested to him that we split the team into two and that newly created teams of seven boys each would play two separate games simultaneously. He wasn't sure what to make of my idea, but he suggested that we ask the boys, which we did.

I explained my plan to the boys and pointed out that with fourteen on a team, nine would always be watching five boys play. I asked if they would like to split into two teams for the day, so that only two would be on the bench at any time. "Yes, yes, we would," they said. "Okay," I said, "let's play."

One of our teams won that day and one of our teams lost. I went over to the coach at the end of the games and I answered a question that even he hadn't asked. "If you're concerned about how to report these scores to the newspaper or to whoever might be tracking such things," I said, "you have my permission to say that you won." Our town's basketball program at that age level doesn't keep standings. What short- or long-term importance did that day's two scores really have? In my mind, none.

It's not whether you keep score—of course you keep score. Rather, it's the importance that you give to scores that makes a difference. That kind of difference in thinking also applies to the debate about whether you are trying to win at all costs. Even if you do not try to win at all costs, you may make poor decisions if you base your decisions on how to win rather than on how to develop all players. You should try to win, but you shouldn't do it at the expense of any child.

Winning with Too High a Price

Few descriptions are more often used to stereotype the "competitive" coach than the phrase "win at all costs." But talk to coaches who have been branded "win at all costs" coaches, and they will say that they are trying to help children become better players, they are aiming for children to have fun, they are in it for the children, not for the score. They want to win, sure, they say, and what's wrong with that?

There is *nothing* wrong with that. The aim of almost every child playing almost every game is to win that game, but too many coaches are inclined to try to win on their terms.

When youth coaches are worried about whether or not they will win, they begin to make misguided choices.

There are proportionately few coaches who want to win at *all* costs. But a vast number of youth coaches are willing to pay a price—namely, the price of not developing all their players. They do this by denying all children a fair chance to play, by discouraging them from taking chances and instilling in them a fear of making mistakes.

When youth coaches are worried about whether or not they will win, they begin to make misguided choices. They bench their less-skilled players. They coach their children to specialize. They go for the immediate reward of that day's score over the long-term benefit of developing all the players and helping them all to nurture their love of the game.

You will recognize these coaches by the way they react when their team is scored against. You will recognize these coaches by the way they talk to their players. You will hear it in their words and you will see it in their body language.

A youth soccer coach in Rhode Island named Jim Buxton wrote a great list for parents of players under age ten, helping them to recognize the difference between coaching kids and trying to win. Distributed by the South County Youth Soccer Association, the list has two sides: what to do if you want to win and what to do if you want to coach kids. (See Buxton's list on page 175.)

Defer Complicated Strategies

Once you've figured out how to get all children playing in the game, figure out ways to make sure the play of the game doesn't overwhelm their development. This means to defer those adult tactics aimed at winning games—defensive strategies, for instance, that stifle offensive players who are trying to learn new skills.

In basketball, these are strategies like the full-court press and half-court trap, with defensive players double-teaming and even triple-teaming the player with the ball. On the other hand, man-to-man defense means every defensive player sticks to one offensive player, with no "ganging up" on a single offensive player. This allows defensive players to concentrate their efforts on one player and thereby to develop better individual defensive skills. It also allows the offensive players to learn at a less frantic pace.

If you want to win	If you want to coach kids
1. Lose track of playing time, or just guesstimate the length of time people are on the field. No one will be the wiser if Martin only gets 20 percent of the time that Sam gets.	1. Have your assistant coach log when players go in and when they come out. Or schedule the playing time ahead of time, so as to be fair to everyone.
2. Let Superstar Brendan, the center half, take any throw-in he wants, especially the ones on Bobby's side of the field.	2. When it's on Bobby's side, Bobby takes it. Teach Bobby how to improve his throws. Don't give him the message that he is not valuable/capable.
3. Don't let left back Murphy take the goal kicks on her side. She can't kick very far.	3. Let Murph "have a go." She will only get better with practice.
4. Have your two backs play about ten feet in front of the net, even when you have the ball deep in the other end. At this age, if they move up, they might get beat by a fast break.	4. When you have the ball deep in the other end, try to get your backs up to mid-field. This way they are able to support the offense. It's riskier but they are more involved.
5. Just use one or two goalies for the season. Develop a best goalie, and keep him or her in there most times. Some kids do not catch very well, and others have no experience.	5. Try to get all of your players to be goalies at some point in the season. Try to have at least four goalies per game. It's a disservice to a kid to lock him or her into one position—especially goalie—even if the child is willing.
6. Make your game plan be "Get the ball to Sandra!" (your best scorer).	6. Don't give anyone the prima donna role.
7. Encourage your players to always boot the ball as far as they can toward the other team's goal. Trapping the ball and short passes are too risky.	7. Encourage your players to be creative, especially in the other team's end. Trap it when possible, then make a pass or shoot.
8. Have one of your players "basket-hang" in their end. There's no off-sides, so use that to your advantage.	8. "Basket-hanging" goes against the spirit of the game. It may teach a habit that will be disallowed elsewhere.

Coaches of select teams love to use full-court presses, traps and similar kinds of defenses because they're figuring out, above all, how to win. So they press kids, which means that those who can't run two miles per hour are forced to run ten. If you think kids make a lot of mistakes at two miles per hour, wait until you jack it up to ten. They'll throw the ball all over the gym.

Children playing under that kind of defensive pressure tend to throw longer passes. Longer passes at that age are less accurate and stay in the air longer. Therefore, they hit their targets less often and are more susceptible to being stolen. The intended receiver of a long pass, if it actually does come his or her way, is often bowled over or charged with traveling while trying to handle a catch beyond his or her control. A lot of turnovers and steals result, in which case the opposing team gets the ball more often which means more opportunities to score. Players learn little about proper half-court offensive or defensive individual skills, and this is the ultimate example of helter-skelter.

I tried an experiment once. I watched a sixth-grade girls' basketball game in which the full-court press was used. I isolated ten consecutive possessions that occurred in a span of five minutes. Nine of those times, the ball never got past half-court or else it went out of bounds. One time, a girl caught it and was fouled. She made the foul shot, though most foul shots taken at this age do not go in. During those ten possessions, that team scored one point and didn't take another shot or make a pass in the offensive end of their court. This is not learning to play basketball. Where is the skill development?

What's Appropriate, What's Not

As coach one time of a seventh-grade boys' basketball game, I encountered an opposing coach who was using primarily full-court press and half-court trap defenses against my team of mostly twelve-year-olds.

I went over to that coach at the end of the game. "We play your team again at your home gym in three weeks," I told him. "I am not going to spend my time between now and then having my guys practice against the full-court press and half-court trap. That's not the best use of their time. Our team plays man-to-man defense. If you will not agree here and now that you will drop those kinds of defensive zone strategies and play man-to-man defense next time we meet, let's cancel that game right now. I'm not going to waste my children's time teaching them how to beat your system. It's a poor system for children at this age."

He agreed, and he kept his word when our team played in his town. His team still beat our team, but that night everyone played a game that was more appropriate for developing young players, more suited to their age group.

Save those winning-above-all defenses for high school varsity, when winning games is your priority.

Make the Practice More Perfect

Once you have established a program that gives everyone a chance to play and sets up game situations that make more sense, take a look at the practice sessions. One of the main reasons children quit sports, experts say, is boredom, and boredom never runs higher than at some of these practices. As a coach, teach skills in ways that are compatible with the needs of the age group with which you're working.

Let the children run part of each practice. Watch how they play. You'll learn a lot about what they want, what they need, what makes them happy.

Practices should keep kids moving and give them a chance to take risks, try out their ideas, be spontaneous and creative. Involve them in decisions. They will play a better game.

Kids don't want to simply do drill after drill in order to learn fundamentals. Why force them to run laps if they can run just as much while playing the game? Let the game be the teacher.

Soccer is a kicking game. Have the kids kick at the coach to hone their kicking skills. While they're trying to knock over an adult, they're really learning about shot accuracy, and they're having fun within a drill concept.

In basketball practices for younger kids, introduce the dribble and the pass. Then have them try it two-on-two, then three-on-three. The idea is to captivate them, to keep them active, to not dwell on anything too long.

For all our organized sports, one of the best games for developing children is tag. The kids are constantly moving and coordinating, reaching, running, devising strategies, diving, getting up. Add tag to any sports practice, and you can't go wrong.

As a boy we played spud: Everyone has a number. You throw a ball into the air. Whoever's number is called has to catch the ball, yell stop and try to hit someone with the ball. When you've been hit four times—S - P - U - D—you're out. Then you have to crawl through an "oven" tunnel and get whacked on the butt as you crawl through. The skills you can learn from this are running, stopping, throwing, catching and crawling fast—plenty of gross motor skill development.

If you're rusty on any of the rules of these playground games, check out *www.gameskidsplay.net*. What fun! You've probably forgotten a lot of these games yourself, but you'll quickly remember how much fun they can be.

My freshman year in high school was my first year of organized basketball. It's the best thing that could have happened to me. I hadn't had any coaching. Therefore, I hadn't had any bad coaching. By the time I got to ninth grade, my body and my confidence were ready to attack this new game. All I had had were thousands of hours playing on playgrounds—tag, spud, kickball, and backyard versions of football and baseball.

Watch How Children Play

The hours spent playing backyard games have been replaced today by formal organized youth sports programs. Something has been lost in that shift.

Children who play formal, structured games generally play games that are designed by adults and are rules-dominated. Children who make up games on their own concentrate on play and action—the rules are made or bent to keep things moving, to keep things fun.

Adults should model their programs on the natural ways children play games. One of the most age-inappropriate games on this count, one that in many ways fails the wants and needs of its targeted age group, is T-ball.

The coach of a T-ball team of seven-year-olds once wrote me a letter asking for advice. At T-ball practice, he said, he had asked the kids what they like best about T-ball. (I wondered why anyone feels the need to differentiate between T-ball "practice" and a T-ball "game," but I digress.) The kids told their coach that the thing they like best about T-ball is going over to the nearby playground and playing on the slide.

At the playground, they hop around, two minutes here, two minutes there. I asked the coach if his T-ball games and practices simulate anything like that. He said no.

Do you know why T-ball was started? My theory goes like this: Youth baseball used to begin at third grade, for eight-year-olds. Youth soccer came on board in the 1970s and soon five-, six-, seven-year-olds were playing soccer. Youth baseball administrators got worried that they would lose too many kids to soccer, so they developed a game for five-, six-, seven-year-olds that included hitting off a tee. They seem to have forgotten, though, that they were designing a game for five-, six- and seven-year-olds, and in T-ball kids mostly stand around.

Out of fifteen kids on the team that's batting, most of the time only one kid is active—the one at the tee. Fourteen others from that team are sitting on the bench—or at least attempting to sit on the bench—when they're anxious to move around. The kids on the fielding team stand around, with adults yelling at them to stay alert. They're all just waiting for a ball to be hit. Pity the outfielders, though, because a hit seldom makes it into the hinterlands. The little outfielders figure that out soon enough, so they're most likely dancing around or drawing in the sand.

T-ball as it is usually structured is entirely age-inappropriate, yet every year thousands of parents sign up their children.

One of the best soccer games for children that I ever watched was three-on-three soccer for a group of seven-year-olds played on a basketball-court-size field—without goalies. The field was much smaller than a traditional soccer field. The teams were smaller. This game is called "small-sided" soccer, and it models an increasingly popular method that is spreading to other sports.

This adapted game is great because all kids want to touch the ball and all kids want to make goals. In the game I watched, no one wanted to keep score, and so many goals were scored that no one could keep track. Now that's age appropriate!

If you have thirty kids in a gym to play basketball, set up groups of three on three and have the kids who aren't playing wait on the sidelines, ready to pass in.

The worst thing you can do for children is to make them stand around with nothing to do but watch other children play.

Who's Winning?

Keeping score is another issue that engenders fierce debate and widespread misunderstanding.

Keeping score is fine, but putting that score up on a big scoreboard with lights is not the best choice for young children's games.

Let the children on your team keep score. This involves them, and it gives those who aren't playing at the time something to do. Hey, it might even teach a little math.

At the start of each game appoint one or two kids as score-keepers. Every time one of the kids asks the score—very often, to be sure—send them to the scorekeepers. At young ages children may argue now and then about whether the score is accurate. That's great! Let them work it out, let them learn how to resolve their conflicts on their own. As kids, we argued about scores all the time. Your silent message as the coach to the kids should be, "As the adult, I'm not all that concerned about the score."

If coaches would listen to the kids more, they'd hear that most of them care far less about the score than do the adults. A coach of ten- to twelve-year-old girls described one of his softball games at a field that did not have a score-board. One of the girls came running in from third base in the middle of the game. "Coach," she said, "my parents just got here and they want to know the score." He told her the score was 15–2. But the girl had one more question: "Who's winning?"

When I was in fifth grade, one of my best friend's fathers was the coach of our Little League team. After the game, we would often get cones at an ice cream shop that was a Boston tradition: Brigham's. I don't recall much about those games, and I certainly remember none of the scores, but I remember very clearly our times together getting ice cream cones.

It's hard to keep the adult ego in check when the score is displayed high on a scoreboard—often in lights—for every-one to see. It drives adult coaches nuts. They begin to coach the score (the outcome) more than they coach the players (the process). Scoreboards drive up the intensity. Parents' eyes are constantly darting over to the numbers.

Take down the scoreboards. If the parents are so worried about the score, let them keep track themselves. In high-scoring games, it'll probably keep them so busy they won't have time to yell—one more advantage. It's likely that keeping an accurate score just won't be worth their time and trouble.

Without the scoreboard to tell the exact numbers of balls and strikes, the precious seconds left on the clock in basketball, football, soccer and hockey, everyone will be a little calmer.

Special Needs

As we talk about programs that should be developmentally appropriate and coaches who need to recognize and respect differences among individual children, it's important to include those children who are sometimes excluded entirely. Children with special needs—from physical differences to cognitive challenges—often find little encouragement in programs that are not entirely committed to welcoming *all* children to play.

All children have differences, even the more "typical" players on a team, and it's important for coaches to recognize and support individual needs. If you are the coach, pay attention to the special needs of your team members and speak with their parents for advice about how to effectively teach and encourage them.

Adults are obligated, whether that adult is administering the system or coaching the team, to be sensitive to these needs and to welcome *all* children. We owe this to every child we take under our wing. Look at them as individuals, not just as a team. Your team may be succeeding, while one child may be struggling.

For some children, the best fit is a team created for children with special needs, such as Little League's Challenger Division and TOPSoccer (The Outreach Program for Soccer). These programs aim to pair a child who has special needs with a child who is developing more typically, and to have them play side by side, often as a pair, during the game.

Other communities offer wonderful team programs administered by the Unified Sports Division of the Special Olympics. On these teams, players who are developing more typically play on teams with players who have special needs. What fun these children often share, celebrating that which they have in common rather than that which separates them. Unified teams may give accomplished interscholastic athletes a chance to rediscover the pure joy of running around and playing a sport for the fun of it.

"I love it, honestly," one high school player told *The Boston Globe* (October 26, 2000) about her participation on the MetroWest Unified Soccer Club that played in Holliston, Massachusetts. Of her teammates with special needs she said, "Their attitude just has such an impact on me. They're always smiling and joking around; they're out there to have fun. Sometimes in high school sports that can get kind of lost in competition."

I suggest that everyone involved in youth sports spend at least one day in their lives volunteering at a Special Olympics event. Look into the faces of these often-inspiring athletes and you will be reminded of the joy of sports, the truest sense of team sportsmanship and camaraderie, and, quite simply, what it means to enjoy yourself participating in athletics.

Here's one rule for adults: If you can't smile 90 percent of the time at games and practices, you don't belong in youth sports. At the Special Olympics, the percentage of time that everyone is smiling seems even higher.

Here's another suggestion: If you really want to take away some of the intensity in youth sports, take adult egos out of the picture—switch coaches halfway through any game. Both coaches win and lose the same game. That way, one team wins and the other loses, but both coaches have won and lost, which should downplay the importance of winning in their minds.

Somebody *Do Something*

Dean Conway, the Massachusetts state coach, tells the story of one of the U-14 girls' soccer games that he coached. The opposing coach, whom Conway met before the game, seemed to "have his head together."

Conway's girls quickly dominated, scoring early and often. The coach on the other side seemed to panic. His only aim was to coach the score, not to help the girls learn how to play the game. All he could offer his players was this beseeching wail: "Somebody *do something!*"

It is that panicky feeling about the score that costs too many players their chance to enjoy the game for the sake of the game, for the love of playing.

●●●

The structures and decisions that create an atmosphere in which children can learn effectively and enjoy themselves must be in place—hopefully, in writing—for all coaches to follow. Those guidelines will reflect the age-appropriate needs of each grouping of young players.

Get out your child-friendly template, and let's do a little of that organizing. The next chapter plots out learning curves and playing rules for soccer, baseball/softball, basketball, football and hockey for children from kindergarten through eighth grade.

Adapting the
Games for Children:
One Play at a Time

*Personally, I don't think five- to
seven-year-olds should play a competitive
league schedule, but the parents always
disagree and they usually win.*

Doug Abrams,
law professor and youth hockey coach

Let's explore in more detail how to set
up teams that embrace the spirit of reform in
youth sports systems that we've been dis-
cussing. This is the fun part, where we play
commissioner of all we survey—much like
Dr. Seuss's Yertle the Turtle. Yertle made all
the lowly turtles in his pond stack themselves
one on top of the other until he had built for

himself a perch high enough to become "ruler of all that I see." I invite you up to that perch, to survey the landscape of youth sports. Let's pretend we are rulers of all that we see.

Of course, we're not like Yertle in every way. Yertle got power hungry, refused to listen to the lowly little turtle named Mack on the bottom of his stack of dozens. Mack was complaining about his pain, and Yertle couldn't be bothered. But when Mack burped, the stack tumbled and Yertle lost his perch and all his power.

We'll play ruler of all that we see, but we'll listen closely to all the little turtles in our kingdom. It's for their sake that we create this world. We'll listen to all the little turtles, their parents and all the other adults.

Let's take a look at five sports—soccer, baseball/softball, basketball, hockey and football—and explore ways to organize games, practices and seasons in order to best serve children from kindergarten through grade eight. Even if your children play only basketball or if you coach only soccer, take a look at other sports sections. Some of these ideas apply to all children no matter which game they play.

Here are some how-to's we'll tackle:

- How to modify field, ice and gym size for small-sided games, and how to adapt the goals of the game, structure of practices and size of teams in order to support the developmental needs of each age group.
- How to establish rules about equal or meaningful amounts of playing time for each child who participates.
- How to keep children active and involved.

- How to set limits on the length of the sports season, and the number and length of practices and games, so that children are not pushed beyond healthy limits.
- How to agree on the importance to be placed on scores and winning-losing totals in order to decide what, if any, postseason playoffs or other events will be scheduled.

General Ground Rules

The most appropriate youth sports systems combine no more than two ages: eleven- and twelve-year-olds but not ten-year-olds, for example. Many youth sports teams are put together with one grade only: a grade-six basketball team, for instance. In other cases, several grades and several ages are mixed.

In talking about three sports in particular—soccer, baseball/ softball and basketball—this book looks at the needs of children in three groupings: lower elementary (kindergarten through grade two), upper elementary (grade three through grade five), and middle school (grade six through grade eight). Teams in your community may mix grade five and grade six together, and such a team will overlap two of the age groupings presented in this chapter.

Children in any grade span more than one year in age from youngest to oldest. Those who delayed entering kindergarten will be on the older end of the span; those who just made the kindergarten age cutoff, or perhaps were granted "early admission," will be on the younger end of the span. Those kindergarten-readiness issues that parents might have looked at when their children were five actually have as much impact when their children are in middle school. Children may enter puberty or turn into teenagers months, or even a year later than their peers. This can have a significant effect on physical strength and athletic ability.

Finally, a word about weekly involvement: My rule of thumb for children younger than thirteen is no more than a total of three "events" each week, an event being a game or a practice.

> My rule of thumb for children younger than thirteen is no more than a total of three "events" each week, an event being a game or a practice.

All that said, the groupings and the recommendations that follow are solely guidelines. They are excellent guidelines, but adjustments will need to be made for individual teams and individual children. My point is that adults must be strict with themselves in deciding how much time children will practice, how many games they will play, what kinds of games they will play and how the results of those games will be treated. Adjustments aside, do not veer too far off this path. If you stray too far, you will violate the very principles that require protection.

When you are criticized for your "outrageous" reform suggestions, which you surely will be, keep yourself strong by remembering what this is for. Good choices for very young players will help ensure that they can become very good older players, physically intact and still energized about playing the game.

Soccer: Kindergarten Through Grade Two

Soccer has been one of the fastest growing sports for years, and with good reason: It allows children to move much of the time in ways that are as natural as play.

In our sports system, soccer can start in kindergarten, though I think first grade is soon enough. While some adults think that training children in soccer at the same time they are toilet training is fine, I'm not one of those adults. Give the kids a chance to watch *Sesame Street* and throw food off their high chairs before they start kicking a soccer ball.

In kindergarten soccer through the second grade, do not separate practice days and game days. For this age group, plan one "event" per week. ("Event" is an important word as I use it here and elsewhere. When I say it, I mean either a practice or a game, or a combination of the two. Any of these sessions is an event.)

In this once-a-week event for the K-2 set, games will not look much different from practices. In fact, I wouldn't make any differentiation. Each event should last no longer than an hour.

During that time, get a bunch of soccer balls, a bunch of kids and a bunch of well-meaning adults together, and you'll see just how many

> In kindergarten soccer through the second grade, do not separate practice days and game days. For this age group, plan one "event" per week.

laughs you can fit into that sixty-minute stretch. Hitting the soccer field with a bunch of little kids on a sunny day is such a treat. So treat it as such.

Do drills if you must, but please don't call them drills. Try the word "activities," which some organizations use. Children, even at this tender age, hear the word "drills" and conjure up all kinds of dread. Make your weekly get-togethers as pleasant as you can by weaving in "activities" with scrimmages as seamlessly as you can. Always break the children into small groups, no more than three on a side, with a maximum of eight players to a team. There are plenty of ideas on the Internet about playing small-sided games. The idea is that each player gets as much time as possible with the ball. The key is that there is no pressure.

> Do drills if you must, but please don't call them drills.

If you're playing another team of eight, terrific. Have two games at once, three to a side. Use the two players who aren't on the field as outlet-pass receivers. In other words, have those two players line up on the sidelines at their team's offensive end. The players on the field can pass the ball to these sideline extras and the extras can pass it back. This gets everyone involved in the game with as close as possible to equal playing time.

The season should be no longer than three months, or ninety days, with no playoffs. If you want a last-day jamboree, fine. All teams play all other teams and then everyone adjourns for pizza and soda. Put the children in charge of keeping the score.

Soccer: Grades Three Through Five

As children move up in any sport, changes will occur. Again, I don't want anyone to think I'm preaching a kind of competition-less free-for-all. Adults will be present, but they need to understand when to pull back and let the children do the organizing and game playing.

At this age, of course, there should be no cuts. Games and practices emerge as separate entities. Ideally, there will be eight children on any one team. There will be three, and up to six, to a side on the field. (Yes, even when they are eleven years old.) Make use of the other children as outlet-pass receivers, again having them stand on the sidelines in their team's offensive zone, ready to take a pass and give a pass back. They're never on the field, but you'd be surprised at the increase in ball handling this affords—a key to future success. Again, give every player as close to equal playing time as possible.

Some teams have two game modifications that can make for great play at this age: (1) Nobody can score until all other teammates on the field have touched the ball first. (2) Nobody can score two consecutive goals. These modifications make the children think more "strategically," if you will. The child who has just put in a goal and then has a perfect shot on a second attempt must forgo the obvious and look around for a teammate.

These are just suggestions. You could create your own ways of getting more children involved. As I watch games or practices, I'm saddest and most frustrated when I see players just standing around. The adults' most important task is to keep all their players moving as much as possible.

At this level, two events per week are fine. That usually means one practice and one game per week. None of these events—neither practices nor games—should last more than one hour. Some coaches like to stretch that one practice into ninety minutes. Don't. An added benefit to keeping each team to sixty minutes is that it frees up valuable field space for other teams, other ages.

The length of a season ought to be three months or ninety days. At this age, ten games and fifteen practices are enough. Scores can be kept in a score book, and the kids can take turns maintaining it. No league standings should be kept either, so no such details are reported to the newspapers. Playing at this age is still for the fun of it, not the fame. There are no playoffs. The last-day jamboree is still a good choice here.

Soccer: Grades Six Through Eight

The amount of time spent on the sport and the number of players to a side both change here. In most communities this age group steps up from elementary school to middle school, and that step up applies to sports, too.

Instead of three players to a side, I prefer to see eight out there, although some leagues insist on moving to eleven versus eleven. If you play eight versus eight, you could keep the team size to about twelve, which is preferable to a larger number. You won't be able to break the team into two separate squads, regardless, but do remember to rotate your players through different positions and allow for as close to equal playing time as possible.

Length of a game at this age is usually 70 running minutes. With eight players on the field at any time, you have a total of 70 minutes times eight players, or 560 playing minutes for the team. Divide that number equally among the twelve players on your squad, and each player will get roughly 47 minutes of playing time.

The season length at this age is still three months or ninety days. Instead of ten games, you can go to twelve, and a maximum of twenty-four practices. Each practice should last no longer than ninety minutes.

Playoffs? Sure. But every team plays until knocked out. There is no selection for playoffs according to the season's record. Keep scores in a score book; the children can do that for you if you want. It's okay to keep league standings, but they ought to be deemphasized.

Basketball

While I can speak with authority on soccer and baseball, basketball is my passion, with thirty years of experience, four of those playing at the pro level. In addition, I have run more than a thousand clinics for players of all ages and have conducted summer camps, while I continue to be paid occasionally as a professional scout.

This next suggestion is important: Children should not play organized basketball before grade three. And, something equally important for the coaches of children's basketball teams to remember: During the games, coaches, please sit down. Coaches who stand up to coach basketball talk too much. When coaches talk too much, they overload the kids with too much information that the children cannot possibly process while running up and down the court.

When you exclude kindergarten through second-grade players from basketball leagues, you make more room in your gyms for those who are traditionally underserviced: boys and girls in grades nine and ten who either were cut from their high school teams, never made those teams or just never wanted to try out for interscholastic teams. Let them have the gym time and let the younger tykes wait their turn. (If you want to read about a great way to give the gyms back to those teenagers, read the story in chapter 9 about the Back to the Past Basketball League in Woburn, Massachusetts.)

Basketball is harder for children to learn than soccer or baseball. It's my observation that children generally can learn soccer about three years ahead of the time they can learn basketball. In other words, your fifth-grade basketball player looks about as "polished" as your second-grade soccer player. Your eighth-grade basketball player looks more like your fifth-grade soccer player.

One of the challenges in basketball is that a lot of the offensive skills require upper-body strength and coordination in the use of your arms, and if you don't have it, it can throw off your balance. There is also much more multitasking required, such as learning how to stop under control without traveling or double dribbling. Young children are not ready to execute such serial skills.

Basketball: Kindergarten Through Grade Two

If you want to involve children in K–2 in the sport of basketball, set up events along the lines of "glorified play groups."

Use small-size balls—28.5 inches in circumference or smaller—one for every child, and let kids shoot at baskets no higher than five or six feet. Have no more than three children "playing" against three children at a time, with the rest of the children standing on the sidelines of their team's offensive end, ready to throw the out-of-bounds balls back into play. Invite the adults on the gym floor to shoot and dribble with the children. One event per week, no longer than sixty minutes, is enough—as long as the kids are not standing around too much. The season should be six weeks at most.

Focus on dribbling skills—these are the least difficult to learn at young ages. Keep your instructions short: ten seconds is a good time frame. Don't preach about teamwork or moving around when you don't have the ball; that level of instruction is over the heads of such young players. At this age, children should spend lots of time touching the ball.

Basketball: Grades Three Through Five

In this age bracket there are no cuts and, please, no drafts, unless they are blind drafts.

Eight children on a team is optimal. Three players against three players is a great ratio. All players touch the ball more than if they are playing five-on-five. Use as many baskets in the gym as are available. You won't always have the whole gym exclusively for your team, but do what you can. The worst activity I see occurs at practices where a team of eight or ten is scrimmaging another team, while baskets sit unused elsewhere in the gym. In these situations, five from each team are on the floor at once, which means three to five others are just watching. Send them to the empty baskets! Let them play.

To further ensure activity and no idle hands, use the kinds of outlet-pass receivers recommended for soccer. Each basketball game in this age range ought to be thirty (stopped) minutes long. That means thirty minutes of actual play, not counting whistles and other time-outs, with a maximum of ten games per season.

One event per week, ninety minutes long, is enough. Sixty minutes will be needed to play the game; the rest can be practice time. Have everybody play equal time.

Until fourth grade, the baskets should be eight feet off the ground. In the fifth grade, they should be nine feet. In the sixth, go to ten feet, and that's where they stay. Those recommendations are supported by the American Sport Education Program, formerly called the American Coaching Effectiveness Program. For communities with gyms that have fixed-height baskets (ten feet high), adaptive equipment is available to create lower hoops.

It does no one—least of all the players on the court—any good to shoot for ten-foot-high baskets when children are only eight, nine or ten years old. They can't reach such high baskets, and they make only about 5 percent of their shots, which is very discouraging to a budding player.

Be sure to use smaller balls at these earlier ages, too. At coaching clinics, I bring along a medicine ball, which bounces and weighs about nine pounds and invariably proves to be a very useful object. I call a few dads up to the court and ask them to dribble, pass and shoot the medicine ball into ten-foot baskets. None can do it. It's like watching a third-grader aim a regulation-size ball at a regulation-height basket. The dads miss their shots, get embarrassed, quickly grasp the point and sit down. The gymnasium is usually filled with laughter, but it's the healthy laughter of adults seeing the fallacy of using grown-up equipment for people who haven't yet grown up.

A caution about officiating at this level: Let some of it go — double dribbles, traveling and certain kinds of fouls will occur frequently. If the referee calls everything, the games are constantly interrupted by whistles, and they seem to take nearly forever to finish.

The season should last no more than twelve weeks. There are no playoffs at this level. Some kind of last-day jamboree as described in the soccer section is fine. Scores can go into a score book; ask the children to assist. But do not report the scores to the local media. Keep no league standings either.

Basketball: Grades Six Through Eight

The intensity ratchets up slightly in this next level. (Remember: Children will put an appropriate amount of pressure on themselves to compete and to play hard.) Team size is ten maximum, but eight is ideal.

On the floor, play five-on-five, the game we all know. There will be five times 26 to 32 stopped minutes (actual playing time) or 130 to 160 playing minutes to divide among your ten players. You must give each a minimum of 12 minutes of playing time, ideally at least 15.

Do not let yourself fall into the trap of giving some kids only two or three minutes of playing time. Those are meaningless minutes. They can't learn the game that way. They didn't sign up to watch everybody else's sons and daughters play, or to watch you coach. They signed up to play. Let them.

No more outlet-pass receivers either. If they're on the floor, they're on their own now.

Practices should be no more than twice a week, for a total of 90 minutes each in sixth grade. In seventh and eighth grade, you can go up to three a week. The ratio of practices to games should be a minimum of two to one.

As for number of games, let's put that at twelve in a season, or about one a week, in a ninety-day block. That means no more than twenty-four to thirty practices, and each practice ought to be no longer than an hour and a half and broken into thirds. First practice fundamentals, then small-sided scrimmages, and then a half-court or full-court five-on-five scrimmage. In the fundamentals portion, every child should have a ball in his or her hands as much as possible. In the small-sided scrimmages, rotate players in for some two-on-two and three-on-three so that players can handle the ball frequently and develop a tactical and cognitive sense of playing the game with others, of moving around on the floor into open spaces, of cutting to the basket.

And please, no complicated playbooks, all those X's and O's borrowed from the colleges and the pros. Coaches at this middle-school level love to work up playbooks of a half dozen to a dozen plays, naming the plays for popular basketball colleges. You'll hear the coach yelling "Kentucky!" or "Duke!"

Watch the children when this happens. First comes that struck but bewildered look in the direction of the coach, then a free-for-all of scrambling as they try to figure where they're supposed to be for the pick or the pass. If you see a child out there not having as much trouble, a child for whom the complicated positioning seems to come easily, my money is on one thing: That child is the coach's child. He knows this stuff because he has to live with the fanatic who's drawing up all these plays.

Teach your charges to play man-to-man defense. Give them the basics for an offense: players moving to open spots and all players keeping their heads up and hands ready. No full-court pressing or traps.

Make sure all your players, of every shape and height, participate in all positions and in all skills. Don't typecast your players according to the positions you think they are best suited for now. That ten-year-old who is below average in size and height may be the tallest, strongest one on your high school varsity squad. Give her a chance at center, too. She may grow twelve inches before her senior year. Don't judge her now.

There ought to be playoffs at this level, but all teams should make the playoffs. It makes everyone feel good about themselves and does not detract one iota from the idea that there is competition and there are winners and losers. By the way, if you have a problem with the idea that every team makes the playoffs, you're almost certainly an adult. The children don't care. If you don't believe me, ask them yourself.

Baseball/Softball

Baseball and softball are two of the most difficult youth sports to coach because the nature of each game dictates that a number of players will wait while others are at bat. That means coaches must be creative. They must look for ways to engage as many of the children as possible.

One policy that should help in game situations: Do not use adults as base coaches for teams with players younger than ninth-graders. In these games, let the children coach the bases, one on third and one on first. However, be sure that they wear helmets for safety. This gives you two more places to put those idle bodies who would otherwise be sitting on the bench waiting to hit. In practices, be sure to organize players into the smallest possible units.

For example, there could be units of three fielders and one hitter. In this grouping, the hitter hits and then switches places with one of the fielders and so forth. The key is to put some motion into what could be a dull afternoon of drills.

T-Ball: Kindergarten Through Grade Two

Most children in baseball and softball begin at young ages by playing the game of T-ball. The basic problem with T-ball is that too many coaches send nine or more players into the field to scoop up the hits coming from one batter. It's the same problem I see in youth football and in youth basketball programs that have more than a dozen or so children on a team. Too many children are just watching, doing nothing, while a minority are active.

The solution for T-ball is to create a modified version of the game. Call it "small-sided T-ball," meaning three or four players in the field while one bats at the tee. Have several of these games going on at once; divide up your playing space as best you can. It's the model we use in soccer and basketball.

Create mini-teams. Get them moving and the children won't be so bored.

Other parameters for this youngest age group will look much the same as they do in basketball and soccer. I suggest one event per week, not one game and one practice. At this age level, there's no need to distinguish between game and practice. If you want, set aside half the time for practice and the other half for more of a game setup. Teach within that game structure. Get together for a one-hour session on the weekend, set up your mini-stations and let the children play. Don't worry about complicated schedules in which each T-ball team plays every other T-ball team. And skip the uniforms. A baseball cap and T-shirt are really just fine.

Ask the children to keep the score and remember to move those younger players around constantly. Never let them get so comfortable in one position that they won't try another. Whatever you do, don't let youngsters or their parents convince you that a child is going to pitch in the big leagues and must get started now. There are no child pitchers in T-ball.

Start easing children off the tee in second grade and allow them to hit pitching, but make that adult pitching or pitching machines. Allow for a maximum of three pitches thrown by an adult, then move to the tee. Have the adult pitcher get each pitch as close to the bat as possible. The idea is to let the kids hit and hit and hit. Let them get comfortable at the plate, comfortable with balls coming in their general direction. Many youngsters are thrown up against difficult pitching at a very young age and never lose their fear at the plate.

Compile no team standings, please.

Baseball/Softball: Grades Three Through Five

After T-ball and its variations, children enter the world of the nine-on-a-field baseball or ten-on-a-field softball team. Each team should carry no more than thirteen players. As much as possible, every player gets equal playing time and an equal chance to play all the positions.

Some children will be uncomfortable pitching, catching and playing the infield. Coaches must recognize this and not force the kids into doing so. Work with them and slowly ease them into it. Let them get comfortable. Children at this level can start pitching to each other, but watch the number of pitches. Remember, baseball pitchers pitch overhand, which puts more strain on their arms. Most leagues recommend no more than six innings per week. In softball, the underhanded pitch does not put nearly as much strain on the arm, so pitchers can be allowed to pitch every day, although it is better to give others a chance.

The season should last no longer than ninety days or three months, with about ten games. The number of practices should be no more than twenty.

Each game should last six innings, as most do now, or an hour and a half, whichever comes first. The practices should last an hour. Begin with activities but quickly get into an active scrimmage mode and move players around frequently. Playing the game is why the team showed up.

No playoffs at grade three, please, but if you choose playoffs for the fourth- and fifth-graders, make sure each team participates so they do not spend the entire season worrying about their standings and whether they will make the playoffs. Stick to the rule about nearly equal playing time for everyone, and skip the all-star teams.

Baseball/Softball: Grades Six Through Eight

Not a whole lot changes as kids enter sixth grade. A dozen players on a team makes sense, as does a six-inning game, or ninety minutes, whichever comes first.

You could increase to twenty games for the three-month season. There should be no more than thirty practices, and none should be longer than ninety minutes each. Playoffs are fine, as long as every team makes them.

In seventh grade, baseball players (usually thirteen years old) go from a small diamond to a bigger one (the softball field stays the same size). The area of the baseball infield goes from thirty-six hundred square feet to eighty-one hundred square feet. Take this into account, giving youngsters time to adjust to the new dimensions.

Football, Hockey and Lacrosse

Football, hockey and lacrosse are different from other sports in that they allow and encourage physical contact as a major part of the game. One of the most difficult responsibilities a coach has in these sports is to teach fair physical contact.

Football, hockey and lacrosse generally draw fewer children in each separate community. Therefore, several communities often band together to form regional teams. In that regard, from day one, these are "travel" team sports.

Football and hockey do not generally "cut" children from teams, but rather have extensive placements according to ability, age and/or weight. That does not make some of those selections any less contentious or political among the adults, but some of the selection criteria are different from those of the sports presented above.

Youth lacrosse is a relative newcomer. Since the early nineties, the game has spread quickly throughout the United States. General concerns about coaching style, length of seasons, intensity of play, inappropriate structures for certain ages, and general attitudes toward winning and losing all apply to lacrosse, as they do to any sport. Though this book does not specifically address the structures of lacrosse, the general recommendations about football and hockey apply to lacrosse.

Football

Among the biggest challenges in youth football are coaching style and expertise. I don't mean expertise about the game of football, but rather an understanding about how young children develop and what their needs are at each age level.

Too often in youth football you find coaches who played high school or college football and have spent their lives watching the NFL. They often do not recognize how inappropriate some of their tactics are, and they might not easily be able to determine how to turn inappropriate tactics into appropriate choices for young children. Coaches need more training in child development.

A large majority of youth football coaches also need to cultivate patience about developing young football players at a slower pace instead of making choices about how best to use them to win next weekend's game.

Football lives in a world populated—I think overpopulated—by nomenclature. Terms like "containment" can befuddle children. There is much lingo, many abstract ideas about field position and tactics. This kind of world is not exactly child-friendly, and coaches must make a concerted effort to make that world easier for their young charges to understand.

One of my major criticisms of youth football has to do with the way practices are conducted. National soccer groups like to remind their coaches to avoid the "Three L's": lines, lectures and laps. Too many youth football practices are notorious for all three of those L's.

The way many youth football practices are conducted, they do not engage and encourage young children being initiated into a new sport. Adding to the problems of how practices are structured is the sheer number of practices that are scheduled. Because football's complexity is difficult for young children to learn, coaches often feel the need to schedule more than three practices, sometimes four or five events a week including the games. It's not surprising to see some young football players in this country have a practice or a game every day.

Warnings about limiting the number of practices and games apply to football as much as they do to any other sport. No good comes from pushing children beyond healthy limits.

In youth football, the size of the field—one hundred yards by fifty-three yards—is the same size as football fields used at the college level and in the pros. A ten-year-old has just as far to run in order to score as does a Super Bowl running back.

For younger children, divide up the football field into four quarters (fifty-three yards by twenty-five yards) and have small-sided practices and games — six versus six. That way, you'll have forty-eight players on the field at once, all moving, experimenting and learning. Isn't that better than twenty-two on the field and the rest of the crew sweating under their pads on the sidelines?

Most youth football leagues have rules about the minimum number of plays that each player must be involved in during each game, and they have methods that ensure opposing teams will keep track of each other. The standards are too lenient, however, often requiring only six to eight plays for each player during a game that may have thirty-five to fifty plays. That involves some children in only one-fifth of the game. That's too little playing time. Raise that standard to fifteen to twenty plays and help everyone learn how to play. My warnings about nurturing a few early-budding "stars" and neglecting the rest of the team apply here. It makes no sense for the future of these players or for the future of football.

I'm not the only one who sees problems that could diminish participation by youngsters at the earliest stages. The National Football League has set aside $100 million for thirteen programs aimed at redesigning youth programs and renewing interest. These programs aim to show children that football is filled with action and fun, and to convince their parents that it's not too violent or risky. "The biggest problem facing football at the youth level is the structure of the practices and coaching," Scott Lancaster, senior director of youth football development for the NFL, told *All-Stater Sports* in 1999.

The NFL has been working with youth programs across the country to reshape drill sessions and take some of the notorious repetition and boredom out of the practices. The aim, Lancaster said, is to add more running and playing to practices, with less sitting around listening to lectures or doing calisthenics and other conditioning exercises.

In a January 22, 2001, op-ed piece in *The Christian Science Monitor*, Lancaster took aim at youth sports systems that are not in the children's best interests. He targeted coaches who have "a style that nears—or at times reaches—verbal or physical abuse." He said the behavior of adults watching all youth sports, not just youth football, has a way of spoiling the fun for the youngsters and turning them off from the games. "At the National Football League, we've been asking ourselves what we can do" about these problems, he said.

One answer is the NFL Flag Program for six- to fourteen-year-old boys and girls. Coed teams play a noncontact variation of football, in which, instead of tackling to stop the play, the aim is to pull off small flags usually worn at the waist. At the national championship NFL Flag competition, the program set up child-friendly rules. Coaches were forbidden from coaching during games and players developed their own plays.

The NFL's Junior Player Development Program aims to involve children ages twelve to fourteen, particularly those who have no previous football experience. Players wear uniforms and learn traditional football skills, including tackling, but no games are played. Instead, the practices aim for a lot of activity and instruction.

The more spontaneity, the more responsibility you can give back to the youngsters, the better the games will be. It sounds like the NFL is working on some good things.

Too often adults lose sight of the needs of young children

at practices and during games. Some young football players are asked to run, sometimes on brutally hot days, under what would be an adult equivalent of forty pounds of protective gear. Would any adult coach or parent watching from the sidelines be willing to do the same?

Any adult attitudes that this kind of physical challenge toughens young kids and makes them more competitive should be severely tempered by healthy choices at appropriate ages. Ideas about "punishing" underachieving players by forcing them to run sprints should be stricken. Coaches who withhold water as punishment should be fired.

Hockey

For ideas about how to adapt the game of hockey to younger ages and how to make the playing time and the practices more effective, more developmentally appropriate and more fun, look to Doug Abrams. If you are the parent of a young hockey player, there is no better authority.

I've mentioned Abrams several times already in this book, and you'll read more about him in chapter 9. In addition to his past as a goalie at Wesleyan University in Connecticut and his present as a law professor, Abrams has coached youth hockey since he was sixteen. That includes fifteen years conducting mites programs for five- to eight-year-olds. Some are at the ripe age of nine before the end of the season. For the past few years, Abrams has also coached squirt teams (nine- and ten-year-olds).

Abrams says some of his mite programs have had weekly in-house games, a regulated number of games against teams from other programs throughout the season, or both. "Personally, I don't think five- to seven-year-olds should play a competitive league schedule," Abrams says, "but the parents always disagree and they usually win."

If the program structure permits, Abrams says, divide the mites into two groups. The eight- and nine-year-old mites are ready for more than the five- to seven-year-olds can grasp, including more games. Additionally, this allows coaches to structure practices and games to meet the particular physical, emotional and cognitive needs of each age group. There's a big difference between five-year-olds and eight-year-olds.

For mite programs, consider one hour of practice time each week, for a season that would run preferably from early November until early March. That hour of practice can include ten minutes of warm-up skating, fifteen minutes of "skill drills" (usually in stations), fifteen minutes of "fun learning games" and fifteen minutes for scrimmaging. Finish practice with a five-minute relay race.

As the season progresses, the coach can increase times for "skill drills" and scrimmaging, and decrease "fun learning" time. USA Hockey, the governing body for the sport, has skills progression guidelines posted on its Web site (*www.usahockey.com*).

Abrams tries hard to make sure all mites stay active all the time during practices. Ice rinks are cold places, so having a few players moving while everyone else's feet freeze is a sure way to lead mites to complain about upset stomachs just before it is time to go to the rink, or to quit altogether, Abrams says. If much of the team is on the bench during a full-ice scrimmage, many mites are too small to see over the boards. They cannot see the action on the ice, and they may even forget there is a scrimmage going on.

Abrams keeps all mites moving all the time during practice in two ways. First, his mites do the "skill drills" in stations— each station focusing on a particular skill, such as stick-handling, skating or passing. Divide the ice into three or four sections, each supervised by at least one coach. To work on most of these skills, younger players do not need the whole ice. Blow the whistle and rotate stations every five or eight minutes, depending on the children's attention span. Players can probably make all the rounds within fifteen or twenty minutes.

Second, Abrams's mites scrimmage widthwise, not length-wise, for much of the season, with full-ice scrimmages saved for later in the year. The older mite group can begin full-ice scrimmages earlier than the younger group. The widthwise format lets the coach set up two or three scrimmages simultaneously, sometimes with three-on-three or four-on-four games. The red and blue lines are out-of-bounds markers. If you don't have enough goalies, the coaches can play. A single lengthwise scrimmage involves only twelve mites and leaves the rest to freeze on the bench, but everybody plays in simultaneous widthwise scrimmages. Early in the season, in particular, these compact scrimmages are better for developing mites because they make it more challenging to skate, stick-handle, pass and shoot in a compact area. Widthwise scrimmaging also maximizes use of ice time, giving players at least twice as much playing time as would one full-ice scrimmage.

By using the entire ice surface most efficiently while enhancing the players' learning and fun, stations and widthwise scrimmaging also allow associations with limited mite ice time to enroll the greatest possible number of children, without placing any on a waiting list or turning any away altogether.

If you are an adult in charge of scheduling ice time, don't do what so many youth hockey associations do. Abrams recommends not always giving choice practice and game times to the oldest and select teams. Mites and other young players often get the leftovers, such as 5:00 A.M. on Saturday or Sunday. Older children and competitive teams usually can better understand why they may have to wake up at 3:00 A.M. and travel in subfreezing weather to spend an hour skating in a cold rink before sunrise. Mites do not understand, and we should not expect them to. Poor choices for mite ice times quickly produce ex-hockey players, Abrams says. Basketball is warmer.

Demonstrate skills for the mites; don't just lecture about them. The mites, too, cannot absorb lengthy chalk talks with lots of X's and O's. Teach the mites the basics of what forwards do, what defensemen do and what goalies do, but leave the collegiate strategy for the colleges. Introduce the basic skills of hockey and basic position play, but then just let the kids play. Many coaches get frustrated when six-year-olds cannot learn a forechecking pattern, but, as Abrams says, the coach's frustration is his own fault.

If you keep asking the players questions and have them talk to you, rather than giving a speech, they will pay attention longer. Whenever you talk to the mites in a group, keep the players on their knees in a semicircle in front of you. Never talk to the team while the players, particularly the young ones, are standing. They won't pay attention if they are milling around, tripping and falling down.

When mites are just starting out, Abrams recommends rotating them in at both forward and defense. He also recommends giving all willing players the chance to be one of the goalies. According to him, children who become specialist goalies at the youngest ages frequently never learn to skate well enough. Allowing all children to experience goaltending's difficulties at a young age also may discourage them from criticizing the goalie in future years. Besides, some mites might learn that they like goaltending and want to stick with it, which would help the program as a whole later on. Rotating the slot, however, requires that parents be willing to share goalie equipment, or that the program have its own set for sharing.

When it comes time for games, USA Hockey has outlawed body checking for mites and squirts alike. "Some coaches," Abrams says, "try to gain a competitive edge by teaching a style of play that approaches body checking and sometimes crosses the line. I do not do this because the line is inevitably crossed during heated games. Teams whose coaches bend the no-checking rule risk injury to opposing players, whose coaches play by the rules and have not taught how to take a check. For the kids' safety, coaches should follow the spirit as well as the letter of the rules. Winning isn't worth cheating."

What I love about Abrams's style, in addition to his common sense, is that he is creative about his mite practices. The following are a few of the "fun learning games" his mites play during practices to develop skating, balance and agility. (Remember that players, even when they're not using sticks, should keep their gloves on to protect their hands from skate blades.)

- *Soccer on ice:* Set up a few games widthwise, with pylons for goals. Red and blue lines are out-of-bounds markers. No sticks. Use soccer balls you're willing to discard at the end of the season because skate blades scratch them.
- *Basketball:* Set up a few games widthwise, and use two large trash cans as goals/nets. (Plastic cans are better than aluminum ones for safety.) No sticks and no dribbling; players just skate with the ball. Players must pass the basketball with every two skating strides. They love to slam-dunk, which is not difficult as long as they are taller than the trash can!
- *Touch football:* The two blue lines are the goal lines; lines joining the face-off dots on the center ice side of the blue lines (marked off with pylons) are out-of-bounds. You can use a regular football or a sponge-rubber football. No sticks. To keep the ball in play, it is a good idea to have the coaches be the quarterbacks. Coaches should make the kids skate a bit before throwing a pass underhand. While part of the team plays touch football on the center ice, coaches can do skill drills with other players at stations in the defensive zone.
- *Baseball:* The coach-pitcher sends the puck to "home plate," where the player at bat stops it with his stick, takes a slap shot and runs (skates!) the bases, which are pylons. Players in the field make an out by stopping the shot and passing the puck to the first baseman, etc. Do not allow sliding because skate blades can cause injury.
- *Obstacle courses, jumping rope, or relay races* also can be helpful and fun.

These ideas and structures need to be adapted and changed as children grow and develop. But hold on to the good ideas that work for the youngest and even the older players. Basketball and baseball on ice do not work well above mite age; touch football is fun once or twice a season with the squirts, and even with older teams; and soccer is great for all, even high school players. Keeping everyone moving is a good idea at any age. Doing some skill drills in stations works well at any age, but squirts and older players usually need to scrimmage full-ice. Continue to be creative and to have fun.

The basic aim of mite hockey, Abrams says, is to introduce skills while letting the players see for themselves that sports is fun and that coaches are good people. "Keep the fires burning" within each child, Abrams says. Mite coaches are successful if most of their ex-mites still love playing hockey as fourteen-year-old bantams and have not joined the 70 percent or so of children who drop out of youth sports by that age.

●●●

With the structural details outlined in this chapter for the most popular organized youth sports, you're almost ready to go out and reform your systems, your leagues or your team. But before you do, a little reality check is in order. How will these changes go over in your youth sports world? In the next chapter, you'll meet people who've been there, done that— and you'll get a sense of what they faced along the way.

CHAPTER 8

The Politics of Youth Sports: Fighting for Change

I find it extremely difficult, nay impossible, to tell a youngster that he or she is not good enough for a team. Heck, these are ten-year-olds! How good can they be at anything yet?

Ric Granryd, director of coaching,
Austin United and South Austin
Youth Soccer Association

Parents yelling from the sidelines and coaches screaming can be dramatic, if not traumatic. However, for some of the highest drama in youth sports, you must go behind the scenes, far from the maddening crowd.

In closed-door meetings, on the telephone, and over the Internet, moms and dads wheel and deal, argue and negotiate, protest and complain in a dance called the politics of youth sports. The idea that this would happen is inevitable in any system run by human beings. Many times the political process itself proves to be productive, but when you're about to suggest changes in your local sports organizations, as I hope you will, be warned: The politics can get uncomfortable, even nasty.

Change is almost never easy. Change makes everyone a little unsettled, so if you are heading the charge to make changes in youth sports, please know the risks so that you may prepare. You may face criticism, even scorn, from people you know as neighbors and as friends. They will question your reasoning. They may question your motives.

"What do you mean we shouldn't keep standings and award trophies? You're killing the competition," they may say.

"Children deserve to play at their ability level. It's never too early to let kids know where they stand in the real world. Some are simply better than others," you may hear.

"What have you got against this league anyway? Do you want to take over? Are you getting back at us because your child didn't make the top team?"

Although these kinds of questions sound antagonistic, they are, in my opinion, fair questions deserving honest answers. Tell people what you believe. If part of your motivation for getting involved is that your child didn't make the top team, be honest. And stay calm.

The divisive issues that arise in youth sports often cut to the core of our emotions as parents. These issues unleash all kinds of guilt, self-doubt, anger and resentment. Think of the red-hot rage that explodes when a mother or father watches his or her child hurt by another player on the field, intentionally or otherwise, especially if that injury draws blood. The instinct to protect is powerful.

Youth sports battles between adults, on the surface, may be about draft rules, elite team selections or playoff line-ups, but the underlying issues are far more complex. Principles and motives are often difficult to sort out. Trying to determine who's right and who's wrong is even trickier.

Try to follow this simple guiding principle: Give yourself a reality check once in a while by looking at the situation, any situation, from the perspective of a child. Maybe that child feels rejected after being cut from another team. Maybe that child has been yelled at by an overbearing coach, or ridiculed by other children for not playing as well as some of the others on the team. The bottom line is that the child may feel that he or she is simply not good enough to play. It is from that perspective that you should decide if your youth sports system is fair, healthy and in the best interests of *all* the children.

You may not agree with that assessment, but please, hear me out as we explore the issues in play and the emotions unleashed in three highly charged youth sports battles. These battles took place in New Hampshire, New Jersey and Massachusetts, but they happen every season in every state. Be assured that somewhere near you right now a political controversy of some sort is brewing in one of your youth sports programs.

I tell you these stories not to expose unreasonable adults who say controversial things about youth sports. In fact, that is the challenge here. The adults you are about to meet, all of them, appear to care deeply about youth sports participation for children. There are no purely good guys and purely bad guys in any of these stories.

Everyone you will meet is motivated by wanting to do "what's best" for children, or at least for their own children. Also, they are all volunteers. They give of themselves and they give of their time because they enjoy working with children. They believe their way is the right way to help children succeed *and* have fun. However, they have radically different ideas about what's best for children and about how the adults in charge should make sure children have what's best for them.

It's important to share their stories, in order that we may continue the debate and, hopefully, learn from these battles and find common ground. I take sides in these stories. I take sides based on the principles, as I see them, that are at issue, even though I cannot know all the details about what happened in each case; these were drawn-out and complicated battles.

Let us have the courage, however, to talk honestly about these issues and to learn from listening to each other. At the end of this chapter you will find some tips that can help you if you choose to fight for change in your community.

Case #1: Elite Teams

One of the most complicated and explosive youth sports battles took place in a small town in New Hampshire over the selection of an "elite" or select youth baseball team. What makes the case so interesting is the clash of philosophies at the heart of it.

Full names are not used in this story because the wounds of the controversy, although several years old, are still raw. Also, all the facts can't be presented in this limited space.

On one side was Paul, the father of five and a coach who believed strongly that the existence of one select or elite baseball team for the town's "better" twelve-year-olds was a divisive element in the overall baseball program. He felt that the adults in charge had tried to build a "stacked" team—including eleven-year-olds and a few ten-year-olds—in order to better compete against surrounding towns rather than to give all twelve-year-olds a fair chance to play at that upper level.

On the other side was Dan, a father and also a passionate coach who said this select team was an admirable part of a healthy and thriving baseball program. Dan said children are happier and have more fun competing at their ability level, that those who were selected for this team deserved to be there. He also said that the others who were not selected were put on teams to play at a level more appropriate for them, and that mixing teams of too many ability levels can be unsafe, particularly when there are powerful young pitchers to be faced. Paul argued that league organizers created similar safety issues when they placed twelve-year-olds who did not make the elite team onto lower-level teams alongside eight- to ten-year-olds, thereby also putting children of vastly different sizes and strengths on the same teams.

As for trying to win, Dan said that wasn't the team's only aim, but he was very proud of how the team performed, even when it dominated its opponents.

Over the many months of this battle, there were heated confrontations between Paul and Dan, a letter-writing campaign and a hotline for parent complaints, league board dismissals and resignations, and lawyers consulted by both sides.

As far as Paul was concerned, there were enough twelve-year-old ballplayers in his town to send two teams into a regional league of upper-level players. The reason that didn't happen, he speculated, was that the egos of the adults ruled. Paul suspected they had figured that having two teams would dilute the "talent," and therefore lessen the chances to win.

Additionally, Paul objected to the fact that a small number of eleven-year-olds and ten-year-olds were deemed good enough to play on this team, and they took spots away from twelve-year-olds who were then relegated to play on lower-level teams.

Paul made some phone calls, including one to the commissioner of the regional league in which this select team played. When Dan found out about that, Paul said, Dan drove up to the field where Paul's team was practicing— screeching tires and all—and jumped out of his car, screaming, "I want you!"

Those who fought against Paul—Dan included—were angered and frustrated by his protests. To this day they say they don't understand Paul's "agenda." They say he went on a "personal mission," defamed members of the local baseball board and created nothing but trouble. They say he didn't do his homework, got his facts wrong and, in the end, got little support from others.

Despite Paul's insistence that two higher-level teams should have been formed, Dan and Scott, the town's baseball commissioner, said the population of twelve-year-olds deemed eligible for that level was small in that particular year, small enough to warrant only one team. They said that creating two teams would have meant including some twelve-year-olds who weren't ready for that level of competition.

"These kids have got to want to have fun, and they've got to want to come to play," Scott said, neither of which happens when ability levels are too far apart. "We don't want kids to come knowing they're going to be humiliated. Peer pressure is a tough thing."

No question about it, peer pressure at that age is very strong, but that's one of Paul's concerns, too. He said he worried about those twelve-year-olds who had to face their friends who had been selected, feeling diminished by being been left out.

In the days before the opening-day ceremony, the select team had played a couple of games, blowing out its opponents by wildly lopsided scores. Paul recalled that it outscored its early opponents 32–1. The controversy began in earnest during the ceremony.

For Dan, the teamwork and the effort shown by the boys were sources of great pride. "I thought it was wonderful," he said, so he announced the scores at opening day, a festive tradition that involves hundreds of children and their parents.

Paul said when he heard the lopsided scores announced, "That's when I hit the roof. This man is proud of that? I just flipped. That was it for me. It began right there."

This is not healthy competition, Paul thought to himself. *It's cheating. It goes against every fiber in me that believes in fair play, especially with kids.*

As a physical education major in college, Paul had played football at the University of Massachusetts and had been a head coach for high school football and an assistant coach at the college level. His biggest beef was that the twelve-year-olds who were kept on lower-level teams should have been given a chance to play at a higher level. That chance, he said, would actually bolster their self-esteem and help better prepare them for the following year should they remain in baseball.

Paul believed that discouraging twelve-year-olds by telling them they weren't good enough to play at the higher level (because the adults were busy building a winning team) could be a fatal blow to some children's enthusiasm.

"No, no, no," countered Dan. The select team during the year in dispute did not even end up winning the district championships. Having one team represent the town that year allowed these ballplayers to play at their "right level," Dan said, "rather than bringing up a bunch of weaker kids and having them suffer. When you play too many weaker kids against strong pitching, they have a terrible year." Paul notes that the next season his town fielded two teams—perhaps "diluting" talent in some people's opinions—one of those two teams actually won the league championship.

Paul went before his town's youth baseball board and made his case. He asked them to vote for changes in how teams are selected, in how children are evaluated. The board voted all right. Paul said the board voted down his suggestions, and then board members took one more vote. They voted Paul out as a youth baseball coach. "It is quite evident," said their subsequent letter mailed to Paul, "that your philosophy of a baseball program is very different" from the league's philosophy.

Dan said Paul was "out of control" at meetings. He said Paul had a "personal vendetta" and "tried to discredit the board."

"We had a couple of heated confrontations," Dan said. "I said, 'You're out of line, you're ruining the work of those adults who have invested time to help kids.'" Paul accused Dan of trying to cultivate elite players at the expense of others.

As the battle raged, Paul sent out letters to about three hundred parents in his town, and surrounding towns, spelling out his arguments and the need for change. He set up a separate hotline to take voice messages. He said he did get several letters and calls from parents who were angry about how the system had treated their son—refusing to find a spot for someone who missed the registration deadline, or allowing a child from another town to compete (which was against league rules), or not finding a place for a boy on a higher-level team who had been named most valuable player at the lower level.

At one point during the months of debate, Paul was invited to join the youth baseball board, which he did. "If you're going to complain, you should do something about it," he said. "Politically, the board meetings were painful. But I stood my ground." Dan said Paul's inappropriate behavior at the meetings eventually forced Dan, a consultant to the board, to walk away.

Paul's major thrust was to convince the league to return to a system of creating two fairly balanced select major league teams in town, not one "stacked" team of the better players. He said he succeeded for two years; the league said it was planning to do that anyway, based on enrollments. After that, the town returned again to one team. Among other things, this shows just how messy and inconclusive these battles can be.

Paul said his efforts did precipitate some changes. He said

the league improved its system for tryouts and also required that an out-of-town player return to play on a team in his own hometown. These days, however, Paul is not involved in the local baseball program. He has decided the only lasting solution is to start another league—"to offer, basically, a better mousetrap." He is motivated by the fact that he has young sons coming up, but he realizes the huge time commitment required and that it is a commitment he may not be able to make.

For his part, Dan lives in another town but still coaches baseball. He said he remains wary of Paul's motives and his tactics and that baseball in the town where they both feuded so bitterly is better off without Paul.

This battle in New Hampshire is about as convoluted and bitter as they get. Even though I have been to Paul's town (he asked me to give a lecture to parents there), I cannot know all the facts in this case. However, even with emotions, bitterness and the personal animosity stripped away, in principle I side with Paul's philosophy.

I believe strongly that too many children pay a price when elite teams are created before children are in grade seven. Granted, twelve years old, which is the age of the sixth-graders in this battle, is on the cusp. But it's still too early.

In this case I would like to have seen all twelve-year-olds provided the opportunity to play at that so-called "higher level." That's the best way to give them all a chance to develop so they can compete in middle school and beyond.

I would not be in a hurry to get eleven-year-olds and certainly not ten-year-olds, no matter how much "superstar" potential they are showing, to move up to compete in an elite league with twelve-year-olds.

The arguments in favor of a select or elite team, of moving up and keeping back certain players, are often heard as arguments about safety, fair competition, and the fact that children are intimidated, humiliated and bored when they are mismatched. I would prefer to see a system that tries to avoid boredom, humiliation and intimidation by changing the way teams are assembled and run.

As for safety concerns, use the lightest weight baseballs as well as breakaway bases and other protective equipment. Importantly, teach young players injury-prevention techniques. Take those steps, and keep just two ages on a team, and there should not be undue concern even if a young Roger Clemens is on the mound.

If you've got a mixture of pitching, maybe you can work your lineup such that your better-skilled hitters face the better-skilled pitchers, such that your less-skilled hitters face your less-skilled pitchers. Less intimidation. More participation. If you and the opposing coach are in this to develop players and to have fun more than you are to win, you'll be able to agree on this ground rule before you start to play ball.

I have no doubt that most of the players on that select team in Paul's town had a great season and a lot of fun, too. That also goes for the coaches. The kids I worry about are those who were labeled during tryouts as numbers fourteen, fifteen, sixteen and lower—those who were cut from an elite team that had room for only thirteen.

How much difference in ability is there between those slotted numbers eleven, twelve and thirteen, and those slotted fourteen, fifteen and sixteen? At twelve years old? There is none—I can guarantee that. There's even less difference when they are eleven and ten years old. Is it really so important, so necessary, to organize elite teams at eleven and twelve years old? I say no.

Ric Granryd, former director of coaching for the South Texas Youth Soccer Association, put it well in "Coaches and Parents: Is It Time for a Reality Check?"—an article that appeared in *The South Texas Youth Soccer Association Shootout* in September 1993: "What is the real rationale behind select teams for kids under twelve years old? I find it extremely difficult, nay impossible, to tell a youngster that he or she is not good enough for a team. Heck, these are ten-year-olds! How good can they be at *anything* yet?"

This book is not a game plan for a wimpier or less competitive form of baseball. My argument puts the interests of the majority of children first. It creates a more sensible atmosphere, one in which the lesser skilled can be comfortable and can develop as players, while the "stars" can also thrive. Scott, the commissioner named above, said his town has had no problems with parents at games. In general, though, a more sensible atmosphere means parents are generally less personally invested, less emotional and less inclined to misbehave.

Case #2: Individual Choice

A testy battle over competitive A and B boys' soccer teams in Washington Township (Gloucester County), New Jersey, rises above most stories in this genre of parental squabbling because this one ended up pulling in even the mayor. Placing himself smack in the middle of the messy fight, the mayor decided on a course of action that often doesn't cross the minds of adults involved in youth sports. He felt he needed to talk to the children.

The battle in Washington Township was essentially a fight over a boy's right to remain on the team of his choice, in this case the lower-level B team, rather than be forced to move up to an open spot on an A team, as was being ordered by the adults in charge of the league. If the player refused to move up to the A team, he was sent out of the program, left with the option of playing intramurals.

This battle came down to, in former Mayor Gerald Luongo's words, a fight over "conscription"—a term used most often to describe a military's mandatory draft. It's a strong word in the context of youth soccer, but, the mayor said, what was happening to the boys in this soccer program was nothing less.

Washington Township, in southern New Jersey, is in the middle of a highly competitive soccer region. Clubs are constantly looking for the strongest players, even outside their townships. The local newspaper, *The Gloucester County Times*, runs small ads in its sports section for the soccer clubs searching for "talent." "Come play soccer for us, and we'll provide professional soccer training," read some of the ads.

As the mayor sized up the controversy, he concluded that young players on any soccer team should have the option to move or not to move. If slots open up on an A team, "You may try out or you may choose not to," said Luongo. "That's the player's prerogative."

The reasons that some of the boys did not want to move up to A are varied. Some, for instance, felt the competition wasn't any better, or actually was less. Why move to a worse

The Wall

TOM MORONEY
The MetroWest Daily News
May 4, 1997

"So, fellas, what's up with those Little League dugouts that you're building?" I asked.

"This is a new feature," said one carpenter, leaning on his circular saw. "On one end of these open-air dugouts, we've been told to build a wall."

"A wall?"

"Yep," he replied. "The end of the dugout closest to the bleachers—where all the parents sit—will be closed off by a wall of lumber and then painted green."

"But why?"

"Why painted green?"

"No, why the wall?"

"That way, the parents won't be able to terrorize the players," he said.

So it has come to this. At Rosenfeld Park in Milford, Massachusetts, adult organizers have moved to protect their players from what has become the biggest threat to their comfort and safety: Mom and Dad.

This wall is being built in Milford, but walls could go into most every dugout, in every city and town across the land. Parents have been cajoled, preached at and fined for their behavior at games.

They've been asked to leave and never come back, and nothing seems to work. Maybe the wall is the answer.

"It keeps the kids focused, and stops the moms and dads from coming over to feed the kids and coach them," he said.

"So the parents here have been a problem?" I asked.

"I don't want to slander or upset anybody," he said.

Fortunately, I feel no such compunction. Once upon a time, parents were helpmates. Their job at games was to hand over a buck now and then so their little shortstops could buy a cold drink at the refreshment stand. Now, the bleachers are breeding grounds for sports agents in the making.

Parents sit there, squirming and fidgeting over everything and anything. Like the superagent in the movie *Jerry Maguire,* stockbrokers, insurance executives, real estate agents—many of them frustrated jocks themselves— keep up a constant patter to the children on the field.

"Let 'em pitch to you, son!"

"Wait for YOUR pitch!"

Or my favorite: "Play your game, son. Stay within yourself!"

And why do you suppose these parents behave as they do? There are several probable explanations: They want their kids to be the best, or they want to prepare them for the real world. But my guess is that most of it has to do with the inflated salaries of today's pro athletes. That you could bear down on your eight-year-old now and one day be known as the biological sire of a millionaire is a temptation many fathers and mothers find difficult to pass up.

Before the wall, Milford baseball officials had tried a fence near the dugout so parents would not get too close. The only problem was that the parents could still see their children and therefore target their yelling and screaming. The wall is designed to prevent that.

"But you know what?" said one of the carpenters building the wall. "Some of them might still find a way."

You can count on that. ■

team? For others, the reason might have involved a coach they didn't want to play for, or a desire to stay in the B level with their friends. Whatever the reasons, the boys and the parents who objected to the mandatory call-up felt it was out-and-out adult manipulation to force these children to move.

On the other side of the debate were parents like Steve Turdo, at the time the boys' travel coordinator, and now in charge of the entire league. Turdo said that maybe some parents were not aware of the rules but that the league always had a policy that B teams are the feeders for the A teams. He noted that the B teams are places where boys develop the skills needed to move up to A. And if they are called to move up, yes, that is part of the deal. "People knew that," Turdo said. "We were very up front about that."

The dispute came to a head and attracted newspaper coverage when some of the boys younger than thirteen ("U-13" in soccer lingo) who had played together on a B team were told to move up to fill open slots the following year on the A team. The boys, and then their parents, objected.

Their argument was this: The league administrators didn't want us as A players before. Now we've come together as a group of B players, and we like playing together right where we are.

Mayor Luongo had been a high school principal. Several months into this controversy, after the soccer board and recreation commissioners had already turned down the parents' requests, Luongo stepped in.

One of the first things he said he did was to tell the soccer parents, "I want to hear from the kids." He had another request: No parents at the session. He asked the parents to drop off their children at the township's municipal building one evening at about 6:00 P.M. and to pick them up at about 7:15.

About sixty-five boys showed up, he said, "All ages . . . some little brothers, some big brothers." The group ranged in age from seven to sixteen. Luongo passed around the portable microphone and listened to the kids' stories. They told him they were afraid to say no to the soccer league's mandatory team drafting rules, afraid they would be blackballed. "They used that word," Luongo said.

Luongo said he saw "a pattern with the way the kids were being treated." He also saw "the stress on the kids . . . the look in the kids' eyes, the body language." The boys told him about being made to feel they were "no good" as players; they talked about being yelled at by coaches. They talked about a "checklist" of skills according to which they were evaluated. "It was almost like a report card," Luongo said. And this: "If your dad was a coach, you went to the top of the line." (Turdo said the charge of nepotism is just not true. Evaluations are done as objectively as possible, and no child is shown favor over another because his parent is a coach.)

There were several other meetings, including one Luongo held with the coaches. Through all the sessions, the township's soccer administration board held firm: The rule says when you're called to serve on the A team, you must serve on the A team. If you refuse, you are disqualified from the travel program; you may play in intramurals if you choose. The players and their parents, the administrators said, knew that rule when they signed up.

Luongo concluded that the system was based on an effort to build the strongest team in the drive toward the high school level, where the local high school boys' soccer team had a legacy of victory. The mayor said coaches at the youth level pointed proudly to the varsity team, pointing out varsity players who had come from their ranks.

"How can we build that excellence," the coaches asked Luongo, "if we just let the boys play where they want to play?" Luongo noted, "The same teams were winning year after year."

There is nothing wrong with striving to win at the varsity level or being proud of your "dynamo" team, Luongo said. What concerned him was the "fallout" at the younger level.

"Very few in high school make the team," Luongo said, likening the process to an inverted funnel. "What," he asked, "about the majority of kids at the bottom of that funnel?"

"At what price do we pursue this excellence for the high school varsity?" he asked. "What is our job? It's to give every child a chance to participate when they are young."

According to Luongo, the caste system in place in the soccer league fed into an "attitude" that some kids assumed. "'Hey, I'm on the A team. You're a loser,'" he mimicked. "You get this among kids. We have enough conflict in this world without creating an atmosphere of entitlement and exclusion among the children."

The soccer board had already turned down the parents when Luongo stepped into the fray. The soccer board is elected or appointed from within its ranks, but the township's parks and recreation commission does have oversight and acts as an appeals board. The mayor went to the parks and recreation commission and asked it to step in and stop this mandatory drafting onto A teams. "To me, this was inequity."

Surprisingly, the parks and recreation commission balked. I say "surprisingly" because the mayor appoints this board. When he discovered the commission would not do his bidding upon request, he ordered it: End the mandatory movement from the B level to the A level. And the board did.

The mayor has since left office and lost track of where the soccer controversy stands. Turdo, now the soccer commissioner, said the rule put in place by Luongo—that no child be forced to move up—lasted about a year. Today the boys are required to move, just as they were before Luongo stepped in, but now parents must sign a document attesting to the fact that they understand the rule about movement to higher levels is mandatory if a coach wants that to happen.

Turdo said few parents have ever contested the rule and that even at the height of the controversy not that many parents objected. "Most people see that it works," he said. Each year, there is a sign-up. The number of youngsters who enroll will, in part, determine the structure of the league. It starts with an A team, with the better skilled players, and then a B team. If the numbers are there, C and D teams are formed.

Contrary to the mayor's take on the situation, according to Turdo there is no undue pressure on any child because they always have a choice. If they are asked to move up and would prefer not to, they can play in the intramurals, which is an in-town league so that teams do not travel to play other communities.

Turdo said he doesn't buy into the notion that these levels of increasingly competitive soccer undermine a child's fun. Rather, it prepares them for a world that is very competitive, a world in which differences in ability are recognized. "Besides," he said, "If you get a bunch of competitive kids together, the more competitive the game you can give them, the more fun they'll have."

In defense of his club's emphasis on the A team, Turdo said if his club didn't have a highly competitive A level, the club would lose its "top" two or three players each year to other clubs in other communities.

This is precisely where I begin to feel sports clubs like the one in Washington Township go astray. Instead of fearing that the two or

Instead of fearing that the two or three "top" players will be lost each year without a competitive A team, the better reaction would be "Why does it matter?"

three "top" players will be lost each year without a competitive A team, the better reaction would be "Why does it
matter?"

Without having every single fact in this New Jersey case, it
seems that the mayor was on the right track. His effort to shut
down the mandatory nature of the movement between levels
is admirable. What's frustrating but oh-so-commonplace is to
see sensible changes like his last only a short time.

Not to pick on Washington Township—because this happens everywhere—but the fundamental problem with
Washington Township's league is that its participants believe
eighth-grade-and-under soccer teams are the varsity high
school farm system. In truth, the varsity team's farm system
is the freshman and junior varsity squads. Any eighth-grade
or younger team should be based on opportunity, participation and choice. Too many of the Washington Township
soccer people apparently believe they should sift the
"wheat" from the "chaff" well before high school.

Winning, these adults have convinced themselves, is a
perfectly fine dynamic upon which to build a program. It is
Darwinian, they may concede, but it works. Except for a
few discontented parents, most of those involved aren't
complaining.

In fact, for virtually every sports program out there, few
adults ever complain. Whether young, old or in-between,
people don't like to complain. That's what makes the testi-
mony collected by the mayor from the children so unusual.
He got a rare glimpse at some of the quiet desperation that
haunts the sidelines and dugouts across the nation in every
youth sport.

My first advice to the soccer club is to put the mayor's order back in effect. No one should be forced to choose between moving up to an A team or being ordered to play intramurals. Children need choices in order to feel comfortable, and they need to be comfortable in order to get the most from youth sports. For some children, playing on a certain team in a certain year—even a lower-level team than a boy or girl might be "qualified" to play on—actually allows them to better develop as players for the future.

Regarding A and B levels of play—the larger question—the distinction is not inherently so bad that we need to discard it. It might not be so bad to group children by ability if—and that's a big "if"—we could start with a clean slate every year. That means each child would be objectively assessed before each season to determine his or her level. The problem is, this clean-slate effect rarely happens in any youth sports system.

Once you've been labeled when you are a young athlete, you're liable to keep that label throughout most or all of your school years. A compromise suggestion, then, is to begin the ability grouping only in seventh grade or older than age twelve. Doing all this divvying up of children before that age is just a giant waste of time and one that creates plenty of headaches for moms, dads and coaches. The primary mission of youth soccer—any youth sport—is to develop better kids, not better high school varsity teams.

Case #3: Trouble with Trophies

Rewards are healthy. Rewards in youth sports are also plentiful. If you have a child who's been in any sport for more than three years, chances are there's a bookshelf or table somewhere in the bedroom holding a platoon of dusty plastic trophies. Just how many trophies does one athlete need? And what would life be like without so many?

The Massachusetts Youth Soccer Association (MYSA) found out the hard way. The association took a step that, in its opinion, would make tournament play more appropriate and more fun for children under the age of ten. In tournaments in which those youngsters participate, usually held at the end of the season, the association mandated that team standings would not be compiled, teams would not be eliminated, an overall "winner" would not be declared and team trophies would not be awarded—unless all the teams got trophies.

The California Youth Soccer Association (CYSA) North, billing itself as the largest state youth soccer association in the country with two hundred thousand members, recently voted to make the same changes in its tournaments for children under ten. "The children are finally big-time winners," said CYSA state coaching director Karl Dewazien in the March 2001 edition of *Soccer America's Youth Soccer Letter*.

The seeds for these changes can be traced back to 1985 when the U.S. Soccer Federation's coaching committee discouraged the idea of awarding trophies and medals to championship-winning teams for players ages six to ten.

It's a great way to tone down the intensity of these events. Unfortunately, not everyone in Massachusetts thought so.

What started as a quiet change in rules became a lightning rod of controversy that was misconstrued and, according to MYSA's state head coach, Dean Conway, "blatantly misrepresented."

The media and others seized on the changes in tournament play as a clear sign that the association was not in favor of keeping score anymore. To Bill Laberis, a soccer coach from Holliston, Massachusetts, who became an outspoken critic of the change, it was political correctness run amok.

"Marxism may be discredited worldwide, but not on Massachusetts soccer fields," said *Boston Globe* columnist Jeff Jacoby in a column that ran June 2, 1998. "Win, lose or draw, every team gets the same reward. Namely, no reward. Good players equal bad players, hard workers equal lazy slugs. Why put any effort into improving your game if all you get in the end is nothing?"

Let's not forget, now, these "lazy slugs" we're talking about are eight and nine years old, or younger. But I digress.

Conway counters that the edict "had nothing to do with scoring. How can you not score?"

"If I was involved with sport, and if I heard a league was passing rules to abolish scoring, I'd be jumping on it, too," he said. "Why call it a sport if you don't keep score?

"We say to the kids, implicitly, 'Yeah, you try to win the game. It's important to win the game. That's why you play. You don't go out just to run around aimlessly. There's an objective, which is winning the game.'

"But when the game is over and you're nine years old, we think it's better to say 'It's over. Forget about it,'" Conway explained. "'Don't be running over to the scoreboard to see if your goals-scored or goals-against average is better than this other team.'

"We looked at the way things were going," he said, "and we said to ourselves maybe the biggest impediment to the development of soccer skill and the enjoyment of the game was the preoccupation, the mania, with winning.

"Our goal," he said, was "calming down the emotions of everybody and trying to make an environment where winning and the ultimate trophy didn't really matter so much as the kids enjoying themselves," Conway added. "Not be the pawns of a manipulative coach, but play a lot of positions, enjoy each game for its own sake."

To that end, games in tournaments for children under the age of ten would be scheduled and played, scores would be kept. At the end of the tournament, teams would have, for instance, played two games on Saturday and two games on Sunday. Throughout the weekend, no matter the results, the games would be played out. No team would be eliminated from participation. There would be no overall winner and, therefore, no trophies.

If tournament officials chose to do so, they could shuffle the Sunday match-ups to play generally stronger teams against each other. Tournament officials could award prizes at the end, but only if everyone who participated in the weekend received the same prize.

"Our feeling was also how many bedrooms in the United States are filled with ribbons and plaques and trophies," said Conway. "Why is it so important to do this?"

The association made these changes for tournaments that involved children younger than ten. However, Laberis, who remains a critic, said it is disingenuous of the association to suggest that it had no intention of expanding the no-standings, no-trophies rule to tournament play up to the age of fifteen. The association backed off, he believes, because of the "overwhelming outcry against what they were doing." Can you imagine, he asked, a freshman in high school wanting to play in such a tournament? Conway said the association did not plan to do that.

Laberis said even children under ten "enjoy it a lot more when there's something on the line for them. What makes them [the soccer association] think kids weren't having a good time when they were competing" (for standings and trophies)?

Signing up for tournament play is an individual choice for coaches and parents, Laberis said, and a choice with which the association should not interfere. But, he said, the association essentially said, "We know what's best for you and we're going to prevent you from doing that [playing in elimination tournaments]."

He said he saw attendance and the "quality of teams" in local tournaments "drop like a stone. Why should a team come all the way from Long Island or Maine [to Massachusetts] to play in a tournament in which their kids don't have the opportunity to win anything?"

Before considering the issue of whether or not a child would travel interstate without the chance for a trophy, here's a bigger question: Why would you, the parent, want a child that young to travel interstate to play in a soccer game?

Condemnation of the Massachusetts association's mandate also came from those who saw the no-trophy policy as a way to deal with out-of-control parents and coaches. If that was the association's intent, Conway countered, the association would not have targeted such a small percentage of the soccer-playing population—that is, only those under age ten and only those teams in tournaments. He also said that the association would not have chosen a venue that is largely out of its direct control, namely season-ending tournaments often run by local soccer groups that are sanctioned by Conway's group to do so.

Also worried were tournament organizers who were afraid participation would decrease and they would lose money. "We said, 'If that's what you're in it for, maybe you should think twice [about why you are hosting this tournament in the first place],'" said Conway. "Secondly, [we said] 'Don't worry. You'll fill up your spaces.'"

The no-standings, no-trophy tournament rule for under age ten has remained in effect for several years now, and, Conway said, at this point "it's basically a nonissue." Although others may disagree, Conway said he has seen no reduction in tournament interest or participation.

The MYSA made a gutsy move, no doubt about it. And there's no doubt that lots of adults and lots of children had wonderful times at elimination tournaments, win or lose—but especially if they won.

There's also no doubt that plenty of parents paid a fee and gave up an entire weekend traveling a great distance only to watch their young child spend most of the time on the side-lines watching the coach coaching and the better-skilled players playing. Indeed, there's no doubt that when that happened young children paid a price.

There's competition everywhere in life; someone wins and

someone loses. So, the critics of the association's mandatory rule said, children should get used to it. I never quite understood that reasoning. Why is it so important that children get used to disappointment at a young age? Isn't there enough time for that as they get older—more than enough time and more than enough disappointment to go around?

It's troubling to think that children who will not "win anything" will not want to play. First of all, it's doubtful this is true. Perhaps it's true of adults, but I don't think it's true of most children. Creative adults should be able to find ways to put a whole lot of excitement and fulfillment into a soccer weekend that does not end with the award of a giant trophy. We must find those ways, for the sake of the children. Developing a love of the game for itself will make their childhoods fun and will increase the chances that they will sustain a passion to play into adolescence.

As far as the MYSA overstepping its bounds, I don't see it that way. Nor do I think all coaches who sign up for tournaments are there to win "at all costs." But if you have eliminations and trophies, you will, by that very act, put pressure on adults to win at the price of not giving every child a fair chance to play and to have fun. The only way to get rid of that pressure is to change the systems and the rules. If the rules aren't mandatory and all-encompassing, you will entice adults to find loopholes—and they will.

Parents and children should have the freedom to choose the kinds of sports programs they want to participate in, but we need strong voices and clear leadership on the part of those in charge of youth programs. Somebody needs to wage these fights on behalf of all children. Under age ten, kids are too young to speak up and fight for themselves. They will follow where adults lead. Too often, adults follow where other adults lead while trying to keep up.

Making Your Stand

You say you want a revolution? As you know from the three case histories discussed, fighting for change is not easy. Even when you think you have made a difference, you may discover your impact can be fleeting.

The essence of any victory is perseverance. You will win some, you will lose some, but making your case is important: These issues must be given voice. I like the sentiment articulated by Paul from New Hampshire in a letter to other parents: "Like we tell the kids all the time when going up to bat—swing at the ball. Don't strike out without swinging."

"It is critical," he told the parents, "that we not sit this one out."

Here, then, are some suggestions as you prepare to stand up and be counted.

1. *Find sources of good information, gather strength and connect with others* as you fight the good fight. One recommendation is the Internet source *www.MomsTeam. com*, a site that offers expert help with difficult questions, as well as chat rooms where you can share your thoughts with other parents. Vent. Bounce your ideas off other people. Practice your arguments before you take them public. Find out what other parents have been through.

Started by Brooke deLench of Concord, Massachusetts, *MomsTeam.com*, as the name implies, seeks
to reach out to moms. Often, "It's really the mother out
there doing the basics," said deLench. "And it's usually
the mothers, too, who don't know how to quite advocate for themselves. The youth sports environment is
really still an old boys' network." Fathers are not left
out of *MomsTeam.com* They are among the expert
contributors to the site and they are also invited to
share. As you prepare to take on youth sports systems,
do your homework. There are plenty of Web sites (I've
also already mentioned the Center for Sports Parenting
at *www.sportsparenting.org*), books and organizations
that can provide you with information. Gather opinions from child development and youth sports specialists. Look for statistics, anecdotes and stories. Put your
ideas in writing. Find examples of programs elsewhere
that are working well. All this is critical to persuading
those who may disagree with you.

2. *Find others who agree with you but may not have had
   the courage to speak up.* Talk to other parents, at games
   or in the grocery store. There is always strength in
   numbers.

3. *Be realistic about the time commitment* and look for
   ways to make the sacrifice as comfortable for you and
   your family as possible. Enlist help. Delegate.

4. *Remember that the "other" side is made up of parents
   and volunteers just like you.* Treat them with respect.
   They have persuasive arguments and good points to
   make. Look for common ground.

5. *Ask your children what they think of your ideas and strategies.* They may offer the most valuable input of all.
6. *Compromise, compromise, compromise.* Youth sports involves so many aspects of our culture, of family life and of personal challenges. Always be willing to listen to the other side. Give a little to get a little.
7. *Encourage your community to use "the power of the permit,"* an idea championed by Fred Engh of the National Alliance of Youth Sports (NAYS). Engh says the permits that youth sports organizations need in order to use community facilities, such as gyms and fields, should not be granted automatically.

   Arguments for fair play, equal access for all children and a fair distribution of resources may find sympathetic ears within local government, including school committees and park and recreation commissions. These people are often, but not always, removed from the politics of the local sports groups, though they are charged with upholding the letter of the law in their communities. That responsibility applies to requirements that must be met by the groups that wish to use the community's gyms, parks and fields. Ask these officials to use their authority to ensure that youth sports leagues uphold fair principles.

   NAYS recommends that programs be developmentally appropriate and "enhance the emotional, physical, social and educational well-being of the children." (I would emphasize of *all* the children.)
8. *Put balance in your life and in your child's life.* Just as sports should be one part of a balanced childhood, so,

too, should your efforts to reform your local youth sports organizations. Take time to play with your children in the backyard and at the playground.

9. *Remember to have fun.* Laugh at yourself a little. It will help others laugh with you. Humor is one of the most effective ways to lessen anger and tension.

10. *Consider building that better mousetrap* if all attempts to change things, to work with the status quo, fail.

●●●

If you have more ideas, or want to share your stories with me, please visit my Web site (*www.bob-bigelow.com*). Meanwhile, for some inspiration about how youth sports can be when people succeed in creating wonderful programs in the best interests of *all* children who play, turn to the next chapter. You're going to like these folks.

Success Stories: Ten Ideas to Inspire You

It got to the point where you almost couldn't enjoy the game because parents were—I don't want to say competitive because I like competition—but they were fanatical about their kids on the ice.

Kim Tinkham, UnitedHockeyMoms

You're almost ready to launch your own revolution, but don't dive into the breach without adequate backup.

In this chapter you'll travel around the United States for inspiration—from the West Coast to the East Coast, from the Florida Panhandle to the Great Plains and back again to my old New England. You'll discover ten terrific initiatives in youth sports reform that you may want to try in your own community.

You'll meet men and women who have created programs that serve children's needs. In so doing, they have come up with ways to stave off some of the problems that spring from systems gone awry.

These are innovators, adults who looked around at the landscapes in their communities, and at their children's games, and came up with better ways. These are people, most of them parents, who have busy lives just like ours, but they reached deep and mustered enough initiative and energy to make a difference.

These people are wonderfully enthusiastic about what sports can offer to children, when things are done right. They enjoy competition when it is fair and when it serves the children first, not the adults.

Some of these efforts are designed specifically to keep parents in line. You can tell that I dream of a day when youth sports systems will be so in tune with children's needs that these parent-monitoring measures will not be necessary. Until then, we really do need these efforts.

Here then are ten youth sports initiatives from around the country. Has this book left some out? Yes, plenty. But that's good news because it means that if you are fighting for changes in youth sports, you have a lot of good company. When you read these stories, I hope you will be inspired.

EDUCATING THE SPECTATOR

Dallas–Fort Worth, Texas

Kim Tinkham is one of the three founding members of a spunky grassroots group who call themselves "UnitedHockeyMoms" (*www.unitedhockeymoms.com*). Don't you love the name? Based in the Dallas-Fort Worth area of Texas, the group organizes clinics dedicated to the proposition that parents who are better educated about the rules of ice hockey will be more civilized and better behaved at their children's games.

"Please don't confuse us with those groups who consider hockey to be a violent sport and want to remove some of the essential components of the game," UnitedHockeyMoms alerts Web site visitors. "We love hockey! We love hockey the way it is supposed to be played."

Suzan Harmon, Stacey Oleksa and Tinkham all met in July 2000 at a hockey summer camp sponsored by the Dallas Stars of the National Hockey League. All three are mothers of goalies, and according to Tinkham that means these moms see the game from a unique perspective. They're not as busy trying to keep track of their own child all over the ice. They watch the game from all sides, and "We just don't want anybody to score on our kid," Tinkham said with a chuckle.

As they talked at the summer camp, Tinkham said, the goalie moms shared a common frustration. At the games they attended, too many parents were getting angry at coaches, officials, the children and each other. Much of the time, that anger was misdirected or the parents were misunderstanding what they saw on the ice.

"It got to the point where you almost couldn't enjoy the game because they were—I don't want to say competitive, because I like competition—but they were actually fanatical about their kids on the ice," Tinkham said.

"What we're missing here is parents learning about the game," Tinkham said. "If they knew about it, maybe they wouldn't yell at the refs so much." Perhaps they wouldn't confuse NHL rules with youth hockey rules.

Some of the worst behavior, Tinkham said, occurs when parents yell at other players for making mistakes or hitting someone, but act as though it's alright if their child does the same. A lot of parents were new to the sport, as program enrollments were booming in the Dallas-Fort Worth area, accelerated by the popularity of the Dallas Stars, who had recently won the Stanley Cup.

The mothers agreed that the most troublesome parents were fanatical and needed to be told, in so many words, to quiet down, keep in their seats and just watch the games. After talking at the camp, the women contacted the governing body for youth hockey in this country, USA Hockey, based in Colorado Springs, Colorado. The organization told the women that USA Hockey supported their mission, but the organization didn't have the time or resources to focus on parent behavior initiatives.

USA Hockey agreed to provide the women its support, though, including links to the organization's Web site, and thus was born UnitedHockeyMoms. The organization is prepared to help rinks nationwide to offer materials and hold workshops for spectators. They will also help to set up support and mediation committees to address disruptive behavior.

UnitedHockeyMoms believes that an "educated spectator" will help ensure that the "highly competitive nature of the game" remains but that the competitors still have fun. The organization offers clinics on three different topics—associate coaching, officiating and CPR. To be a certified United-HockeyMom, candidates must pass all three courses and must be vouched for by the directors of the hockey rinks where their children play. "If the director knows the mom in a negative light, that means she's complained. She has problems," said Tinkham. "We don't want somebody who wants to join our organization because they think they'll have a leg up to complain. We want to be part of the solution."

Since the certification takes time and the group formed only in the summer of 2000, as of the winter UnitedHockey-Moms had only four certified members, but the members have a list of volunteers helping them in other ways, including hockey registrations and program orientations. Hockey Moms also sit in on mediation sessions when sanctions for adult behavior issues are decided at local rinks.

Upon certification, a member is given a UnitedHockey-Moms jacket. Members are encouraged to roam the rinks and, if they see trouble, to act. Troublemakers are approached and asked to step to the side so that the Hockey Mom can explain to them, in polite terms, that their yelling and screaming are not welcome.

UnitedHockeyMoms also holds a mandatory orientation for parents at their home rinks at the beginning of each hockey season. Parents who want their children to play are asked to sign a spectator conduct code, a pledge that they will behave. The three founders say this has led to a decrease of complaints of bad behavior at their home rink, the Blue Line Ice Complex in North Richland Hills, Texas.

Tinkham advises all parents to consider three things if they want to improve youth sports: (1) Get involved and make yourself available to the "powers that be," (2) be willing to learn about the sport, and (3) be a person who is able to walk up to another adult and talk to them calmly about their misbehavior.

Walking up to unruly parents in ice rinks is gutsy, I say. Tinkham says that no one she or her comrades has ever approached has refused to listen. Some have suggested the chat be postponed until the end of the game—which is fine by the Hockey Moms. By then, Tinkham said, most have cooled off anyway. That's often because "they know who we are."

A MANDATORY BEHAVIOR PLEDGE

Jupiter and Tequesta, Florida

Jeff Leslie is a certified public accountant, the father of four children and a man who deserves at least a footnote in the modern history of youth sports reform.

Leslie is president of the Jupiter/Tequesta Athletic Association in Florida, a group of adults that organizes baseball, softball, basketball, tackle football, flag football and soccer for about six thousand children in the adjoining communities of Jupiter and Tequesta, north of West Palm Beach.

As president of the association, Leslie led the charge to implement a mandatory behavior pledge for all parents: Sign it, or your children can't play.

The move by Leslie and his fellow board members toward a mandatory pledge grew out of their increasing frustration over the number of incidents of adult misbehavior at youth games. By 1999 they were talking in earnest about implementing a tough zero-tolerance policy. The group had held hearings every time a complaint was lodged about a belligerent or abusive parent.

"It was getting out of control," Leslie recalled. About twice a month the volunteers had to spend their time holding hearings to address a parent who had stepped over the bounds. Some were unruly or disruptive, others screamed obscenities, threatened a coach or a lawsuit.

"Numerous times we felt we were within inches of an adult-to-adult physical confrontation," Leslie said. "Sportsmanship had just gone out the door."

Parents also were "pushing hard at young ages," taking an attitude that their child was destined to be a scholar-athlete and the association better not get in their way. Leslie said some parents were "bringing their kids to tears."

The group decided it could not simply continue to hold hearings. It needed to become proactive, to find ways to cut down on the problems and encourage parents to police themselves. The association decided to put together a parent education program.

It turned to the National Youth Sports Coaches Association (NYSCA), whose coaching classes the association had been requiring their coaches to attend for ten years. "Do you have any materials or ideas that might help?" NYSCA responded that its umbrella organization, the National Alliance for Youth Sports (NAYS), led by Fred Engh, had just put the finishing touches on a parent education program that included an educational videotape and a parent behavior pledge. The program is actually offered by another NAYS organization, the Parents Association for Youth Sports (PAYS).

Leslie's group sent an announcement to the local newspaper, asking if the paper "wouldn't mind" running the item. His group wanted to make sure that parents knew they would be required to attend and to sign the behavior pledge in order for their children to play. No one counted on what would happen next.

The Associated Press picked up the item, with emphasis on the mandatory pledge for parents, and soon Jupiter/ Tequesta's bold new requirement made news around the nation and around the world. Just about every major television network, newspaper, magazine and talk show wanted the story.

The Jupiter/Tequesta association had picked February 15, 2000, as the date for the first parents' education session. The idea had been to hold the session in a room in association headquarters, but the sheer volume of requests from reporters to cover the event told the group it needed more space—a lot more. A call was made to the local minor-league baseball venue, Roger Dean Stadium, and stadium officials offered their facility.

So, on February 15, with a large number of TV crews and reporters present, the Jupiter/Tequesta Athletic Association held its first "course" for parents. More than twenty-five hundred parents attended. The night began with a nineteen-minute videotape. Leslie also addressed the crowd. He reminded his audience of the incidents that had occurred in communities close by. Recently, for example, a soccer coach had head-butted a sports official at a game, sending him to the hospital. "We wanted to tell them, 'Look, guys, this could happen right here, to you.'"

The final component of the session was the signing of the pledge. Jupiter/Tequesta organizers took the PAYS pledge and added a clause to say that all who sign promise also to adhere to the Jupiter/Tequesta association's rules. The event was a publicity coup. As far as Leslie knows, it was the first time any youth sports group in the country had made a behavior pledge a requirement for parents in order for their children to play. No parent, he said, has refused to sign the pledge.

More than a headlines-grabber, said Leslie, the effort was effective on the home front. In the baseball season that fol-lowed, only three hearings were needed, compared to more than a dozen the season before, and all three hearings involved minor infractions.

A survey completed a year after the course and pledge requirements went into effect showed that 60 percent of parents who responded said they witnessed a positive change in parent behavior. Fifty-one percent said they felt more committed to their child's participation, and 62 per-cent said they felt empowered to stand up against negative acts (76 percent indicated that they had sometime in the past felt uncomfortable because of other parents' behavior at a game).

Leslie said he is proud of how his group has worked to lessen hostilities. He goes to games now, and he'll overhear parents saying to each other, "Hey, before you scream again or misbehave, remember that pledge you signed."

Any advice Leslie would offer to others? "Yes," he said, "make sure you have the resolve to insist that all parents take the class and sign the pledge. It has to be that way."

GIRLS (AND BOYS) JUST WANT TO HAVE FUN

Medway, Massachusetts

Tucker Reynolds is a self-described country lawyer and father of three whose claim to fame is something he called "library soccer" in the small town of Medway, Massachusetts.

"Library soccer" is a version of the game in which everyone except for the children on the field are quiet, as if they were in a library. That way, according to Reynolds, players don't have to deal with all the noise parents often send their way. This sounds like those "Silent Sundays" you might have heard about, when youth sports groups put a gag order on parents. In that sense, Reynolds appears to have been ahead of his time.

It all started in the spring of 1994 when Reynolds decided to get involved in the town's soccer program. At an organizational meeting, he jokingly recalls, he got up to take a break. When he came back, he already had been placed in charge of starting an instructional league for four- to five-year-old boys and girls. This is where it gets, well, funny.

In his role as the instructional-league czar for the next five years, Reynolds supervised weekly events during which young soccer players would learn some basic skills and, hopefully, have a lot of fun. There would be time set aside each week for a little "library soccer." Nobody would be allowed to talk except for the children. To make sure that happened, Reynolds walked around with a roll of duct tape, threatening to tape the mouths of any parent who was yelling.

He never actually taped anyone else's mouth, he said, although he did tape his own a few times to underscore his point. Many times, when he approached a rule-breaking parent, he would peel off the tape and threaten, all the time explaining why. He did see a lot of rolling eyes at first, but once he talked to parents, they seemed to understand the value of leaving the children alone.

Reynolds impressed upon the adults a couple of ideals he said they may not have recognized. The first is that soccer is a game of continual action, so the situations on the field are constantly changing. "It's a game of instinct," he said. "And in order for children to develop those instincts, they need to do it on their own."

Because the game is constantly moving, words from parents often reach the ears of little children after those words are helpful. For example, if someone yells "Shoot the ball," by the time the child processes that command, the ball may be somewhere else and the child no longer has the shot. Instead of realizing that the command came in too late, the child may process the sequence as a failure on his or her part.

"The child may think, 'I feel bad because I haven't done what Grandpa told me.' It takes the fun away from the game," Reynolds said.

Another factor, Reynolds said, is that "99.9 percent of the time when a parent yells out something, they're wrong. They're just flat-out wrong" about what they say because they don't know the game.

Partly because Reynolds's use of duct tape was so grounded in good coaching, nobody in the league office complained. His efforts were always intended, also, to make the point with humor. "If somebody wasn't laughing, I'd make sure I went over and made the point to them so they understood the humor," he said. We're often too serious, even when it comes to trying to put more fun into children's games.

In addition to "library soccer," Reynolds also got creative with his weekly soccer events, making them more fun for the players. He held "Hawaii Day," for example, giving each player on the field a plastic lei. The kids played soccer while Reynolds blasted Don Ho's greatest hits from a boom box.

"I'd call them to huddle around," he recalled. "And I'd ask them if anybody knows what soccer and Hawaii have in common. Nobody would know. I'd say we should ask their parents, and none of the parents would know. And then I'd tell them: Soccer and Hawaii have absolutely nothing in common. We have Hawaii Day for one reason and one reason only: to remind us to have fun."

"People forget what it is to be a kid," Reynolds said. "And whether you see it as a curse or a blessing, I'm still a kid."

NO ADULTS NECESSARY

Woburn, Massachusetts

Twelve miles north of Boston, in the city of Woburn, every Thursday night during the winter a sports league gets together in the Kennedy Middle School gym.

When the local newspaper did an article on the league the headline read, "Back to the Past League," which is a great intention. The league's official name is the Ninth and Tenth Grade Intermediate League, and it's been running for the past twenty-two years. In that sense, it's not new, but what happened six years ago was a breakthrough: The league essentially dispensed with the adults.

"What I'm hearing is that there aren't too many teams around like this," said Woburn Recreation Director Thomas Jones.

There are four teams, each with nine freshmen and sophomores, for a total of thirty-six players in the league. They play one game of basketball each week, and they do it without adults coaching on the sidelines and very few, if any, standing there watching. The norm here is that parents have just two jobs: drop off and pick up. Most everything else is handled by the players.

"It's gotten to the point now that the kids who are the captains of the team are sort of like the board of directors," Jones said. "They make the rules for the league and so forth."

The boys who participate often tell Jones it's the best fun they have all week. They are generally the players who get cut from the junior varsity and varsity basketball teams, or simply decide not to play at the interscholastic level. Many have good athletic skills.

For example, each basketball team has two captains for a league total of eight. In the 2000-2001 session of the league, three of those eight captains had been on the school's golf team that had recently won a state title.

Because a number of them are golfers, Jones told the boys they could have their choice. The winning team in the play-offs could get trophies or golf shirts. The boys overwhelmingly chose the trophies because, as Jones explained, "For most of them, this is the first and only time they'll ever get a trophy." While I do not recommend trophies at younger levels, these players are in high school. Let them gather their trophies to their hearts' content.

Jones eliminated adult coaches from the league six years ago primarily because he was having difficulty filling all the slots. "We were always scrambling," he said. "So one year I thought we'd just let the kids do it. 'Let's give it a shot,' I said. It could have been a disaster, but it turned out to be quite the opposite."

Not only the boys are having fun. The sports officials, who are paid, tell Jones they look forward to going to a gym where they don't have to put up with yelling and screaming from adults on the sidelines. "The refs tell me it's the easiest league in the world," he said. No surprise there.

And talk about playing for the love of the game. As the playoffs approached at the end of winter 2001, one of the four teams had a dismal 0–7 record. However, when you asked the boys on that team if they were depressed or even frustrated by their poor showing, you got an answer that may have surprised you.

According to Jones, "I think the 0–7 team is actually having the most fun because the other teams are now trying to outdo each other for the best record. So they like to jab each other as the playoffs get closer. The 0–7 team just plays."

Close to 80 percent of the players in the league in that session were sophomores, Jones said; therefore, the league would end for them at the end of those playoffs. "But they've already asked me if they could continue with an eleventh-grade program," said Jones, who was mulling the idea when I saw the league in action.

Imagine that. Boys older than thirteen, some of them getting their driver's licenses, some with jobs, and most of them still want to make time on Thursday nights for a little basketball with friends. Now isn't that the way it should be?

ROOT, ROOT, ROOT FOR THE HOME TEAM

Bloomington, Minnesota

Talk about pioneers. In the world of youth sports reformers, Arnie Johnson of the Minneapolis, Minnesota, suburb of Bloomington has to rank near the top of the list.

He is seventy-nine years old now and retired from his job as a supervisor at Minneapolis Honeywell, but it was in 1953 that he made his mark on youth sports. Johnson was coach of a traveling baseball team of fifteen- and sixteen-year-olds when he was faced with one of the job's most unpleasant tasks.

He had to cut five of the boys who had tried out for the team in order to narrow his roster to sixteen. "I can remember they were very unhappy, with tears in their eyes," he said. "I never wanted to do that again." Johnson made up his mind right then and there that he wouldn't.

The very next year he presented a plan to Bloomington officials for the formation of the Bloomington Athletic Association (BAA). Its guiding light would be the guarantee that every child who wants to play will play. That first year, thousands of children signed up to play baseball, depending on where they lived, in one of the four sections of the community—east, west, north and south. And that's the only place they'd play for the season.

Concentrating the play within these four zones helped build a sense of community in each place. It also meant that neighborhoods would push for more ballparks in close proximity. One of Johnson's goals was that no child would be more than one mile from a ballpark. "We were able to do that," he said with obvious pride.

The winning teams in each of the four areas, within their specific age groups, would play the winners in the other areas at the end of each season. It was the only "travel" allowed. Johnson also insisted on strictly enforced rules that every player would have a minimum amount of time in every game. There would be no tryouts. Children would play regardless of their ability. If they could not afford the fee to play a sport, there would be scholarship money available. Those same principles apply forty-eight years later.

The people of Bloomington loved the idea when Johnson came up with it—and they still do. Today the Bloomington Athletic Association serves close to six thousand young athletes—boys and girls—in twelve sports year-round.

Johnson retired as director of the BAA twenty-five years after he started the organization. He went on to start another sports group—"Born Again Jocks," retired men and women who get together to play golf, softball, bocce, volleyball or to bowl.

To this day Johnson is praised for his work with children. "I was walking down near the lake and saw a young father with a baby," Johnson recalled. "The guy looked at me and I looked at him, like we knew each other. And then he said, 'You're the man I played baseball for.' I love to hear that."

Frank Pikala, who put in eight years as director of the BAA after Johnson left, said the founder never forgot his purpose. "Arnie recognized the fact that the kids needed a place to play," said Pikala. "That's what it's all about."

CHANGING PERSPECTIVES

Stanford, California

Jim Thompson came to the world of youth sports with an unusual background. He had worked previously with children who had emotional and behavioral difficulties. He came away from that experience with a powerful set of tools that would help in his future work as a reformer of the ways that adults think about children's organized sports.

Jim remembered his childhood on the playing fields of North Dakota as enjoyable, nearly idyllic times. Years later, on the playing fields of Palo Alto, California, while helping coach his son's teams, he saw a great contrast with that joy he had experienced as a child. Thompson saw children who were unhappy and stressed. What had happened?

It's that question and its answers to which Thompson has committed himself as founder and director of the Positive Coaching Alliance (PCA), a nonprofit organization affiliated with and located at Stanford University's Department of Athletics.

Thompson and his staff have developed an approach to reforming youth sports that he says combines models found in sports, business and education. PCA offers what it calls its "local partners program" to any youth sports organization. For a fee PCA will send out a team to conduct leadership and education workshops in a community. PCA also supports an extensive bank of materials that are available at its Web site (*www.positivecoach.org*).

At the heart of PCA's workshops, indeed the group's philosophy, is the not-so-modest goal of changing the "win-at-all-costs coach mental model" to a more constructive "positive coach mental model."

Training for coaches and parents is a good second step, PCA says, but the first step is to "get inside their heads" and make sure they have an appropriate "internalized job description," to ensure they look at their place in youth sports in healthy ways.

Winning is still important, according to PCA's model for change, but it's not the only goal. "This is not anticompetitive at all," Thompson said. The group seeks to "redefine what it means to be a winner," away from the scoreboard and toward goals that include trying your hardest and learning from—not fearing—mistakes.

The difference, Thompson said, is that the win-at-all-costs coach has one goal: winning. The positive-model coach has two goals: winning and teaching life lessons. PCA also reminds youth sports organizations to encourage mothers to consider coaching: "Many women have an intuitive understanding of the elements of Positive Coaching but may not believe they know enough about the technical aspects of the sport."

To break down an entrenched win-at-all-costs mental model, Thompson's program asks coaches to think of such concepts as "honoring the game" and helping players to develop as citizens with a sense of belonging to and respecting their community, brimming with self-confidence and internal motivation. Together, these goals are what Thompson and his staff call "life lessons" that children can learn from positive participation in sports.

One of the primary missions of a coach is to help the child keep his or her "emotional gas tank" full so that child will be prepared to take on not only the game, but life as well.

"But the relationship between the coach and the players is not the only problem," Thompson said. "There's also the problem of parents abusing and physically attacking officials, getting in fights with themselves, parents browbeating their kids. So it's gotten to be kind of an ugly scene."

So PCA took what it was teaching the coaches and began trying to teach the spectators the same positive approaches.

PCA looks at youth sports on several levels. First is the internal organization and how coaches, players and parents relate to each other. Second, PCA looks at how the youth sports organization functions in the context of a community. What is the "culture" of the organization, its values and its goals, within the context of the city or town it serves? How can that culture encourage positive behavior?

On the third level, the youth sports organization and its members—coaches, parents and players—are looked at in the context of society in general, including what Thompson calls the professional sports entertainment business, the world of professional sports in which so many adults and young players form their impressions about the role of sports.

"You entertain by winning, so the win-at-all-costs model really is the driving force," Thompson said. "But youth sports is an educational development experience, and therefore totally different metaphors, totally different ways to go about what you're doing" should apply. In the long run, "we hope to have some impact on that larger culture," he said.

Thompson concedes that his is an ambitious plan. Already, though, a scant two and a half years into what he envisions as a ten-year effort, Thompson said he is seeing results. Anecdotal evidence is coming in. The Pleasant Hill Baseball Association in California is a good example.

Officials of the league called on PCA at a time when there were fifteen to eighteen incidents of parent or coach misbehavior occurring in a total of nine hundred games played by all the teams in one season. The next season, after the PCA staff offered its program, the number of incidents dropped to six.

THE CUSTOMER KNOWS BEST

New Hampton, New Hampshire

Jeff Beedy is a leading-edge thinker because he was one of the first in the field of youth sports to focus on what the children were saying about their wants and needs.

It was after attending the New Sport Experience Camp, Beedy's summer camp in Maine, that my own ideas about youth sports began to percolate. The camp was an eye-opener for me. As I walked around and observed, I was constantly reminded that the children were the customers and that we, the adults, needed to keep that in mind. What is best for the customer?

In 1997 Beedy published his book, *Sports PLUS: Developing Youth Sports Programs That Teach Positive Values.* One of the book's major ideas is to use sports to teach children values that will be useful to them long after their days in a baseball or soccer uniform are over.

Beedy's emphasis on "warm-up" and "cool-down" meetings before and after games is a great example of that ideal. Instead of focusing on the score, coaches are encouraged to set other goals during these sessions, such as individual goals that are reachable. One would be getting on base safely once during a game; another, making a catch. With the focus no longer simply on the final score, games offer the children something valuable whether they win or lose.

With a doctorate in education from Harvard, Beedy is now headmaster of the New Hampton School in the town of the same name in New Hampshire. One of his more recent projects puts him again at the forefront of creative sports reform. The initiative is called "GoodSport," an after-school program designed for children in grades four through six, which uses sports as a foundation from which to help children achieve a number of other goals.

Two of those goals don't have a lot to do with sports: to become better readers and to become better people. The latter is a constant in any of Beedy's projects. Today such efforts are often called "character education," based on the belief that you can help children to develop morality and values by how you teach them.

GoodSport is built around a curriculum Beedy has developed to be used by teachers and others after school in a variety of settings. The program can last up to three hours, or can be tailored to shorter sessions. Children participate in a variety of group activities. They play sports like soccer, basketball, whiffle ball or softball, and they read. They also keep journals and participate in group discussions about what they've read or written. In a segment titled "You Make the Call," they work out solutions to a variety of sports-based dilemmas. The idea is to use a child's interest in sports as a tool, as a way to get him or her interested in other areas, such as reading.

The city of Lawrence, Massachusetts, is one place where GoodSport was piloted. The Lawrence YMCA, the Lawrence Public Library and Beedy's group teamed up. The program was offered three afternoons a week at the YMCA from 3:00 P.M. to 6:00 P.M. According to Beedy, reaction from city officials and from the children was overwhelmingly positive.

Many reasons recommend a program like GoodSport. One of the benefits that is rarely mentioned is how it puts sports into perspective. Side by side with reading and character education, sports may lose some of its glamour, but children begin to see that it is simply a part of one's life. They learn to use sports to their advantage whether or not they play on a team, earn a scholarship or make sports a career.

RECONNECT WITH YOUR FAMILY

Wayzata, Minnesota

Barbara Carlson is a former elementary school teacher and the mother of four children who teamed up with a university professor to create one of the most wide-ranging and ambitious reform programs going. It's called "Family Life 1st" (*www.familylife1st.org*), and it's a group dedicated to reconnecting family members to each other in the most basic of ways—primarily by making sure there is family time.

This effort is not all about youth sports, but the intent to reconsider our overbooked lives makes this program a "must" on my list of ways to stop schedule madness.

Carlson lives in the Minneapolis suburb of Wayzata. For years she had been active in various volunteer groups in the Wayzata School District, which encompasses parts of eight communities. Many of these programs were aimed at efforts to build a better sense of community. Carlson served, for example, as supervisor of a program that assigned high school students to community service projects.

In 1998, working with a local community group, Carlson invited University of Minnesota professor William J. Doherty to speak. Doherty had just written the book *The Intentional Family*, which Carlson said warns us all that families must make intentional connections—they must work at being together—or they will fall apart. (Doherty has since written another book, *Take Back Your Kids*.) In Wayzata, Doherty found a receptive audience. According to Carlson, "Everyone liked him so much that we decided to invite him back the next year."

When he returned, Doherty talked more about over-stressed and overscheduled families. School and community officials also realized that organizations contribute to the problem by offering more and more activities for children without underscoring for parents the toll on family time.

Carlson, on her own, had noticed that a busy schedule, as much as people complained about it, seemed to be the new status symbol. It wasn't whether you had a lush green lawn or a luxury car in the driveway. If your children had soccer games, a music recital, a ballet practice and maybe a football scrimmage to top off the same day, that was something worth bragging about. That bragging usually came out in conversation: "If you think you're busy, just look at how busy *I* am!"

Doherty, the professor, told Carlson and others in town that he was looking for a community in which to try some of his ideas about how to reconnect the family unit and take back some of that misplaced time. Carlson formed a steering committee and Family Life 1st was launched. "It was really to see what we could do as a community to be more family-oriented," Carlson said.

Carlson noticed one benefit right away. The very existence of the program made families realize they were not alone in their struggles to get everything done that needed doing every day. Some parents drew strength from the group, finding the support to go to a coach and say, "'Look, our son or daughter won't be able to go to this practice because we have a family wedding' or something else that is important," according to Carlson.

"Our real operating principle is that there are no villains," she continued. Parents as well as the other adults who run all these activities are just trying to do the best they can," she says. The goal is to find balance.

A year after the program was launched, action groups were formed, each to focus on a certain issue, including youth sports. Family Life 1st also developed an intriguing "seal of approval" program. By meeting certain guidelines, any group or organization in Wayzata's district may submit an application for a seal of approval. These could include churches or, as Carlson describes them, faith communities, theater groups and youth sports organizations. Once they apply, these groups are evaluated by Family Life 1st to see if they meet guidelines that put a premium on family time.

To earn the seal, the group must allow Family Life 1st to poll the adults whose children are in the group. If 80 percent or more of those polled agree that the particular group is living up to the ideal of putting the family first, the seal of approval is granted. The approval, however, must be renewed each year to make sure those principles remain in place.

That process may take time. It may be necessary for Family Life 1st to work with the group, ironing out new policies and helping to eliminate those policies deemed contrary to nurturing the family unit. Family Life 1st urges leaders of sports programs to be clear with parents about the time they will be asked to invest and the money they will be asked to spend.

Family Life 1st may also advise sports programs, for instance, to hold one longer practice each week instead of two shorter ones, a change that could give a family another opportunity to eat dinner and spend an evening together.

The seal of approval program is so new that, as of the spring of 2001, Family Life 1st had granted only one. Interestingly, it went to Wayzata's youth football program. It is surprising to me because the stereotype of football is that it takes large chunks of time away. Somehow the football organizers were able to work out a schedule that made sense for families. "They worked very hard," Carlson said.

Family Life 1st emphasizes two-way commitments. "Just as we ask coaches and other supervisors to be fair to the family, we tell the family members that they must be fair to the coaches. If your son or daughter is going to sign up for a sport, it is their responsibility to be there when the team meets."

Family Life 1st got a big boost when *The New York Times* featured the group on June 13, 2000. Since then, Carlson and Doherty have fielded calls from around the country, even from other countries. "Bill has spoken in Portugal," Carlson said. "You might not think of Portugal as having trouble with this issue of overscheduling. It just shows me that all families are just too busy."

INTERNET TO THE RESCUE

Kingston, Rhode Island

Dan Doyle is a man with an extensive sports background and a love of the games. He was an assistant basketball coach at Brown University and then head coach at Trinity College in Connecticut. These days you can find him at the Institute for International Sport on the campus of the University of Rhode Island in Kingston. As founder and executive director of the institute, Doyle, along with his staff, develops and supports a number of initiatives steeped in the ancient and classical notions of sportsmanship and fair play.

His group created National Sportsmanship Day, an annual event that involves an estimated 6 million student athletes from the elementary grades through college. From this event, Doyle got the inspiration for his latest project.

As he and his staff worked with schools to help them set up local events for sportsmanship day, they continually heard from adults who wanted basic information about how to keep their children healthy, safe and having fun playing sports. They had questions about what foods to eat and what substances—weight enhancers and the like—to avoid.

At the same time, Doyle was having conversations with another passionate sports reformer in his own right, Rick Wolff, a former professional baseball player, author of several books on youth sports and the host of a weekly sports parenting radio show on WFAN-AM in New York City.

Together Doyle and Wolff came up with a plan for an Internet service that would strive to answer questions large and small from all parents in search of information. They call this Web resource the Center for Sports Parenting (*www.sportsparenting.org*). The Web site was launched on March 6, 2001, to coincide with National Sportsmanship Day.

The way the resource works is simple. Parents—or anyone else for that matter—may log on to the site, choose from a panel of about twenty experts in various fields of youth sports, e-mail questions to the appropriate expert and expect an answer within a week or two.

The expert panel includes pediatricians, coaches, athletic directors, sports and child psychologists and psychiatrists, even a nutritionist and an attorney. Visitors are invited to e-mail questions about the psychological and physical challenges of raising athletes—whether they are in elementary school, middle school, high school or college.

The center also plans to research and post current news on psychological and medical issues in youth sports, as well as to offer monthly online chats about the issues adults face raising or teaching young athletes. A bulletin board option allows visitors to share ideas with each other, and the center also plans to conduct its own polls.

Doyle said he hopes that answers from this "clearinghouse" of experts will one day be instantaneously available whenever someone logs on. As parents ask questions and get answers, both the questions and answers will be inventoried in order to create a supply of answers that will be stored for future reference.

I was flattered when Dan called and asked me to join the panel. I quickly accepted, of course, and now you can find me at the Web site as well. The important thing about the project is that it doesn't overlook the one thing that is often missed as we struggle to do better by our kids: Sometimes we just need the right information.

TELL ME WHAT'S HAPPENING

Jefferson City, Missouri

Doug Abrams is a law professor at the University of Missouri-Columbia and has coached youth hockey at all age levels for thirty-two years. He teaches juvenile law and family law, and he helps the state legislature draft bills to improve the health and safety of Missouri's children. He recently coauthored a twelve-hundred-page book, *Children and the Law*, which is already required reading in about three dozen law schools, including Yale, Columbia and the University of Pennsylvania. Doug played goalie for Wesleyan University in Connecticut and set an ECAC Division III record for most saves in a game (sixty-four), a record broken ten years later by one of his own hockey students.

Doug's involvement in coaching began early. He was a high school senior on Long Island when an adult hockey organizer asked him to supervise a team of youngsters. Doug's been coaching ever since. When he moved to the Midwest in 1989, he introduced mid-Missouri to youth hockey by founding the

Jefferson City Youth Hockey Program, and he served as its president for eleven years. The Jefferson City rink, 35 miles from his home, is the closest one for 120 miles in either direction. With Doug as president, "equality" became the program's byword—every interested youngster is permitted to enroll, no youngster is cut or put on a waiting list, and every youngster is placed on a team and gets fair and meaningful ice time every game. The program develops its beginners, and most teams finish strong in their leagues each year. For families needing financial assistance, the program maintains a scholarship fund and provides used equipment donated by players Doug coached in the 1980s. By the time he stepped down as president of the Jefferson City program in 2000, enrollment had grown from 19 players to more than 175.

Abrams has seen his share of bad behavior by parents at youth sports events. In fact, he became so disgusted with their antics locally and nationally that about two years ago he began what has become a unique service.

Using the Lexis and Westlaw databases and the Internet, Doug collects tales of adult misbehavior at youth sports games around the country. His search words are simply "youth sports." Each day about a hundred newspaper and magazine articles are delivered into his computer system. From that number, there are usually one or two articles that focus on an incident of adult misbehavior.

"I'm looking for outrageous behavior," he said. "I'm also looking for articles where writers talk about the way things ought to be," Doug said. "And there's no shortage of either."

Once he has selected his daily offerings, he sends them out to an e-mail list of several dozen people around the country, including the parents of every player on the youth hockey teams he coaches. Many of his recipients are coaches themselves, who can forward the articles to their own teams' parents, helping to create a national network.

Abrams says he hopes people will read these articles and say, "Wow, I thought I had heard everything." The idea is to hold up a mirror, to use the articles to show parents the extremes adults can go to when they let their emotions take over.

"I want parents to be so disgusted at what other adults do that they won't engage in such behavior themselves," he said. "Recognizing a serious problem is the first step toward finding a solution."

Abrams said he thinks that in any youth sports program, the majority of parents are well-behaved and often suffer in silence. Reading the stories may empower them "to stand up to the few who ruin the fun for everyone else," he said. "The power of shame goes a long way."

Doug (*AbramsD@missouri.edu*) is always willing to add a new name to his e-mail list, and the results of his media campaign are encouraging. The list grows each week. Many parents of his players come over to him at games and practices to say how much they appreciate reading these stories, he says. Their strong support shows him that the list is working.

● ● ●

So there you have it: ten initiatives that go a long way toward making a difference in youth sports. I'm always interested in hearing about these kinds of efforts. If you know of an interesting program, please log on to my Web site (*www.bob-bigelow.com*) or send an e-mail (*Bob@Bob-Bigelow.com*).

In the next chapter you'll see what lies ahead for the young athlete who enters the world of interscholastic sports. You'll learn about some of the disturbing trends that middle school, high school, college and professional sports authorities are seeing.

CHAPTER 10

Going the Distance: Beyond Youth Sports

*Now I sometimes see kids who
are frightened to try something outside the
coach's "system" in case they get scored on
and get stuck at the end of the bench.*

Bobby Orr
NHL Hall-of-Famer

Ever play silly games in your head? Try to envision the Wizard of Future Sports Rosters looking down on the fields and the gyms and rinks where children play. In this silly game, that wizard is shaking his head and having a good old laugh at the things some adults do in the name of future success in sports.

You can almost hear him shouting from

on high: "What is going on down there?" So much of the frenzy, the pressure, the dead-serious effort that adults are putting into decisions and games played by their children is fodder for laughter—and dismay.

What's it all for? Does it make for better athletes? Happier athletes? Think about it.

If all this intensive effort, training and specialization at young ages do not produce more skilled, more productive adult players—and believe me, they don't—then why are we trying to figure out who are our "best" ten-year-olds?

Consider today's sports professionals or those who have retired with their passion intact. Do you know what some of our greatest sports stars are speaking out about and working hard on these days? Are they calling for more specialization or longer schedules in order to better prepare young players for the highest levels of sports? Are they suggesting children make sure they get onto elite teams? That's not what I hear them talking about.

At the National Hockey League All-Star Game in February 2000, "The Great One," Wayne Gretzky, clearly one of the most talented players in the history of the game, told reporters that the game needs the reintroduction of that terribly abused three-letter word: F-U-N.

Gretzky drew on an image of the way hockey was played in the days before superorganized youth systems took over. "One thing we have lost is what the Jean Beliveaus, the Bobby Orrs and the Gordie Howes of the world had: creativity and imagination," Gretzky is quoted in a February 7, 2000, USA Today article. "That creativity was basically founded by the fact that they would go on ponds and skate for six, seven or eight hours a day, choose up sides and have two nets and no goalies."

"We need to get back to the basics of just having fun," Gretzky said in an Associated Press story at the time of that All-Star Game. "That would go a long way toward getting back a lot of the imagination in our game."

Speaking of Bobby Orr, he's working on those same goals. Together with another Hall-of-Famer, the former New York Islanders' Mike Bossy, Orr works with the Chevrolet Safe and Fun Hockey Schools in Canada. Orr skates on the ice alongside the children, talking with them and showing them how to have fun playing the game.

"I still have the same love, the same passion for hockey that I had as a kid," Orr told *The Toronto Sun* (February 3, 2000). "I get a kick out of being part of this." But Orr also told the newspaper he has concerns about what he sees happening today in some youth sports systems. "We have to get back to letting the kids grab the puck and go with it."

"Now I sometimes see kids who are frightened to try something outside the coach's 'system' in case they get scored on and get stuck at the end of the bench," Orr told the newspaper. "I know that coaches feel the need to win or they lose their jobs, but is this any way to introduce our kids to hockey and develop not only skills but a love and a passion for the game?"

"Some of the happiest memories I have are of my days in minor hockey," Orr is also quoted in an article that appeared on the SLAM! Sports Web site, "but for many kids that's not the case and that's wrong. When that happens we fail, and we're failing in many cases."

What is so powerful is that these are the players who were

good enough for the pros and the history books. And what are they focusing on? Creativity and fun. A love of the game.

A Bitter Loss

Canada had to swallow a bitter pill in the 1998 Olympic games in Nagano, Japan. It was the first time Canada's hockey professionals, not the amateurs, had competed in the Olympics, and the first time Canada came home without a medal in hockey.

In a newspaper series that year, *The Globe and Mail* (Toronto) quoted youth hockey coaches describing fathers who put their fourteen-year-old players on steroids to bulk up in order to improve their shot at professional careers. The series cited the focus on elite teams and insanely long seasons as factors contributing to the deterioration of the game. The series concluded that more young players were burning out or simply losing their passion before they reached the point when that passion is needed most. The newspaper further reported that the win-at-all-costs philosophy at the lower levels also shifts attention away from much needed instruction for young players and practice of the fundamentals.

For some of us, watching an NBA game these days is disappointing. Teamwork? Intricate ball-passing maneuvers? These talents feel more and more like remnants of another generation. Expansion certainly has had something to do with the caliber of play. But many of the players making it to the NBA today don't have the requisite maturity to play in the league.

Part of this is a direct result of the ways in which players have or have not been taught at the youth levels. There's little doubt that you could find professional players in every sport who would line up to say much the same thing.

When Sports Stars Become Parents

When professional sports players become sports parents themselves, it is refreshing to hear them talk about their experiences and the advice they dole out to their own children and to the other adults around them.

Consider this image frozen in the minds of hockey fans everywhere: Mike Eruzione, the boyishly energetic captain of the 1980 "Miracle on Ice" U.S. Olympic hockey team, scores the deciding goal in the historic 4–3 win at Lake Placid. The previously indomitable Soviet Union's Olympic hockey team is eliminated. The United States goes on to win the gold. Unbounded joy and a medal ceremony ensue, with Eruzione in the middle of it all.

Fast forward twenty-one years: The Soviet Union doesn't exist anymore. Mike Eruzione is married with children, living in a Boston suburb, and working as director of development for athletics and as assistant hockey coach at his alma mater, Boston University. He also coaches his children's youth sports teams.

One day in December 2000, Mike found himself behind the bench as coach of his son's pee-wee hockey team. Well into the third period, Mike's team was losing 4–1.

Parents in the stands were booing and hissing the official, but there was a twist. Those loud parents were there for the team that was ahead by three goals. So obnoxious were their

insults and catcalls that, during a stop in the action, Mike sig-
naled the official and said, "My team is not taking another
face-off until those people are gone." Two men and one
woman were ejected.

As Mike recalled, the woman wasn't finished. Still angry at
the official for what she saw as poor officiating, she walked
around the circumference of the rink to get closer to the official and flashed him an obscene gesture. "To be honest, I was
shocked," Mike said. "I've seen some crazy behavior but
three people got thrown out of that game—and *their* team
was *winning*."

Those like Eruzione who have reached the highest levels
in their sports often are among the least hands-on as parents.
Perhaps that is because most have no need to relive athletic
glory through their children's lives. They've had glory on
their own terms. Now it's their children's chance to live their
own lives.

Modern baseball's home run king, Mark McGwire, is
another good example. He says that parents at Little League
games should be seen and not heard. "You wouldn't even
know I'm there," McGwire told columnist Michael Knisley
of *The Sporting News* (June 21, 1999) about his role as spectator at the baseball games of his son Matt, the boy so many
of us remember hugging Dad at home plate after home run
number sixty-one. "Look, I know I'm a good dad. He knows
I will always be there for him no matter what."

Asked how much coaching he gives Matt, McGwire
responded, "Zero." You must be tempted, he was told. "Not
at all," McGwire responded. "He's too young. All I tell him,
which every father should tell his son about the game, is 'See

the ball and hit it.' That's all you should tell a young kid."

Are you listening, sports parents?

This is not to suggest that elite athletes just wake up one day as adults and, presto, they're at the top of their game. They train and play hard for years before they make it to the pros. But there is an appropriate time and place for that intensity.

In the years when that intensity increases—after youth sports and into middle school, then high school—adults often continue to make misguided choices on behalf of children, both those who simply need recreation and those who have their eyes on a higher prize.

The Wonder Years

Adults can ruin the fun and get in the way of success for so many children playing youth sports. So what happens to children as they reach their teenage years, head toward high school, then college and adulthood?

What are the issues in youth sports that carry into these later years and help determine who will continue to play, who will get left out and who will pay the price of all that has happened during childhood? What are the consequences that youth sports experiences have on those who do make it to high school varsity, college athletics and the pros?

As children move into middle school, they often encounter for the first time a system of interscholastic athletic teams. This does not signal an end to our mission to prevent cuts at an early age, to guarantee children meaningful playing time and to ensure that these games are fun. Quite the contrary.

Middle schools should not be seen as feeder systems for

high school sports teams. The freshman and junior varsity high school teams are the feeder systems for varsity. Even through junior varsity, the aim of sports teams should be to develop as many players as possible, to fatten the base of players ready for the varsity level.

At the varsity level, winning games trumps playing time. The goals of varsity athletics should continue to foster sportsmanship and life skills, but winning goes to the top of the list, too.

Before that, however, coaches and athletic directors, despite the inevitable protestations from gung-ho parents, should be doing all they can to draw in as many students as possible. That goes for all school sports teams.

Earlier chapters explored the effect that misguided adults can have on children who are caught in a youth sports caste system (A's, B's and so forth). You've read about children who, from young ages, are denied an equal chance to develop, children who quit sports long before they have a chance to see if they might be great players.

If the weeding-out process has not already taken its toll before middle school and adolescence, perhaps that is when some of the most unwise cuts are made. Middle schools, traditionally grades six through eight, generally serve eleven- to fourteen-year-olds. These are children at the start of or in the middle of puberty, that great determining force when it comes to athletic ability.

Huge differences in abilities and sizes are seen among children in middle school, and there are no certain ways to predict future athletic success even in high school, which is just a few years away. Do not eliminate players now. Do not discourage them at this age. You may be sending away your future varsity stars.

Additionally, the middle school years, perhaps even more than other times, are critical years for figuring out where you belong within a group, for building a sense of self-worth and self-confidence, for determining your passions. Decisions made by adults in charge at this level have a powerful impact on children's sense of belonging and discovery.

The good news is that some middle schools across the country are taking wonderful steps to encourage and support wide participation in school sports and other activities, to keep their students active and involved as they head toward high school.

Making the "Funnel" Wider

When Pete Foley, athletic director for the middle school and high school in the town of Weston, Massachusetts, talks about school sports, he talks about "fattening the base" in middle school in order to increase the pool of players at the high school level.

On the suggestion of one of his coaches fifteen years ago, Foley initiated "the core team concept" at Weston's middle school.

"Say we have thirty-four kids out for soccer," Foley explained. "We try to put the top sixteen kids on a core team. Then we might take another nine kids and call them the Red Team. The other nine will be the White Team. On Mondays, the coach takes the core team as well as the Red Team to the game. On Thursdays, he takes the White Team along with the core team."

Players on the White and Red Teams will not get as much playing time as those on the core team, but they could be put in, here and there, when needed. The idea is that they have a chance to see some playing time as opposed to simply being cut.

On those days when the core team is not playing, Foley will sometimes combine the White and Red Teams and send them to play a team at another school. One of the most difficult challenges is to convince other schools to do the same. "For whatever reason, they'll cut their soccer teams down to eighteen kids and leave it at that. I won't be able to send my White and Red Teams because they won't have anybody we can play."

Even though these efforts may look fair and reasonable, Foley said he hears sharp disagreement from time to time from parents who wonder how their young "stars" will be ready for varsity competition if their ranks aren't winnowed down in middle school. "The criticism I hear a lot is 'How are you going to build winning teams?'" he said. His answer? "That's precisely what I'm trying to do."

In middle school basketball, Weston doesn't have core teams. There are no cuts, which means the school carries large numbers on its squads. Foley recalled the last game of a season for a basketball team that had thirty-one players. Weston's coach figured that the opposing team would bring along its B squad. That way, Foley said, the schools could split into two teams each and play two separate games. The other school showed up with only its A team. Suddenly the

Weston coach had to figure out how to get thirty-one players into the same game. After all, it was the last game of the season and many of the parents had given up an afternoon of work to be there.

The coach managed to pull it off, getting all thirty-one players into the lineup that day. The Weston team lost the game, but finished the season above .500. At the post-season pizza party, two parents approached the coach to complain that their children had not played enough minutes because, they argued, there were just too many kids out there.

Foley said he sometimes ends up having "long, philosophical talks" with complaining parents about the aim of middle school sports—that is, to explore, to participate and to develop in middle school, not just to prepare for high school teams. That debate is familiar to many middle school administrators who have faced similar questions on their own turf.

New Methods Blossom

Meet youth sports reformer Ed Canzanese, assistant principal and athletic coordinator for the Rosa International School, which enrolls eight hundred students and is the newest and third middle school in the Cherry Hill, New Jersey, school district.

Canzanese began his reform efforts with a simple observation: "We were eliminating more and more kids at the middle school level every year from participating." His research showed that up to 60 percent of all middle schoolers in Cherry Hill trying out for sports teams were being cut.

For activities that were ostensibly designed to include children, this was a disturbing trend. Canzanese also found some middle schools around the country that had adopted no-cut policies for some teams.

In 1998, as the district was getting ready to build a third middle school, Canzanese took his passion for reform to the school board. He argued that the policy of cutting athletes at the existing middle schools was having a detrimental effect on children and on the future of the high school teams.

Canzanese asked for and received permission to draw up a new system. He decided there would be two categories of sports in this new middle school: those that allow cuts (basketball and baseball/softball) and those that don't (soccer for boys and girls, field hockey for girls, cross-country and track-and-field for both genders, and wrestling for boys). It is difficult, he said, not to cut players from basketball and baseball. So many try out for relatively few spots on the roster.

Canzanese said the results of his no-cuts efforts are encouraging. The participation rate in the old middle schools, with cut policies, was 17 percent of all children in sports. In the first year under his new policy, 270 of the 600 in the new middle school played sports, an increase to 45 percent of the student body.

Canzanese said he believes that a no-cut policy will help send to the two high schools—Cherry Hill East and West— a bigger crop of more skilled athletes, which would serve to strengthen those teams. Is he right? It's too early to tell, according to Ira Kosloff, the athletic director at Cherry Hill West. However, Kosloff said, "I think spiritually, philosophically, it's the way to go."

The no-cuts policy change wasn't easy for Canzanese to get by parents. The resistance from some, he said, was "monstrous." There were letters to the local paper, petitions, angry demonstrations at board meetings. Parents of the more skilled athletes, in particular, worried that competition would be watered down.

"It was absolutely a philosophical difference," Canzanese said. "I never took it personally and they never meant it personally."

Eventually things worked out so well that parents at the two other middle schools began clamoring for a no-cuts policy, and they got it. He's also getting calls from other communities in New Jersey and even from out of state for advice.

His advice to those who would reform sports programs in their cities and towns: Start small. Attack the problems within your own little sphere and create a model there first. If you can show people that your ideas work, you have a better chance of moving them out into the wider world.

Oh, Pioneer

A celebrated reformer of middle school sports is Jerry Goldsberry, principal at Plainfield Community Middle School in Plainfield, Indiana, who has been following a no-cuts policy in his school since 1990 when the building opened.

Among the teams with no-cuts policies are swimming, wrestling, cross-country and perhaps the most stereotypically exclusive clique of all: the cheerleaders. That distinction helped earn the school a story in *People* magazine.

Those cheerleading squads are the size of some small companies—close to a hundred each year. That gives some communities pause when the hordes show up for football games, until they realize all the additional gate and refreshment receipts about to come their way, including from families who show up to watch the girls cheer.

Plainfield, said Goldsberry, wants its students to feel included, not shut out. "We want students to be engaged as active participants. We want them to feel they are capable rather than feel they are incapable."

Basketball is one of the sports with cuts. Indiana, after all, is hoop country. The sheer number who try out can be daunting. One year a hundred seventh-grade boys tried out, not to mention the numbers at the sixth- and eighth-grade levels. "We figured that if we divvied up playing time, each boy would get about ninety seconds in each game," Goldsberry said.

In response, the school created an A and a B squad of a total of about twenty players, but it also created an extensive intramural program that accepts all who join and divides that number into teams that play each other after school. "We looked at what we could do to keep kids connected," he said. Sometimes grade-level participants in one of the sports might get together for their own event: a sixth-grade track meet, for instance.

Goldsberry has seen the success spill over to the high school, in terms of individual stories. One boy did not make the middle school interscholastic basketball squad but kept playing in intramurals and went on to become the starting center on the high school varsity team that won a state tournament.

Goldsberry occasionally hears from parents who question whether this inclusive approach hurts the development of competitive athletes. "People need to understand that there are opportunities for everyone." In addition, an individual's desire to excel should not be at the expense of someone else's chance to participate.

Keeping as many children as possible interested in and involved with sports participation is a critical responsibility of school systems. High school coaches and athletic directors may not all be certain of the statistical or qualitative benefits of middle school efforts on their varsity teams. Some of them emphasize that there is no getting around the need for successful high school athletes to add outside training, more competition and camp programs to a season's work on the school team. In that respect, they are uncertain about the effects of no-cuts policies at the middle school level.

"Today, to compete in basketball you have to play AAU [American Athletic Union, which offers competitive play outside of schools]," said Christopher Sweeney, assistant athletic director at Plainfield High School. "To play football you have to go to football camps, you have to lift weights, you have to do all sorts of out-of-season things if you expect to compete. These things, in themselves, will often times weed kids out."

The man has a point. Researchers would do well by looking at all of these questions in order to provide us better data on how choices and policies at younger ages affect the pool of talent that makes it to the varsity level. But we don't need statistics to tell us what we know to be true. Regardless of how middle school sports policies affect high school teams, wider participation in athletics during adolescence can mean only good things for children at that age. On that point, these policies are clearly victories.

The High School Years

At the high school level of school sports, conflicting needs and goals often have significant impact on the entire student body—from the varsity athletes to those students who do not participate in athletics at all. We need to consider both if we are to continue to make the best choices for all our children.

There is excitement for many parents and young athletes as they step into the brave new world of high school sports. This can be the place where sports careers get started. Media coverage often begins in earnest. College is on the horizon. State championships are on the line.

An entire community gets invested in the results of high school games. Ever been to a Thanksgiving football game in New England? Some of those rivalries go back generations. The games are usually sold out, as alumni and former football players gather to watch the new boys on the block.

The number of students participating in high school athletics is growing at the start of this new century, partly because the number of overall students in high school is on the rise. A baby boomlet has reached our high schools. Many communities are building new high school buildings to keep up with the population expansion.

Those increased numbers make it hard to determine the effects—in terms of attrition—that youth sports may have on the numbers who continue to play sports in high school. New sports, lacrosse being the prime example, are also adding to overall participation, as is the increasing number of female students who compete.

Most of the teenagers who participate in high school sports

are a great group, enthusiastic boys and girls who bring honor and excitement to their schools and communities. The same is true for most of the parents, whether they bake for the booster club fund-raisers, offer to carpool or show up for the games to give their support.

High school athletic directors and coaches also see some of the troubling side of youth sports carry over into their high school gyms and onto the fields. Increasing numbers of athletes and their parents arrive with a disturbing sense of entitlement, according to some athletic directors. Too often they expect the staff to cater to their wishes, as the parents continue to hover over their developing sports "stars." Some of that attitude also has rubbed off on the children.

We can talk about various shades of this problem — egos, unrealistic expectations, obsessions with college applications and scholarships or professional careers — but at the heart of many of these issues remains a clash in philosophies, similar to the clashes we see in organized youth sports.

High school sports, the administrators say, should focus on developing players who are there to learn the ideals of sportsmanship. You want to win games, for sure, but not at the expense of higher goals.

William F. Gaine, deputy director of the Massachusetts Interscholastic Athletic Association, which oversees the state's high school sports, pulls no punches in this regard. He says that more and more youngsters are coming into the high schools these days "tainted." "In my opinion the norm that has been defined in the sports culture is contrary to the mission of interscholastic athletics," he said. "We are fighting a battle that almost can't be won."

Strong words. What Gaine means, of course, is that the pressure to win, if not at all costs then certainly at far too many costs, is ingrained in the culture. It is so trumpeted by the youth and club teams from which these students emerge that they need nothing short of a reeducation when they reach high school athletics.

Strong forces are bearing down on these teenagers. At the top of the list are parents. Gaine said that too often the spectators at high school games, usually the parents, see no difference between the environment at a high school game and that at the NBA, NFL, NHL or other professional leagues where adults with contracts play each other in giant entertainment complexes.

And so the spectators at high school games boo and yell, they scream at the refs, and they hurl comments, often expletives, at everyone—coaches and players included.

Gaine has more than a few unkind thoughts about the media that cover high school sports and treat the games and players as they would professionals. The notion of high school sports as banners of sportsmanship, grace and fair play, he says, too often disappears behind that coverage.

Nancy O'Neil, athletic director for Lincoln-Sudbury Regional High School in Massachusetts, has seen the impact of parents in search of athletic futures for their children. Sometimes, she said, they shop around for the right high school based on the caliber of the athletic facilities.

"Since I've been in it," O'Neil said, "the parent over-involvement has increased and, I believe, become problematic." Winning is paramount to such parents, she said, because they believe it is critical to helping their children advance to the next level or catch the eye of a college recruiter, or more.

"A focus on winning as opposed to the improvement of skills, things like that, that's the crux of the problem today," O'Neil said. "When kids come to us [as freshmen], we're seeing some of the damage that comes out of this kind of philosophy."

In the Lincoln-Sudbury district, which is nestled in a swath of affluent suburbs west of Boston, young athletes sometimes are recruited by and lost to private schools that have better and newer sports facilities, according to O'Neil. That exodus increases the pressure on public school districts to hold onto students by building better facilities of their own.

Top-notch athletic facilities are wonderful to play in and great for spectators, but we should never ignore the cost to the school population at large or the communities in general of an imbalanced perspective on sports financing.

Investments and Returns

Budget priorities are always under scrutiny in school districts. Often not discussed is that a few sports get the lion's share of athletic budgets. The typical rebuttal to the charge that football receives a disproportionate amount of the sports budget is that football actually makes money for the school with gate receipts, refreshment sales and the like. But at what price?

John Gerdy, a college-sports reformer and a former professional player with the Continental Basketball Association, raises the issue of budget fairness in his book *Sports in School*. He challenges educators, taxpayers and parents to "reconsider whether our tremendous investment in athletics continues to be a sound one.

"To continue to blindly invest significant resources in an activity that falls short of meeting its educational objectives," he says, "is irresponsible."

Don't misunderstand Gerdy. "Competitive athletics has the potential to build character and contribute positively to the well-rounded education of our nation's youth," he says. "Sport's ability to bring a community or school together cannot be overestimated. Undoubtedly, our schools and communities would be much less vibrant without such programs."

Expanded intramurals and physical fitness programs, however, would better meet the needs of a larger number of students, according to Gerdy. "If community and education leaders were committed to using athletic participation as a tool to improve public health, school systems would be strengthening, rather than weakening, physical education requirements and appropriating increasingly scarce public education dollars to these programs (intramurals and the like) rather than to the football or basketball teams.

"If we were interested in deriving the greatest health return on dollars spent on athletics, more resources would be spent on broad-based, participatory, intramural, club and physical education programs than on the current programs designed to cater to a small population of elite athletes."

Interscholastic athletics can offer wonderful experiences to a school and to the individuals who play, but Gerdy makes important points, and it is our challenge as communities to consider the need for expanded physical education classes, intramural sports and community recreation programs for high school students in order to reach the masses, not just the select players.

Disturbing Consequences

Many athletic directors and coaches are seeing other consequences that youth sports have on high school athletics. Overuse and other physical injuries, burnout and plain old fatigue also take a toll.

By the time they reach high school, students who began in youth sports at an early age have played hundreds of games. Sometimes a student simply says, "I've had it," but other students continue to play, if only halfheartedly, the games having become more like a chore or a job.

Nancy O'Neil, the Lincoln-Sudbury athletic director, says she blames some of this on overscheduling in youth sports. "I think some of the programs are over the top. They run too long," she said.

O'Neil has also seen disturbing consequences for some young athletes who quit, especially for teenagers whose childhoods and identities have been wrapped up in youth sports. Their self-esteem is damaged and, she says, "They wonder 'What's going on here? What am I even here for?'"

Some youth sports "veterans," particularly those who have played extensively on select teams, are surprised and even disappointed by some of what they find in interscholastic sports at the high school level.

Children who are used to playing thirty-plus games in a basketball season discover their freshman schedule has been whittled to fourteen games. There are even rules—can you imagine that?—at the high school level, usually monitored and enforced by state high school athletic federations, about how early a sport season can begin, how long it can run, and how many games and practices can be scheduled.

Sometimes the high school uniforms are a letdown. The duds were often fancier and newer at the youth sports level, particularly for elite teams.

Perhaps the most familiar image from youth sports that arrives pretty much intact is the frenzied parent, overreacting and misbehaving at games. Those who are involved in high school athletics say no sport is exempt.

"Field hockey is a good example," said Pete Foley, the Weston, Massachusetts, athletic director. "It's almost comical. I see a guy out there in a Brooks Brothers suit, a three-hundred-dollar pair of wing tips and a beautiful overcoat. And the guy's working up a sweat running up and down the line yelling at a ref or yelling at his kid."

Missing Out on the Action

If youth sports systems are too selective at young ages, high school athletics programs also consistently do little to pull nonparticipants into the action and activity.

High school students too often take a look around at their school community and find no place that welcomes them to play. If they are not chosen for one of the high school teams—perhaps they didn't even try out—there is little else left for them.

They may have sized themselves up as not "good enough" for the school teams or perhaps they are not interested in investing the amount of time required for practices and for games, not to mention the pressure that often comes with that territory. Intramural sports are nonexistent in many high schools, decimated in others by budget cutbacks and a lack of faculty willing to stay late to supervise these activities.

Instead of fighting for more ways to include and interest teenagers in physical activity, school districts often take a pass. When was the last time you heard about a heated battle to increase athletic funding for students in the vast middle or lower tiers of athletic ability? Yet these teenagers are often precisely the ones who need the most encouragement if they are to plug into a lifestyle of physical fitness.

A letter I received from a bright young man from my hometown of Winchester, Massachusetts, reminded me how often adults fail to find alternatives for children who don't make the cut.

Adam Storeygard, a physics major at Harvard University, was in high school when he came to hear one of my talks about youth sports. After that, he wrote me an intriguing letter about his experiences in soccer.

He fell in love with the game in the first grade. By third grade, he was on a travel team. He continued to play happily until his sophomore year in high school, at which point he was cut from the travel soccer team, the only such team in his town for players of his age. Suddenly Storeygard didn't have an outlet for his soccer passion.

"Knowing how badly I wanted to play the sport that I love, the head of the soccer club offhandedly offered to enter a second team in the league if I could find the players," Storeygard recalled. "I immediately accepted the challenge. I talked to every former player I could recall from previous seasons. I ended up making a lot of phone calls and talking to a lot of people at school."

After all that hustle and hard work, Storeygard put together a team of about a dozen who would go down in the annals, at least among his friends, as "The Scrap Team." They had a schedule of ten games that season, with other towns or cities in eastern Massachusetts. Getting all twelve to show up for the same game of eleven versus eleven was difficult, and as a result the team forfeited nine out of its ten games. The players who made it to any given game still wanted to play, so the other teams would invariably lend Storeygard's squad a few players—usually, Storeygard said, the least talented. These reconfigured squads played every game scheduled for that season.

The only game that was not forfeited was the tenth and last one. The required number showed for Storeygard's team. They lost in a heartbreaker, 1–0.

Now comes the best part. In his letter Storeygard concluded, "I had completed the most enjoyable soccer season in which I had ever competed. . . . The games," he wrote, "really didn't need to be that competitive to be fun."

Terrific story. At the heart of this team were a dozen high-schoolers ready, willing and able to play—if only given the chance. Sure, all of them didn't always make it, but that's to be expected in high school as other activities take up your time.

It is a credit to Storeygard that he pulled off his Scrap Team season, but a shame that administrators and other adults, including those who draw up sports budgets, do not find more ways to encourage similar kinds of opportunities for teenagers.

The College Experience

The number of children who continue to play sports once they enter high school drops dramatically. Exact numbers are difficult to determine with certainty, but national groups estimate that about 35 million children participate in organized youth sports. An estimated 6.5 million play sports once they enter high school, primarily in interscholastic athletics rather than community-based sports programs. An estimated three hundred thousand college students, fewer than half of whom receive any aid for athletics, participate in college sports programs. Obviously, a child's chances of getting an athletic scholarship are very slim; that child's chances of making it to the pros are slimmer still.

Those in charge of college athletics say they, too, see some of the consequences that have carried over from youth sports and continued through high school: burnout, entitlement, lack of effective player development.

Kathy Delaney-Smith, with nineteen years as coach of the women's basketball team at Harvard, is frustrated with some of the attitudes. "I am battling all of the huge egos created from youth sports who were not taught teamwork, who were not taught how to lose, who were not taught how *not* to be the star," she said.

An athlete who comes into a college program with attitude can put a strain on a coach's time, Delaney-Smith said. "Where did they learn leadership? Do I have to spend a year teaching them not to whine about the officials? How about loyalty to your coach? Are you going in the locker room bad-mouthing your teammates and coach? No one's teaching

that. So when I get them, it's the first time anyone has said
'Stop that stuff.'"

Remember What's Important

The youth sports player who is aiming for college athletics
or the professional level will need to get serious and work hard
at some point. For the "serious" athlete, so to speak, or for any
child playing any game just for the fun of it, I have the same
advice. Don't confine yourself to one sport too soon. Don't
play so much that you lose your passion to play. And don't let
adults take away the fun or make you afraid to make mistakes
in a game. With risk often comes the greatest glory.

For youth sports systems, my advice is to let the children
play as much as they can for as long as they want. Eliminate
the youth sports caste systems that entrap children at such a
young age. Put off weeding out "the best" and benching or
cutting "the rest" before anyone's athletic ability can be accurately evaluated. Do not sacrifice any child's future, or the
future of sports at a higher level. Do not take a chance that
you are cutting or benching a future star. Give all children
the opportunity to shine.

If you are an adult coaching a team or if you are a parent
organizing your child's sporting life, do not compete with
other adults through your children. Back away when you
should, give them the time and the space to be children first
and young athletes second. Put off all those extrinsic awards
and novelties, and encourage the joy of play.

A great little story appears on several Internet sites and was
originally published in the fall 1998 issue of the American

Youth Soccer Organization's *In Play* magazine. The story comes from Larry Hughes, a Phoenix, Arizona, coach who describes a game he officiated for players under age eight. The playing field was located near the approach for planes and helicopters landing at Luke Air Force Base.

The young players, he said, were all doing their best to advance the ball toward the goal when, suddenly, they heard the whirling noise of four helicopters moving in unison.

"The play stopped dead in the middle of the field," Hughes reported, "and all looked to the sky to see these beautiful flying machines—all, that is, except for one player with one thing on his mind: to score. He dribbled his best through and around all the gawking players and the referee and shot the ball into the net. Needless to say, he was celebrating big time, shouting 'I scored! I scored! I scored!' His celebration was cut short when one player said to him, 'So what? You didn't see the helicopters.'"

• • •

Whether you are a child or an adult, please take time to enjoy all the wonderful aspects of a childhood in balance—youth sports among them. Take the time "to watch the helicopters." You may not get another chance.

Here's a final piece of advice from a *San Francisco Chronicle* story. It comes from a father who coached his team to victory in the California Soccer State Cup tournament but was replaced by a professional coach.

"For me, something in youth sports is really wrong," the newspaper quoted John Wondolowski. "If we are screwing up our kids, let's stop it."

FREQUENTLY ASKED QUESTIONS

In this section Bob Bigelow answers some of the questions he often hears from sports parents. A few of these questions and answers were excerpted from The Center for Sports Parenting Web site at www.sportsparenting.org. You may direct your questions to Bob and other members of that expert panel, which addresses issues including sportsmanship, injuries, difficult parents and coaches, nutrition, athletic development, and children with special needs. Bob also may be e-mailed directly at Bob@Bob-Bigelow.com.

Keep Coaching All In the Family?

Q. I have been coaching my seven-year-old in baseball and basketball for two years. Oftentimes when I make suggestions to him, he gets defensive and upset. How do I know if I am being too demanding of him?

A. Coaching your own child can be a challenge. In this case, my suspicion is the child has already received plenty of advice and suggestions (need I say "critique"?) from you. His defensive posture is probably a signal that it's time for Dad/Coach to lighten up.

A couple of questions and suggestions: Do you praise or positively reinforce the actions and accomplishments of your son and his teammates? A five-to-one ratio of praise to *constructive* criticism for all team members is a must. An added benefit to the adults—you'll have more fun! As the saying goes, "Catch them doing something good." Since your son seems to have tuned you out, arrange for another one of the adult coaches to offer advice. The same words, with a different person imparting the message, may be better received.

Since these are seven-year-olds, are you keeping things incredibly simple? In organized youth sports for children ages three to fourteen years old, adults should not try to introduce age-inappropriate concepts and strategies to children who can't (and won't) get it.

For instance, in basketball—which shouldn't even be organized into games and practices until third grade—are you trying to introduce strategy and concepts such as "plays"? If you are, please quit now and set up some dribbling relay races instead. The kids will have more fun doing this than listening to you lecture on the definition of a power forward or other terms that are useless for young ages.

Finally, my rule of thumb is no more than two consecutive years of coaching your own child. Remember, this could be six to ten "seasons" of different sports that your child has to spend listening to your coaching pearls of wisdom. After that, it's time to let developing athletes listen to someone else's voice. If you'd like to continue coaching, start anew with a younger child or return after a hiatus of a year or two when your voice and advice sound fresher.

Constructive Coaching Criticism?

Q. I'm a first-year assistant Little League coach who had a recent run-in with a parent. I was coaching third base at a practice game when one of the players at bat struck out. I yelled his name in order to get his attention because I wanted to tell him where the ball was so he wouldn't make the mistake again. When he didn't look at me, I yelled his name again. He kept walking toward the dugout without noticing, so I yelled his name again.

After the inning, the boy's father pulled me aside and said, "You will never belittle my son like that again!" I was shocked. I didn't know what he was talking about. The father followed me into the dugout and lectured me on how to give positive reinforcement. I tried to explain that I was only trying to get his son's attention to give him this positive reinforcement. (I don't believe I yelled in a harsh or mean way, but I was at third and wanted the boy to hear me.)

The more I think about the incident, the more upset I get. I never raise my voice at the kids on the team, and my philosophy is that having fun is more important than winning. The situation has taken the enjoyment out of coaching, and I'm considering quitting altogether. Now I'm hesitant to say anything in front of parents because I don't know what's going to get them upset. Should I get used to parents being like this? If so, how do I handle any future conflicts?

A. This letter brings up one of my biggest pet peeves in organized youth baseball and softball—the use of adults as base coaches. I firmly believe that the children, from third through sixth grades, should be asked to "coach" on the basepaths and the adult managers and coaches should remain in the dugout, on the bench and away from the field of play as much as possible. Why this seemingly radical approach? Several reasons:

1) The game belongs to the children who play. The adults who coach and watch are guests at these activities. What better way to let the kids learn the game than to put them on the basepaths to help move runners along and assist in stealing bases. Too often I see adults, mostly adult men, flashing fancy and ridiculously confusing signs in order to showcase their "coaching" skills. I call this the "Look Ma, watch me coach" syndrome. (They must imagine they're in Yankee Stadium.)

2) Placing the players as basepath coaches gets two players off the bench every inning. In six innings—a fairly common length of these games—that's a minimum of twelve players used in this way. This keeps more players active. If their turn in the batting order comes up, replace them at the base with a teammate who won't come up for a while. Another bonus: The children will pay more attention to the game; after all they're now "coaching."

3) This keeps the adult coaches near the bench, where they belong. Away from the action, the adults can provide positive and corrective reinforcement to players in a more private setting. This is much more effective than yelling across the field, at the highest decibel level and in negative tones: "Jimmy, I *told* you not to swing at the high

ones!" This "hindsight" reinforcement—way too often negative, accusatory and arbitrary—is the primary reason to keep adults out of basepath coaching.

Now, let me address the first-year coach who asked this question. Yes, my friend, you were well meaning, but wrong. You tried to correct the batter's mistake from seventy to 100 feet away. Trying to be heard by the child at that moment in time was the coach's mistake; the coach didn't consider the effects of his words. The child was feeling dejected and probably did not want to hear any adult point out his mistake publicly. The batter's father misread the coach's loud words (repeated twice, and louder the second time as the child walked farther away) as belittling rather than helpful, which I'm sure had been the coach's intent.

Coach, you did "raise" your voice. You had to, to be heard from a long distance. Apologize to this father immediately and tell him you did not think through the possible consequences. As a new (and hopefully contrite) coach, you're also learning.

If adults must coach basepaths—they shouldn't—the only words uttered from their mouths should be positive and supportive. Save the constructive criticism for private one-on-one talks, away from teammates and sideline adults, either in between innings or as quick tutorials after the game. This creates a better learning environment for the child and fewer embarrassing moments for all. One last thing: Make sure children used as basepath coaches wear batting helmets. Screaming line drives as coaches look elsewhere are always a possibility.

When Is a Child Too Competitive?

Q: Phil is a teammate on my son's basketball and soccer teams. Phil is very athletic and competitive. Although Phil is a quiet kid, he has made good friends on the team. Phil plays to win. His athleticism really takes beautiful form when he's at his best. When we win, Phil is happy and open. Yet when we lose, Phil is withdrawn, quiet, sullen, and depressed. At twelve years old, is this behavior healthy for Phil and for the team? Should the coach intervene? Should anyone intervene? Phil's parents are good people, and I wonder if someone should mention something to them about Phil's behavior when we lose.

A: I'll first make the assumption that Phil's coach has winning, losing and players' development in healthy perspective for a twelve-year-old level. This can be a big assumption these days, especially for select/travel/elite teams. If not, chances are good that the coach also will be taking losses too hard, which means the coach probably wouldn't recognize problems with his/her players' reactions to losses.

Certainly a good coach would have noticed the downcast look by Phil after each loss. At this point, only a few positive words of sincere praise are all Phil is likely to hear. ("Great job of helping on defense." "Nice effort passing to the open man.") A reiteration of similar words to Phil's parents by the coach before they leave might help ease their anxiety for the ride home. If, as the writer states, Phil's parents are "good people" and good sports parents, they should let Phil initiate conversation about the loss during the ride home. The presence of siblings, teammates or friends will mitigate a gloomy atmosphere. Seven-year-old siblings could care less about a game that's over; it's time for big brother to pay attention to them.

A coach who is mature and insightful plays the most important role here. At the next practice (hopefully there are at least two before the next game), the coach can take Phil aside beforehand to discuss methods to help Phil develop as an individual and a team player. Mention two or three things that Phil can recognize as needing improvement and that he and the coach can monitor and evaluate throughout the season. These age-appropriate skills and methods will help Phil turn his attention more toward the "process" (the improvement of individual and team effectiveness) and away from the "outcome" (winning or losing).

The good coach will also keep Phil's parents informed of his progress toward these goals, to help encourage the parents to consistently gear their youth sports conversations around issues of process, not the team's record. Questions such as: "What do you think you're doing better this season?" or "Who do you think is the best passer on your team, and why?" provide nice accelerants to meaningful parent-child chats about sports participation that carry far beyond wins and losses.

Be assured that Phil will not cure his post-loss gloom immediately, but he, with consistent and fair attention from parents and coach, will soon move toward a healthier outlook.

Will Son Grow into Baseball Success?

Q. My son is ten and enjoys playing several sports, including basketball, soccer and baseball. He is short for his age but is physically strong and muscular. He will probably not be very tall, so we feel baseball will be the best game for him. We are not looking for him to get a scholarship, but we would like him to continue playing the game through high school if he chooses.

He plays second base and has pitched a little. While he should be very strong, he is not. When we suggest doing a little practice, he says "Don't you think I'm good?" In his mind he is the best player on the team and therefore doesn't need any practice. He wants to pitch but will need to practice to do so. He also needs to practice his hitting.

My wife and I would like to see more enthusiasm when we send him to summer camps. While we want sports to be fun for him, we know that the competition is fierce and it only gets more so in later years. We just don't want him to be disappointed later for not putting in the effort now.

A. You raise one of the most frequent parental concerns: Will my child fall behind? The simple answer is no.

A ten-year-old boy within the fiftieth percentile of height and weight is four foot six inches and sixty-nine pounds. At that height and weight, on average, a ten-year-old boy is not going to be strong and muscular.

Your son will obviously be much taller and heavier in five or six years. Just as your son's height and weight cannot be predicted, certainly his athletic talent and sport preference cannot be predicted. By saying that you feel your son is best suited for baseball, you've labeled him prematurely. Your son has so far to travel in sports, not only physically but cognitively and emotionally. The best thing you can do for your son is to keep him interested in, and fascinated by, all of the sports he plays and allow him to gravitate to the sport(s) he enjoys.

If he appears overconfident or even cocky, your son can join the 200,000 other ten-year-old boys in this country who act the same. As the father of two sons, I know firsthand that cockiness is not an uncommon trait for ten-year-old boys!

Please be guided by your son's lack of interest in summer camps. He may be interested in going to a more general-interest sports camp (archery, rock climbing, mountain biking), which would expose him to other endeavors. Ask him if he would like to go to a general-interest camp or a specific sports camp other than baseball.

Hopefully your son's leagues are structured for ten-year-olds rather than miniature sixteen-year-olds. As he gets older, your son will create his own opportunity for competition that will seek a natural level.

Please don't worry now about where your son is going to be at twelve, fourteen, sixteen or eighteen. Enjoy his being ten. Neither of you will get that chance again.

Should You Let a Child Quit a Sport?

Q. We have invested a lot of time and money over the years for our son to play hockey. This year, even with his eighth-grade school activities, he told us he just *had* to play. Now he's halfway into the season and says he wants to quit. Should we let him quit or make him see his responsibility through?

A. First, given the suddenness of your son's decision, I recommend you approach your son's coach. Ask if your son got along with his teammates, if there's been any bullying or razzing going on, or if the coach has noticed your son losing interest. If none of these is true, I would think your son is experiencing some "hormonal independence." At the age of thirteen, boys become more involved in other activities and interests, including other friends and the opposite sex.

Since some children can be very close-mouthed with their parents at this age, you may want to ask the coach to intervene. He or she may be able to talk to your son and find out what he likes and what he doesn't like about the sport. But make sure this is a coach who will understand the situation versus one who can't see past the fact that your son doesn't want to help win the championship. Remind yourself, too, that this is your child's hockey "career," not your career, despite all the investment of time and money on your part.

Because sports such as hockey tend to have long seasons, there is a great deal of burnout. If, after your assessment of the situation, you suspect your son is burning out, then it's time to move on to another activity. If you can allow your child to quit a sport and you can say, "We had a good run, let's go find something else," then you've done a good job. He may need a rest. He may even decide to go back to the sport when his energy and enthusiasm return.

Encouraging vs. Obnoxious—Fan Etiquette

Q. My wife says she doesn't want to go to any of my son's soccer games with me because she doesn't like it when I yell and cheer for our son. I say I am just being encouraging; she says I'm being obnoxious. Who's right?

A. The way I gauge whether you are an encouraging fan versus a distraction is the way experts gauge exertion level when jogging with a partner: You know you are running too fast if you can't carry on a normal conversation with the person next to you. Likewise, when watching a youth sports game, if you can't carry on a normal conversation with the person next to you then you're probably paying too much attention to the game. When your focus is on every pitch, every slap shot, or every pass or dribble, you're too darn invested in the game. If there's no scoreboard and you always know the score, you're too darn invested in the game. Pull back and relax.

If you are going to say something, always be positive and encouraging. Never criticize—even quietly—your child's performance, some other child's performance, or the coach's or the official's performance. Negative comments may start out spoken softly among friends, but as things get more intense the comments generally get louder. Another good rule of thumb: Always cheer for good plays, even those made by the other team.

Avoiding Burnout

Q. My ten-year-old daughter plays three or four seasons of soccer a year. She still loves it, but I worry about burnout. Yet I don't want to make her sit out a season because I worry she'll fall behind. Should I let her continue such a schedule?

A. First, there is no reason to worry your daughter will fall behind at this age. However, there is reason to worry that she won't like the sport by the time she's fourteen. If your ten-year-old likes soccer and she plays it well, chances are she'll be able to play other sports just at well.

By the time she's twelve years old, she should be exposed to three team sports and three individual sports. Team sports give her a chance to meet other kids and to try out something new. Individual sports (golfing, swimming) are activities she can potentially enjoy for the rest of her life.

Before the ages of thirteen or fourteen, there is no reason any child should specialize by playing one sport all year round.

Fostering Teamwork

Q. My eight-year-old daughter is a terrific skater and a stronger hockey player than many of the boys on her team. The coach always encourages her teammates to pass it to her so she can make the goal. I'm sensing that some of her teammates are beginning to resent her 'star status.' How can we encourage our daughter to be a team player when the coach won't?

A. Let me preface this answer by saying it's not surprising that your daughter is better than many of the boys on her team. Up until the age of twelve, girls, for the most part, are taller and heavier than boys. They also seem to be better able to grasp cognitively abstract concepts. At thirteen, testosterone starts to kick in, and the boys begin to catch up and surpass the girls in height and strength.

In terms of making sure your daughter is a team player, I recommend that you talk to the coach—not before or after a game when he or she is distracted—but in a separate meeting. Tell the coach that you want your daughter to develop her skills as a defensive player as well. This will serve two purposes: She will develop a different set of skills on the ice and that will also put her into a position of assisting her teammates to score goals, which will de-emphasize her star status.

Any good coach will understand that the greater goal is to develop well-rounded skills and knowledge of the game, something children cannot do if they are always pegged into playing the same positions.

When Should You Start Your Child in Sports?

Q. When is my child old enough to play organized sports?

A. If your child is going with a bad coach in a bad system, he or she will never be old enough. However, there are good systems and there are good people out there. Your job as a parent is to find them. Generally, at the team levels, first grade is fine, if, and this is a big if, the games and the systems are structured age-appropriately.

Beware of coaches who focus too much on the score. Beware of all-star teams. Beware of coaches who take the games too seriously. A good rule of thumb: Before your kids get there—a year or so before—go to a game and see if this is something you want them to be a part of. If you don't like what you see, call and ask why it's happening. You could always choose not to enroll your child, but the better solution is to try to change what exists.

Too Many Kids, Too Little Space

Q. We have too many kids signing up for youth basket-ball and we don't have enough gym space.

A. My suggestion is, don't cut the children, but cut the number of times a week you play and practice. Start with your youngest age groups.

If it's still a problem, you may have to eliminate those youngest age groups all together. If you have to eliminate first- or second-grade basketball, which should be quite infor-mal, in order to make way for the preteens and teens, this is a better trade-off. I would prefer that the fourteen- to sixteen-year-olds get more structured time, given their ages, given their needs and given their out-of-school temptations.

How to Deal with Poor Coaching

Q. What do we do about bad coaches?

A. I'm assuming by a "bad" coach you mean someone who treats the children disrespectfully or yells at officials. "Bad," in my book, does not mean someone who didn't make the championship or insists on letting even the lesser-skilled players play. Given that, here's what I recommend:

1. Make sure you have some allies who can recognize and attest to the same bad behaviors.
2. Approach the league coordinator or age group commissioner who may often be a coach on the same level. (An important note: This person may also be a bad coach, or may be friendly with the coach in question. If this is the case, obviously he or she won't be too sympathetic. So bypass this person and head to the league president. If the league president is also friendly with these people —and this happens—then you need to gather up enough allies and bring your grievances to a board meeting, which will generally be open).
3. If this doesn't work, start your own league or get your children involved with another activity.

REFERENCES

Abrams, Douglas E. and Sarah H. Ramsey. *Children and the Law—Doctrine, Policy and Practice.* West Group, St. Paul, Minn. 2000.

Ad Hoc Committee on Sports and Children of the International Federation of Sports Medicine and the World Health Organization "Sports and Children: Consensus Statement on Organized Sports for Children," *Bulletin of the World Health Organization,* 1998.

Allen, Kevin. "The Great One's Outlook," *USA Today,* February 7, 2000.

American Academy of Pediatrics. "Intensive Training and Sports Specialization in Youth Athletes," *Pediatrics,* July 2000.

Bar-Or, Oded, ed. *The Child and Adolescent Athlete.* Blackwell Science, London. 1996.

Beedy, Jeffrey Pratt. *Sports PLUS: Positive Learning Using Sports.* Project Adventure, Inc. 1997.

Belluck, Pam. "Parents Try to Reclaim Their Children's Time," *The New York Times,* June 13, 2000.

Brown, Jim. "An Epidemic of Burnout," *Georgia Tech Sports Medicine & Performance Newsletter,* November 2000.

Century, Douglas. "The Boys of Summer Get Younger All the Time," *The New York Times,* March 11, 2001.

Coakley, Jay. *Sport in Society: Issues and Controversies.* Times Mirror/Mosby College Publishing, St. Louis, Mo. 1986.

Cohen, Tom. "Getting Back to the Basics," Associated Press, appearing in *The Boston Globe,* April 9, 2000.

Cook, Jon. "Bobby Orr and Mike Bossy Team Up for Kids," *SLAM! Sports,* April 4, 2000.

Cowen, Richard. "Town Moves to Avert Bad Behavior on the Sidelines: Parents of Athletes Must Vow to Be Good," *The Record* (Bergen County, N.J.), November 19, 2000.

Cowin, Jackie. "Teens Unified by Spirit of Fun," *The Boston Globe*, October 26, 2000.

Deacon, James. "Rink Rage," *Maclean's*, March 26, 2001.

De Lisser, Eleena. "Abusive Fans Lead Amateur Umpires to Ask Courts, Legislators for Protection," *The Wall Street Journal*, August 1, 1994.

Doherty, William J. *Take Back Your Kids: Confident Parenting in Turbulent Times.* Storin Books, Notre Dame, Ind. 2000.

_____. *The Intentional Family: Simple Rituals to Strengthen Family Ties.* Avon Books, N.Y. 1997.

Engh, Fred. *Why Johnny Hates Sports.* Avery Publishing Group, Garden City Park, N.Y. 1999.

Erardi, John. "Pelé, Panel Criticize Select Teams," *The Cincinnati Enquirer*, January 18, 1998.

Fausset, Richard and Nedra Rhone. "Man Headed to Jail After Attacking His Son's Coach," *Los Angeles Times*, January 26, 2001.

Fidlin, Ken. "No. 4 Sees a Troubling Trend in Kids Hockey," *The Toronto Sun*, February 3, 2000.

Gerdy, John R. *Sports in School: The Future of an Institution.* Teachers College Press, Columbia University, N.Y. 2000.

Giardina, Anthony. "Kids Are Us," *Gentlemen's Quarterly*, June 1998.

Goldstein, Warren and Elliott Gorn. *A Brief History of American Sports.* Hill and Wang, N.Y. 1993.

Goldstein, Warren. "The Seasons of Childhood," *The Boston Globe Magazine*, April 6, 1997.

Granryd, Ric. "Coaches and Parents: Is It Time for a Reality Check?" *STYSA* (South Texas Youth Soccer Association) *Shootout*, September 1993.

Greenberger, Scott S. and Ellen Barry. "Manslaughter Charge Brings Not Guilty Plea," *The Boston Globe*, July 11, 2000.

Harper, Timothy. "Sideline Saddams," *Sky*, April 1997.

Hellmich, Nanci. "Kids' Bodies Break Down at Play," *USA Today*, November 6, 2000.

Hemery, David. *The Pursuit of Sporting Excellence: A Study of Sport's Highest Achievers.* Human Kinetics Books, Champaign, Ill. 1986.

Hines, Scott and David L. Groves. "Sports Competition and Its Influence on Self-Esteem Development," *Adolescence*, Winter 1989.

Houston, William. "Game in Crisis," *Toronto Globe and Mail*, April 17, 1998.

Hughes, Larry. "What Really Counts," *In Play*, American Youth Soccer Organization, Fall 1998.

Hutslar, Jack. *Beyond X's and O's: What Generic Parents, Volunteer Coaches and Teachers Can Learn about Generic Kids and All of the Sports They Play.* Wooten Printing Co., Welcome, N.C. 1985.

Hyland, Tim. "Dad Protests Team Cuts," *The Capital* (Annapolis, Md.), August 24, 2000.

Jacoby, Jeff. "PC Police Are Spoiling It for Kids Who Play Soccer," op-ed, *The Boston Globe*, June 2, 1998.

Janda, David. *The Awakening of a Surgeon.* Sleeping Bear Press, Chelsea, Michigan. 2001.

Karp, Josie. "Welcome to the Quiet Fields," *The Boston Globe*, August 24, 1993.

Katz, Bob. "Parents Behaving Badly," *Parents*, October 2000.

_____. "What Is a Hockey Game Worth?" *The New York Times*, July 12, 2000.

Kelly, Dennis. "Parental Agony on Sidelines," *USA Today*, June 6, 1995.

Knisley, Michael. "A Lesson for Little League Dads," *The Sporting News*, June 21, 1999.

Lancaster, Scott. "Fixing Kids' Sports," op-ed, *The Christian Science Monitor*, January 22, 2001.

"LBC 3rd/4th Graders Own Talent to Vie for Suburban League Title," *Derry News* (New Hampshire), December 29, 1995.

Leo, John. "We're All Number 1," *U.S. News & World Report*, June 22, 1998.

Malina, Robert M. "Talent Identification and Selection in Sport," *Spotlight on Youth Sports*, Institute for the Study of Youth Sports, Spring 1997.

Malone, Stephen. "Back to the Past for Rec Hoop League," *The Woburn Daily Times Chronicle*, January 18, 2001.

Marotta, Terry. "Go Find Your Own Passion," op-ed, *The Woburn Daily Times Chronicle*, October 10, 1997.

McKee, David. "How to Win the Battle Against Soccer Burnout," *The Bay Stater*, February 1999.

Micheli, Lyle J., M.D., Rita Glassman, and Michelle Klein. "The Prevention of Sports Injuries in Children," *Pediatric and Adolescent Sports Injuries*, vol. 19, no. 4, October 2000.

Minnesota Amateur Sports Commission. "Breaking Barriers: Keeping Youth Sports Safe and Fun," brochure written by Cordelia Anderson and the Minnesota Children's Trust Fund, 1994.

Nack, William, Lester Munson and George Dohrmann. "Out of Control," *Sports Illustrated*, July 24, 2000.

National Youth Sports Safety Foundation, "Emotional Injuries," fact sheet and National Youth Sports Safety Month press release, April 2001.

Nevius, C. W. "Child's Play No More: The Pressure on Kids and Coaches in Youth Leagues Has Reached a Level that Would Be Laughable if It Weren't So Destructive," *San Francisco Chronicle*, December 10, 2000.

_____. "High Hopes Usually Lead to Hard Fall," *San Francisco Chronicle*, December 10, 2000.

Ode, Kim. "Parents Should Know What the Score Really Is: The Child Is Always More Important than What Is Happening on the Field," *Minneapolis Star Tribune*, May 24, 1998.

Outerbridge, A. Ross, M.D., and Lyle J. Micheli, M.D. "Adolescent Sports Medicine: Changing Patterns of Injury in the Youth Athlete," *Sports Medicine and Arthroscopy Review*, vol. 4, no. 2, 1996.

Sakamoto, Bob. "Family Is at the Core of Jordan's Dream," *Chicago Tribune*, April 15, 1990.

Schofield, Dan. "Phooey on PONY," S.A. *Kids Magazine* (San Antonio, Texas), August 1997.

Seefeldt, Vern and Martha Ewing. "Participation and Attrition Patterns in American Agency-Sponsored Interscholastic Sports," Sporting Goods Manufacturers Association and Michigan State University, 1989.

Shank, Wendell J. "The Future of High School Football: Will the Tradition Continue?" *All-Stater Sports*, vol. 4 no. 4, 1999.

Sherrington, Kevin. "Unkindest Cut of All," *The Dallas Morning News*, January 4, 1998.

Tanner, Lindsey. "Doctors Advise Against Young Kids Specializing in One Sport," Associated Press appearing in *Daily Times Chronicle*, July 14, 2000.

Thomsen, Ian. "Go-o-o Home!" *Sports Illustrated*, June 29, 1998.

Tofler, Ian, P. K. Knapp, and M. J. Drell. "The Achievement by Proxy Spectrum in Youth Sports," Child and Adolescent Psychiatric Clinics of North America, October 1998.

U.S. Department of Health and Human Services. "Promoting Better Health for Young People Through Physical Activity and Sports: A Report to the President" from the Secretary of Health and Human Services and the Secretary of Education, Fall 2000.

Vinella, Susan. "Select Teams' Goals Bench Some Kids," *Dayton Daily News*, July 7, 1997.

White, Nancy. "Game Misconduct," *The Toronto Star*, March 17, 2001.

Woog, Dan. "CYSA-North Bans Tournaments," *Youth Soccer Letter, Soccer America*, March 19, 2001.

RESOURCES

The following resources offer information on general youth sports issues and research, sports parenting advice, e-mail access to experts, chat forums and bulletin boards, electronic newsletters, and articles (both current and archives). Most of these Web sites address a variety of youth sports issues, but they are listed here under general categories.

You will find me at, Bob Bigelow, at *www.bob-bigelow.com*.

Programs for Parents, Coaches and Administrators

American Sport Education Program (ASEP)
P.O. Box 5076
Champaign, IL 61820
www.asep.com

National Alliance for Youth Sports (NAYS)
2050 Vista Parkway
West Palm Beach, FL 33411
www.nays.org
(includes Parents Association for Youth Sports [PAYS])

National Institute for Child Centered Coaching
Family Development Resources
3070 Rasmussen Road
Park City, UT 84098
www.thenurturingprogram.com

North American Youth Sports Institute
4985 Oak Garden Drive
Kernersville, NC 27284
www.naysi.com

Positive Coaching Alliance
Department of Athletics
Stanford University
Stanford, CA 94305
www.positivecoach.org

Sports PLUS Institute
Positive Learning Using Sports
P.O. Box 219
New Hampton, NH 03256
www.sportsplus.org

Online Resources

Center for Sports Parenting
University of Rhode Island
P.O. Box 104
Kingston, RI 02881
www.sportsparenting.org

Coaching Youth Sports
Richard Stratton, Ph.D. (Editor)
Virginia Tech
201 War Memorial Hall-0313
Blacksburg, VA 24061
www.tandl.vt.edu/rstratto/CYS

MomsTeam.com
60 Thoreau St., Suite 288
Concord, MA 01742
www.MomsTeam.com

Youth-Sports.com
10945 E. San Salvador Drive
Scottsdale, AZ 85259
www.youth-sports.com

Sports Issues/Research

American College of Sports Medicine
401 W. Michigan St.
Indianapolis, IN 46202
www.acsm.org

American Academy of Pediatrics
141 Northwest Point Blvd.
Elk Grove Village, IL 60007
www.aap.org

Institute for the Study of Youth Sports
Michigan State University
Department of Kinesiology
213 IM Sports Circle
East Lansing, MI 48824
http://ed-web3.educ.msu.edu/ysi

National Council of Youth Sports
7185 S.E. Seagate Lane
Stuart, FL 34997
www.ncys.org

National Youth Sports Safety
Foundation, Inc.
333 Longwood Ave., Suite 202
Boston, MA 02115
www.nyssf.org

SportDISCUS
116 Albert St., Suite 400
Ottawa, Ontario K1P 5G3
www.sportdiscus.com
(sports articles search engine)

Youth Sports Research Council
Rutgers, The State University of
New Jersey
130 College Ave. Gym, Room 206
New Brunswick, NJ 08901

The Institute for Preventative
Sports Medicine
P.O. Box 7032
Ann Arbor, MI 48107
www.ipsm.org

Sportsmanship and Character

American Sports Institute
P.O. Box 1837
Mill Valley, CA 94942
www.amersports.org

Athletes for a Better World
1740 Barnesdale Way N.E.
Atlanta, GA 30309
www.aforbw.org

Center for the Study
of Sport in Society
Northeastern University
716 Columbus Ave., Suite 161 CP
Boston, MA 02120
www.sportinsociety.org

Character Counts! Sports
Josephson Institute of Ethics
4640 Admiralty Way, Suite 1001
Marina del Rey, CA 90292
www.charactercounts.org/sports/sports.htm

Center for Character and Leadership
The Culver Academies
1300 Academy Rd.
Culver, IN 46511
www.culver.org/characterandleadership

Citizenship Through Sports Alliance
10975 Benson Drive, Suite 350
Overland Park, KS 66210
www.sportsmanship.org/main.html

Joseph Matteucci Foundation for
Youth Non-Violence
P.O. Box 20397
Castro Valley, CA 94546
www.jmf4peace.org

Institute for International Sport
University of Rhode Island
P.O. Box 104
Kingston, RI 02881
www.internationalsport.com
(sponsors National Sportsmanship Day)

Mendelson Center for Sport,
Character & Culture
University of Notre Dame
202 Brownson Hall
Notre Dame, IN 46556
www.nd.edu/~cscc

National Collegiate Athletic
Association
201 South Capitol Ave., Suite 710
Indianapolis, IN 46225
www.ncaa.org/sportsmanship
(includes the Sportsmanship and
Ethics program)

Girls and Women in Sports

American Alliance for Health,
Physical Education, Recreation
and Dance
1900 Association Drive
Reston, VA 20191
www.aahperd.org
(includes the National Association
for Girls and Women in Sport)

Tucker Center for Research on
Girls and Women in Sport
University of Minnesota
203 Cooke Hall
1900 University Ave. S.E.
Minneapolis, MN 55455
www.tuckercenter.org

Women's Sports Foundation
Eisenhower Park
East Meadow, NY 11554
www.womenssportsfoundation.org

Interscholastic and Collegiate Sports

A-Game
P.O. Box 34867
Los Angeles, CA 90034
www.a-game.com

National Federation of State High
School Associations (NFHS)
P.O. Box 690
Indianapolis, IN 46206
www.nfhs.org

National Collegiate Athletic
Association
700 W. Washington St.
P.O. Box 6222
Indianapolis, IN 46206
www.ncaa.org
(includes the National Youth Sport
Program at *www.ncaa.org/edout/nysp*)

Physical Education and Fitness

American Alliance for Health,
Physical Education, Recreation
and Dance
1900 Association Dr.
Reston, VA 20191
www.aahperd.org
(includes the National Association for
Sport and Physical Education)

Gatorade Sports Science Institute
617 West Main St.
Barrington, IL 60010
www.gssiweb.com

PELINKS4U (Today's Physical
Education Online)
709 E. Manitoba
Ellensburg, WA 98926
www.pelinks4u.org

Sportscience (sport research/
Internet publication)
www.sportsci.org

Officials, Administrators and Coaches

American Sport Education Program
(ASEP)
P.O. Box 5076
Champaign, IL 61820
www.asep.com
(includes the National Federation
Interscholastic Coaches Education
Program)

National Alliance for Youth Sports
(NAYS)
2050 Vista Parkway
West Palm Beach, FL 33411
www.nays.org
(includes the National Youth Sports
Coaches Association [NYSCA] and
the Academy for Youth Sports
Administrators [AYSA] and the
National Youth Sports Administrators
Association [NYSAA])

National Association of Sports
Officials
2017 Lathrop Ave.
Racine, WI 53405
www.naso.org

Miscellaneous

International Association for
the Child's Right to Play
www.ipausa.org

Family Life 1st
www.familylife1st.org

Games Kids Play
www.gameskidsplay.net
(rules for playground games)

United Hockey Moms
www.unitedhockeymoms.com

www.WholeLifeHealth.com
(articles on holistic living and
health care)

YMCA
101 North Wacker Drive
Chicago, IL 60606
www.ymca.com

Canadian Resources

Canadian Association for the
Advancement of Women and Sport
and Physical Activity
N202-801 King Edward Ave.
Ottawa, Ontario K1N 6N5
www.caaws.ca

Canadian Centre for Ethics in Sport
2197 Riverside Drive, Suite 300
Ottawa, Ontario K1H 7X3
www.cces.ca

Coaching Association of Canada
141 Laurier Ave. West, Suite 300
Ottawa, Ontario K1P 5J3
www.coach.ca

Sport Canada
Department of Canadian Heritage
8th floor, 15 Eddy St.
Hull, Quebec K1A 0M5
www.pch.gc.ca/Sportcanada

ABOUT THE AUTHORS

Bob Bigelow is a former National Basketball Association player who lectures across the country about how to restore a healthier perspective to youth sports. Since 1992 Bigelow has delivered more than four hundred talks to coaches and parents, and has spent years researching the sociological, psychological and physiological impacts of today's systems of youth sports, in which an estimated 35 million children participate in the United States each year.

Bigelow was an NBA first-round draft pick and played four seasons in the league, for the Kansas City Kings, San Diego Clippers and Boston Celtics. He played college basketball at the University of Pennsylvania for Hall of Fame coach Chuck Daly. While playing for Winchester High School in Massachusetts, Bigelow was named one of the top fifty players in the country. He is a part-time NBA scout. Bigelow earned a B.A. in history from the University of Pennsylvania and an M.B.A. from Babson College in Wellesley, Massachusetts.

He lives in Winchester, Massachusetts, with his wife and their two sons.

Tom Moroney is a columnist with the Community Newspaper Company, a chain of ninety suburban newspapers in eastern Massachusetts. He is also a radio talk show host and part-time television reporter/commentator in Boston. His column has won numerous awards. In 2000 he won both the Best Serious Columnist and Best Humorous Columnist honors from the New England Press Association.

Among his favorite columns—some of which appear in this book—are those that focus on parents' antics in youth sports. "I never get tired of hearing about how some coach went berserk because his team of ten-year-olds had somehow been cheated, or how other coaches push their young charges to do such extraordinarily difficult things in the name of winning."

Moroney graduated from Holy Cross College. He began his writing career as a sportswriter and then became a news reporter, bureau chief and editor. Moroney has also written for *The Boston Globe* and *People* magazine. Contact him at: *lleehall@aol.com.*

Linda Hall has been a writer and editor since she graduated, summa cum laude, from Boston University. She covered a variety of suburban lifestyle and local government issues as a reporter and bureau chief for the *Middlesex News* (now *The MetroWest Daily News*) in Framingham, Massachusetts. She worked as an editor both at the *Middlesex News* and at *The Providence Journal* (Rhode Island). Her freelance stories have been published in *The Boston Globe*.

Linda has experienced many aspects of youth sports parenting, from team tryouts to pressure-packed games to overbooked schedules. She has enjoyed good times, but she has long been concerned about problems that appear each season. "I have watched children's coaches kick bleachers, parents flash obscene gestures and capable young players sit on a bench for an entire game.

"Too often, my vision of what youth sports should be about was not the experience I discovered at games. I hope this book gives a voice to parents who struggle with similar feelings."

Linda and Tom are married and have two sons. They live in a suburb west of Boston. Contact Linda at: *lleehall@aol.com.*